ALAN BEITH

A VIEW FROM THE NORTH

*Life, politics and faith seen from
England's northernmost constituency*

Published by Northumbria University Press
Trinity Building, Newcastle upon Tyne NE1 8ST, UK
www.northumbriauniversitypress.co.uk

First Edition Published 2008

British Library Cataloguing in Publication Data. A Catalogue Record for this
book is available from the British Library.

ISBN 978-1-904794-27-1

Designed and printed by Northumbria Graphics, Northumbria University.

Typeset in Sabon

Northumbria University is the trading name of the
University of Northumbria at Newcastle. 219786B/08/08

In memory of Barbara and Chris

Acknowledgements

I am grateful to Andrew Peden Smith of Northumbria University Press for encouraging me to write this book, and for calmly supervising its production. Bryan Kirkpatrick was a most helpful designer, and Sophie White tied up many loose ends. I owe particular thanks to those of my staff who gave up their own time to help: Gill Cheeseman typed most of the manuscript, together with Sylvia Crane, and Dr Clare Mills helped with research and administration. The index was meticulously prepared by Andrea Hertz, who also helped with proofreading. Canon David Adam, former Vicar of Holy Island and a widely-read author on spirituality, kindly read and commented on the chapter on 'Faith in the North': he bears no responsibility for any errors resulting from my reckless compression of two thousand years of history into a few pages. Emeritus Professor Jon Wisenthal of the University of British Columbia – a friend since our days at Balliol – proofread the whole manuscript. My wife Diana sacrificed a summer holiday to allow the book to be written, and encouraged me at every stage. I am grateful also to the very many people who have helped me in elections and in my work as MP, and to all the people who have given me such an interesting life, especially the electors of the Berwick-upon-Tweed constituency.

Alan Beith
Berwick-upon-Tweed, August 2008

Image Acknowledgements

Chris Auld Photography
Henry Brewis
Historic Chapels Trust
Michael Goonan Scenic Photos
Berwick Liberal Democrats
Liberal News
Clare Mills
Parliamentary Recording Unit
Joe Payne, *Berwick Advertiser*
Allan Wainwright
Sophie White

Evening Standard
The Guardian
Liberator Song Book
Methodist Recorder
The House Magazine
The Times
Times Educational Supplement

Every effort has been made to obtain necessary permission with reference to copyright material. The publisher apologises if, inadvertently, any sources remain unacknowledged and will be glad to make the necessary arrangements at the earliest opportunity.

CONTENTS

— 1 —

BEING NORTHERN

Like a compass needle, I am drawn by the magnetism of the North. It is where I have lived my life, and it is where I started. Well, we thought it was the North. Viewed from Northumberland, Manchester looks like the Midlands, and Cheshire even more so. But we knew that we were Northerners. We had baths, not 'barths', and probably not as often as the Southerners – and the Midlands started somewhere around Stoke-on-Trent. Beyond the Midlands lived better-off people who had their dinner at teatime, or even later, when they called it supper, which to us was toast and dripping, or fish and chips after the pictures. Such were the simple stereotypes of childhood.

I was born in 1943 in a tiny 1840s coal miner's cottage in the already growing village of Poynton. The event was celebrated in the Poynton-with-Worth Working Men's Club across the road, by my Dad, James Beith, with his 'Dad's Army' home guard pals. By this point I think he must have been suffering from nervous exhaustion – he was worried to death about my mum, who found it a painful experience and had no wish to repeat it. Precisely how my 'only child' status was preserved was not a subject discussed in front of children or, indeed, at all.

We had ended up in Cheshire because of the war. My dad was a packer in a Manchester textile merchants who were also developing 'war work' on heated flying suits for pilots. Their premises had been bombed in the 'blitz', as it was always known, and the firm had been allocated a requisitioned former sportswear factory in a very pleasant former mining village 10 miles south of the city. My mother, Joan Harty, had worked as a secretary in the firm, where she met the kindly man from the dispatch department. They fell in love and married in the middle of the war, with all the difficulties of assembling enough borrowed material and ration coupons for a wedding dress and a bridesmaid's dress. Latterly my mother had been working in the nearby Avro factory where Lancaster and Shackleton aircraft were being built. Pregnancy was fortified by rice pudding from the canteen: I seem to have inherited my mum's temporary craving for this unjustly spurned delicacy.

Mum and Dad were quite different, but surprisingly compatible. Dad worked all his life in the same job for the same firm, sewing up bales, packing up parcels and sending out orders, eventually becoming the dispatch department foreman. He had been born in the Gorbals in Glasgow, and all his forbears were Scottish, having migrated from Paisley to Glasgow when the bottom dropped out of handloom weaving. His father had worked as a printer, but latterly worked on the docks, and moved in 1905 from the Clyde to Manchester's then busy docks at the terminus of the Ship Canal in Salford. My Dad later packed goods which went through those same docks, and his lifelong unfulfilled ambition was to travel as one of the few passengers on the cargo-carrying 'Manchester Liners', across the Atlantic to Canada and through the St. Lawrence seaway. The anticipated breaking of the ice in the seaway set a timetable for one of the busiest parts of the year in the dispatch department.

In those days, Baxter, Woodhouse and Taylor Ltd. was a family firm in which the bosses were all Taylor brothers. They were always referred to, and addressed by employees, as 'Mr Eric', 'Mr Norman' and 'Mr Bill'. My Dad's attitudes were moulded in that environment, which was not heavily unionised, not very well paid, but marked by a great deal of mutual respect and concern between bosses and employees. My Dad, who was good at woodwork, made dolls' houses for the bosses' children. When he became ill with bronchitis and emphysema, they sent my parents on a holiday to Switzerland to see if the Swiss air would help him. When I got to university they provided a bursary for 'Jimmy's lad'. He died in his fifties, when I was 20; the factory closed for the morning and hundreds came to his funeral.

He was a lovely man, who greeted everyone in the same friendly way, and seemed to be liked by everyone. He cycled to work and called at the Farmers' Arms for half a pint of mild on the way home, and had two halves there before Sunday dinner. With this unfailing routine, nobody ever heard of him being drunk. As a child I used to hear women talk about their husbands coming home drunk, and it sounded alien and scary. My Dad had very few ambitions, other than to care for his family: as a 13-year-old, when he left school, he had been disappointed not to get a job working with carthorses, and he was really upset when he failed to get into the war-time Auxiliary Fire Service because he failed the medical. My singular lack of prowess in either football or rugby (he was a Salford Rugby League fan) was rather disappointing and puzzling to him, but he reckoned that 'getting on at school' was enough to make up for it. He had no particular ambition to get a better job. It was my mother who had ambitions, and Dad supported her in pursuing them. He was devoted to her, and would often cycle up the road with grocery shopping in his raincoat pockets and a bunch of flowers for her balanced on the handlebars. They enjoyed ballroom dancing, and as a child I would be taken with them, learning to do the waltz or the military two-step in 'progressive' dances (in which you keep changing partners), which involved dancing with kindly ladies whose busts would be above my head. At the New Year's Eve dances Dad looked rather special in the well-worn dinner jacket which I continued to use for some years after him.

Mum's life had been dominated by living through two wars, rationing, and the depression, which left her father periodically out of work. The death in 1941 of my cousin Jack Harty, who was a leading seaman on *HMS Hood* which went down with over 1,400 men, was a severe blow to her – although he was her nephew, he was close to her in age. She moved house (or, more usually, moved rented rooms) 17 times during her childhood, as the family migrated between Manchester, the Black Country and even Blackpool in pursuit of jobs. One Christmas things were really bad: there was no food and no coal, so Mum as a girl of about 10, and therefore half-fare, was sent on the halfpenny tram ride across Manchester to her Auntie Nellie's to 'borrow' a few pieces of coal for the fire. Mum's father was quite able, but inclined to spend money rather quickly when he got it, often on buying drinks for everyone in celebration of the latest job only to find that it did not last very long. His unemployment forced her to leave school at 14: she had been getting high marks and the school wanted her to stay and sit the school certificate exam, but money was needed. She got temporary jobs, learned shorthand and taught herself typing, and came to work in the Manchester office of the firm where my Dad worked. After I was born she stayed at home until I was well settled at school, and then worked part-time on the post office counter. This sparked an interest in retailing which was to culminate in her taking over a small shop selling watches, clocks, jewellery and gifts. As a child I remembered the anxious discussions about renting this shop with a flat above in which we were to live. Borrowing money was something we just did not do: we had always lived in rented homes, first a five-shilling (25p) a week cottage, then a small 10/6 a week semi. The landlady called to collect the rent in cash from Dad's wages every Friday. The shop business was starved of capital, and when the possibility of buying the shop came up, the bank manager would not agree to even a small loan. Years later it came out that the manager was having a long-running affair with the chief cashier, financed by helping themselves to the bank's money. 'I always knew there was something up', said Mum. Despite these limitations, she made a modest success of the shop, and it gave us a little more comfort and a few extras like holidays. Mum was talented at display – dressing the window occupied her for most of the night several times a year, but the results set a new standard for the village. She was also talented at buying and stocking things that would prove popular for Christmas gifts. Men would come into the shop at 6pm on Christmas Eve desperate for my mother to suggest something for 'the wife' – with luck Mum would already know the taste of the lady concerned.

Wednesday was closing day, which my Mum spent in Manchester going round the jewellery wholesalers and repairers. She would be accompanied by her favourite sister, my Auntie Doris, who was a big influence on me. Auntie Doris lived only about 12 miles away, near Altrincham, but her visits to us involved three buses in each direction and many long waits at cold bus stops. No one in the family ever had a car, although Auntie Doris and my uncle were actually buying the semi-detached house in which they had lived since it was built in the 1930s. My uncle was a railway porter who later became a shipping clerk in a timber firm, and was very frugal, although he liked to have a good suit made. In school holidays I got taken on these Wednesday trips to Manchester, which opened up a world of big department stores, majestic but soot-blackened buildings, tea at the exotic-seeming Kardomah café, and boring waits while earrings and necklaces were ordered by the gross. The wholesalers were mostly Jewish, and my mother had great respect for their business skill, their family life and their religious observance: 'closed next week for Yom Kippur, Mrs Beith' they would announce.

The shop was fascinating, but very hard work, and Dad and I helped out. We were open all hours, and the shop bell controlled us. The vegetables or the fish under the grill for tea would be abandoned for a customer unless one of us took over. On quiet days my Mum would attempt to decorate, and just as she was single-handedly lining up a full length of pasted wallpaper on the stairs, the bell would go. Alas, she never made a lot of money out of the business, and she was left with very little when Dad's terminal illness forced her to sell up, but she enjoyed it, and we would have struggled without the extra income. The run up to Christmas was so busy that there was no time to prepare for a family celebration, so for several years we used to book in to a boarding house in Blackpool. We would share a car at 8 o'clock on Christmas Eve with friends of Auntie Doris who ran a chip shop and brought the week's considerable takings with them in a canvas bag. The big attraction was ballroom dancing at the Tower Ballroom with Reginald Dixon at the organ, and there were bracing walks on the wind-swept promenade.

Leaving aside such interludes, I was having an uneventful childhood in a pleasant community. TV and cars were things that only better-off people had. For many years, my only experience of TV was watching the Coronation in 1953 with most of the rest of the road in a house where they had won the football pools – not the £75,000 'first dividend' which everyone kept hoping for, but £600, enough for a TV and a holiday. I was very impressed by the Coronation, and even more so when I got the chance to go to London while the decorations were still up, and the Queen and the Duke of Edinburgh could be seen as they undertook carriage tours of various parts of the capital. This was all down to my Auntie Alice, my mother's other sister. She worked as housekeeper and chauffeur for a bachelor director of the *Daily Herald*, which meant that I could stay in his flat opposite the Science Museum, where I spent fascinating hours during my two childhood trips to the capital. The trip involved putting me on the train at Manchester, with my Dad tipping the guard half-a-crown to keep an eye on me and hand me over to Auntie Alice at Euston. Auntie Alice would take me to Lyons Corner Houses and London shows like *Oklahoma* and *Paint Your Wagon*. She would send me programmes from big events autographed by stage stars.

My other glimpses of a grander life were based on the fact that my best friend's dad was the chauffeur for the Town Clerk of Manchester, and if he came home after a function driving the official car, having nowhere to put it, he would park it outside our house. Like the buses it had Manchester's coat of arms painted on the side: *Concilio et Labore* was the motto, although I had no idea what it meant. Otherwise, cars were mostly driven by people who my mother thought were looking down on her.

Our perception that we were Northern was heavily reinforced by our radio listening, in which there was a sharp distinction between the news, read as it was by wonderfully plummy BBC voices like Alvar Liddell, and the slice of the day that was devoted to the BBC North Home service. From this we got our regional news and weather forecast, as well as all the entertainment programmes which were produced from Manchester and reflected Northern life, like *Club Night*. Wilfred Pickles' *Have a Go*, Al Reed's wonderful portrayal of Northern characters, and what was then to me the impenetrable *Wot Cheor Geordie* from Newcastle. It was a language I was to learn and love later. Children's programmes had a Northern opt-out once or twice a week, and featured Violet Carson, later to be the formidable character star of the early days of Coronation Street, Ena Sharples. Even high culture had a regional flavour, with what was then the BBC Northern Orchestra (now BBC Philharmonic) heard regularly.

All of a sudden, the North started to appear in the films. Previous British films had featured actors who spoke like Trevor Howard and Celia Johnson (although I still love *Brief Encounter*, and it was actually filmed in Lancashire). Then along came films about Rugby League and Ken Loach's *Kes*. And then came the Beatles, whose singing accent was not completely Americanised and bore the stamp of Liverpool: Northern became fashionable. But that is to jump ahead.

— 2 —

BEING EDUCATED

It must have been something like a whirlwind that hit the education system in the decade following the Second World War. At one and the same time, schools coped with a rapid 'baby boom' expansion in pupil numbers, a major reorganisation of secondary education, the raising of the school leaving age from 14 to 15, and the recruitment of a large work force of new teachers, trained in colleges hastily set up in whatever premises could be found. A significant number of these new teachers were men who had returned from the war. They took the opportunity they had never previously had to go to training college and take up teaching, in place of a previous manual or clerical occupation. Many of them, and many of the newly recruited women teachers, were not graduates but would certainly have gained university places if they had been born in my own generation.

We were lucky: in our rapidly expanding village, the Victorian board school had been replaced in the 1930s by the latest thing in school design – a matching pair of E-shaped single-storey buildings, one for the junior school and one for the secondary school. Long, open-sided verandahs connected the classrooms and led to the separate toilet blocks. There were playgrounds and large playing fields, along one side of which were grass mounds covering air-raid shelters – a reminder of the war, and temptingly forbidden territory. My wife

Barbara later compared this apparent luxury with the school she attended in another village a few miles away, a one-roomed 1870s school with a curtain to divide the two classes. It had chemical toilets, visited weekly for emptying by what the children called the 'custard cart'.

But even our extended premises were soon outgrown, and several classes decamped to the Methodist Sunday School across the road. Classes were large – 40 was normal, and in the year in which we took the 11-plus exam, there were 52 children in our class. Order was maintained by the teacher's force of personality, by the device of sitting every boy next to a girl in the hope that calmer influences would prevail, and by the regular administering of caning on the hand for offences which included talking out of turn. I used to claim, as a badge of honour, that this had befallen me 18 times, but in reality I think it was a total of 18 strokes, exaggerated for effect. Girls were almost never the recipients of this treatment. This seemed to us boys to be a gross injustice, since they usually had some role in whatever mischief was going on.

With such numbers we must have been a challenge to the teaching staff. And we were a diverse bunch, although not in the modern ethnic sense: the only non-white faces I ever saw in my childhood were in a visiting group of West African teachers who came round the school. Nor was there much religious diversity: there was a handful of Catholics who stood outside the school morning assembly until we had sung our hymn and said our prayer. Socially, however, the housing mix of the area allowed for considerable diversity. The many rows of miners' cottages had been sold off cheaply when the pits closed, and could be rented from local families who often owned the one they lived in and another along the row. There had been very extensive council house building by the local rural district council, and some 'overspill' council housing by the City of Salford, sending people to a new life in the country. A lot of private housing was being built, from the standard semi-detached houses to a few rather grand houses along a private road in the park. There were working farms, mainly small dairy farms delivering their own milk. Farm children brought an earthy reality, an understanding of the natural world and dialect speech into the school mix.

It was not a trouble-free utopia. There was a horrific case of a young teenager who murdered his parents. The father of a girl in my school class went to prison for larceny (itself a mystifying description – what on earth was it, I wondered?), and I well remember my mother drumming into me that although it was a bad business, I must not let anyone speak unkindly to, or about, the girl herself – she was going to miss her dad, none of it was her fault, and she would have a hard enough time without other children being nasty to her.

I am still impressed by what the teachers achieved. The only one I could not get on with at all was in the nursery class, which we all attended full-time from the age of four: that was because we were supposed to go to sleep on camp beds for half-an-hour in the afternoon. I never once went to sleep, despite the fact that in later life I would have been glad of the chance, and have occasionally found it hard to resist. The school was large enough for the headmistress to be non-teaching. She was very firm, and once had me lined up outside her study for the offence of wiping my mouth with the back of my hand after eating my school dinner. 'You come from a good family', she said, 'and I expect better manners'. I shall always be indebted to her for taking a group of us nine-year-olds on the bus to Manchester to hear the Hallé Orchestra in the Free Trade Hall, in a programme which included Richard Strauss's *Till Eulenspiegel*. There was not a lot of music in the school, but this trip laid the foundation for a life-long interest, and for a love of the music of Richard Strauss which was re-awakened many years later. She also loved the pre-Raphaelite painters and took us to see their work at Manchester City Art Gallery.

I probably did not fully appreciate the extent to which education was about passing the 11-plus, or 'the scholarship' as it was generally known. The secondary modern school next door looked exciting enough to me; it had science laboratories, and serious football; people seemed to like it there, and it would be an easy transition. Two-thirds of my friends and class-mates would go there, with a few transferring later to the grammar school by a mysterious '12 plus' process designed to identify potential which had been missed. When the day came to take the 11-plus, a certain nervousness seemed to attend my dad's 'cheerio and good luck' and my mum got me an even better breakfast than usual. An awesome silence descended upon the rows of carefully spaced desks in the parquet-floored school hall, and we set about papers in arithmetic, English and verbal reasoning (the purpose of the last being a total mystery to me at that stage). There had not been such a silence in the hall since the headmistress announced that the King had died, and we were all sent home. We had once lined up in the centre of the village to see the King pass through in an open car on his way to visit Woodford aerodrome, and I still recall him as a pale (and probably ill) man in a big black overcoat.

The sequel to the 11-plus day came at the end of term, when those of us who had passed were lined up on the stage to be applauded by the rest of the school, including those who would not share our success or our opportunity. In Cheshire roughly one-third of children always seemed to pass. For the girls, that meant going to Macclesfield County High School for Girls, a state grammar school. For the boys, the prize sounded altogether grander – the King's School. Suddenly the discussion at home was of saving up to buy a blazer, rugby shirts and a leather satchel. Education was getting serious.

In today's system I would never have got to the King's School, because it is now a wholly fee-paying school (although it does have an increasing but limited number of bursaries). Whether the high school which now takes the local pupils from 11 upwards would have given me comparable opportunities I have no way of knowing.

King's School dates from the sixteenth century, from the reign of Edward VI. In the reorganisation of 1945 it had managed to remain wholly independent while contracting with Cheshire County Council to provide for all the boys in the area who passed the 11-plus. Although it maintained its own fee-paying preparatory school, the main school had hardly any fee-paying pupils. It was, to all intents and purposes, the local boys' grammar school, with a wide six-stream intake, but it also had some of the traditions of the independent sector. This meant that rugby, a sport in which I never excelled, was compulsory, and football relegated to the playground. In the Borders, of course, as in South Wales and Cornwall, rugby union, like my dad's rugby league, has none of the 'posh' cachet it has elsewhere. In rugby I found it safer to play a rather inactive role as full-back and opt for swimming whenever there was a choice, despite the frigid temperatures of the local public baths and the fact that, with all compulsory sports being after school, swimming meant not getting home until 6pm. It could be 7pm if you were too slow getting dressed and missed the hourly train.

I presume it was the school's status which enabled it to attract several schoolmasters of very high ability. Several of those who taught me had Firsts from Oxford or Cambridge, and devoted energy and time well beyond the call of duty to imparting to us an interest in and excitement about their subjects. Their methods of teaching varied considerably, and in some cases would not have passed muster in the new training colleges, but what mattered was their knowledge, commitment, and ability to pass on their enthusiasm. The school plays in which I took part were directed by David Brierley, who went on to run the Royal Shakespeare Company. That was not the whole picture, of course: there were poor teachers, teachers who could not keep order, and teachers who had given up interest either in their subject or in their pupils. In my fourth year I had a maths teacher whose entire interest was in maintaining the quality of the cricket pitch. He usually left to attend to the grass after scribbling a few calculations on the blackboard for us to attempt in his absence for the rest of the lesson.

The headmaster was rather a figure of fun: what he did with his time was unknown to us, although it may have been keeping the finances in order and keeping the governors happy. On two occasions, however, he made an impact. One was better remembered by my late wife and her sister, because it was the girls from the High School who were the more impressed: news came to him of more than usually riotous behaviour by some of the boys on the train home. He managed somehow to race the train in his car to the next station. All King's School boys were ordered off the train, given a stern lecture, and left to explain to their parents why they had been made to wait for the next train and were late home. The second was after the school hall had been almost completely destroyed by fire. Assembly was held outside: by this time I was Deputy Head Boy, and my job was to blow a whistle and secure silence, whereupon the Head would emerge from inside the building to conduct the proceedings. Excitement and curiosity about what had happened was intense, and would have completely distracted us all for days had the Head not had the wisdom to announce that the entire school would file past the opened doors of the ruined hall, in an orderly fashion, to see the damage for ourselves. It was a rare example of common sense coming to terms with schoolboy curiosity.

The daily train journey turned out to be a pretty significant factor in my life. It was not merely that I developed the environmentally friendly habit of travelling by train whenever possible, for work or pleasure. The transition from steam to diesel had an even more significant consequence. For the first couple of years our journeys to school were by steam-hauled trains made up of four or five coaches divided into single compartments without connecting corridors. This was not considered by the authorities to be a safe environment for young ladies to travel to school, especially as some boys had been in the habit of hiding in the luggage racks until their apparently empty compartment was boarded by girls, who were then tormented for the rest of the journey. So the front two carriages were reserved for girls, and boys and other passengers travelled in the rear carriages. On the evening return journey the girls' carriages stood in a bay platform, and were attached to the train just before it departed. Segregation was the order of the day.

All changed when steam was replaced by diesel trains, which had open bus-style carriages. Segregation could not be maintained, but behaviour generally improved, and there was no longer the threat for girls or younger boys of being marooned in a compartment with bullies and tormentors. Better still, you got to meet girls. I still keep a scale model of a dark green diesel unit, because it was on such a train that I met and fell in love with Barbara, with whom I was to enjoy over 30 wonderful years of marriage. She lived in a more remote spot and had to cycle two miles to her station, the next one down the line. As our romance grew we took to getting the later train home, which was quieter, to enjoy a precious quarter of an hour together before going our separate ways to tackle homework and exam preparation.

In another way the train journey points to a difference in the way secondary education affected us. No one was driven to school by their parents. We went off on a train, into our own world. It was a world which some of our parents had not experienced at all, and it was one to which they were rarely admitted. They were allowed on sufferance for speech day, school plays and musical performances, and I suppose for parents' evenings, although I have no recollection of my parents actually going to one. It was not, in more recent parlance, 'cool' to be seen with your parents around the school. All educational thinking suggests that this is a very bad state of affairs, close links between school and parents being essential to supporting educational attainment. But it simply was not like that for us: school was our world, and having a world which was our own was part of growing up.

Meanwhile, what were we learning? In the first two years, it was the whole range of subjects, but after three years in the school there was a rigid division between those who went into the science stream and those in what were bizarrely called the 'modern' forms, where English, history, and languages made up most of the curriculum. For some of us this separation came even earlier; boys who were thought to have the potential to enter Oxford or Cambridge scholarship exams missed out the third year and went straight into the two-year preparation for 'O-level' (as what became GCSE was then known). This certainly benefited me in the long run, but it was fairly disruptive at the time. As well as causing me to miss rather important bits of biology and leaving odd gaps in my knowledge of history, it started a decline in my grasp of mathematics which was accelerated by the inadequacies of the aforementioned cricket pitch-obsessed maths teacher. Skipping a year also had social consequences: you were suddenly amongst boys a year older, and you were desperate to be one of them, or at least not to appear to be the baby of the form. My genuine interest in many of the subjects had to compete with the need to be part of a more nonchalant coffee-bar culture of pretended sophistication in which excessive diligence in study was not fashionable. Success, if any, had to be achieved without visible effort. I shall always be grateful to the English master who saw what was happening and took appropriate action. As I walked casually in to school from the train one morning, having enjoyed coffee and toast to the sound of the latest Bill Haley or Gene Vincent record in a snack bar en route, every boy I met seemed to be delivering the same ominous message: 'Mr Burt wants to see you on your own straight after assembly.' I duly and apprehensively presented myself to this thoughtful, rather other-worldly man who was my guide to the poetry of Shakespeare's tragedies and the mysticism of George Herbert's verse. To this day I cannot precisely remember what he said, but the general import was that I was well on the way to throwing aside my own potential and the sacrificial efforts of parents, aunts, uncles, teachers, etc., as well as wasting the ratepayers' money which had sent me to this establishment. It worked. Thank God for people who give timely warnings. Would that there were more of them.

It was nearly too late for O-level German. An idle master had left my own indolence in the subject unnoticed, until my poor mark in the German mock examination made it impossible to ignore .'You will fail', said the German master. There was no hope of progress in the remaining weeks with a teacher in whom I had no confidence at all, so I got Stopp's *Manual of Modern German* out of the library and raised my game to a decent pass standard in about six weeks. Alas, for maths it was too late. A mental block had developed to the working out of mathematical concepts. I thought I understood them, but I could not demonstrate this to the satisfaction of the examiners. It left a potentially fatal gap in university entrance qualifications. The gap was hastily filled with the help of the very kind head of Biology – an enthusiastic Methodist – who gave up two lunch hours a week, and brilliantly compressed his subject to enable me to pass it in two terms. It not only filled the qualification gap: it gave me a small, much-needed if limited insight into the world of science which the school's rigid separation had denied me.

My determination to pass German was partly based on a desire to prove the German master wrong, but it also reflected a love of languages. It was a love for understanding, speaking and reading the languages, although it was not supported by an adequate determination to learn grammar and vocabulary. Latin and German, with their relatively formalised grammar, were not the languages I coped with best, although I passed them both. With six years of it at school, my French, although adequate, should be much better than it is. That is partly down to lack of practice – France seemed a long way from us in the North, and I never got to France, or indeed to anywhere abroad, until I was 20. Welsh intrigued me, because I heard people speaking it when we took holidays in a rented caravan in the Lleyn peninsula in North Wales. I got myself a book, watched afternoon Welsh-language programmes on Granada TV, and went to a Welsh chapel in nearby Stockport. Although I have never lived in Wales, I now speak the language better than most of the others I have tried to learn, and my eccentric persistence in learning it opened many doors to friendships, hospitality and musical experiences in Wales and amongst Welsh-speaking people in England. It also gave me some of my first experiences of being interviewed for television, and I have continued to do occasional interviews for Welsh-language programmes, with some last-minute revision on the Welsh words for devolution, coalition, privatisation and other concepts which did not feature in text-book or chapel Welsh. And then there was Norwegian, first picked up on family holidays in Norway. It is our nearest foreign country in the North East, then readily accessible with ferry services from the Tyne and flights from Newcastle. Later plans to spend a sabbatical at a Norwegian university were set aside for politics. In preparation for this, I had been doing some work on my Norwegian in the language lab, but I could do with more vocabulary and more practice. I remain dissatisfied with the very low level of basic proficiency in languages which is accepted in Britain; it puts so many British people at a disadvantage, and restricts both business and cultural opportunities. It has nothing to do with any inferior capacity for languages: I believe it results from lack of motivation and need. In countries whose language is little spoken elsewhere, like the Netherlands and the Scandinavian countries, high levels of proficiency in English are achieved with no greater amount of time and resources than are given to French in British schools. The need for communication drives the learning process.

As well as a love of languages, and even more significantly in terms of impact on my life, the King's School was the main means of encouraging a love of music, and in particular a love of playing or performing music. Early in my time at the school we gained a dedicated and enthusiastic head of music. Out went the unlearned tonic sol-fa wall charts, and in came a wide range of instrumental tuition and musical activity, both orchestral and choral. If we were willing to learn an instrument we had access to superb professional teachers. I learned the trumpet from Arthur Lockwood, who had been principal trumpet in the Hallé and was principal in the BBC Philharmonic (then the BBC Northern): he had recorded Handel's *Let the Bright Seraphim* with Isobel Baillie. The school orchestra was led in concerts by Barry Griffiths, who taught stringed instruments and went on to be Leader of the London Symphony Orchestra. By the time I left school, I had taken part as an orchestral player or occasionally as a choral singer in all the major oratorios, including the Bach passions, four Gilbert and Sullivan operettas and several concerts, as well as taking both O- and A-level music, the latter squeezed into the first year of sixth form as a supplement to my main diet of A-levels. It was a wonderful grounding for which I have been grateful throughout my life.

As O-level and then A-level approached, there came the heavy concentration of work which tended to cut out many social activities and segregate the academically ambitious from the rest of our age group. Much of the work I found intensely interesting and exciting: I was fascinated by the way writers used the English language, from the poetry of the speeches in Shakespeare's tragedies to the graphic perspective of the landscapes described by Thomas Hardy. The political and religious conflicts of sixteenth and seventeenth century England were fascinating and stirring, and the development of our system of government through the massive social changes wrought by the industrial revolution laid the foundation for an interest which was to take over my life.

After A-level the benefit of the 'skipped' year kicked in. I still had a year in which to do Oxford or Cambridge scholarship exams. It would never have occurred to my parents, or to many people in our village, that this was something I would have the chance to do. It is entirely down to the vision and encouragement of teachers that such an option was opened to me. The Heads of English, History and French set about training the pupils they believed could succeed. They chose 'horses for courses' by getting us to apply to colleges to which they thought we were well matched. They had never tried for Balliol before, but they encouraged me to apply in the belief that it was a college on the look-out for determined applicants from a working-class background – one of the better fruits, perhaps, of the Marxist beliefs of Christopher Hill, then History tutor and later Master of the College. They were right, and after a freezing December week in rooms in the College and a forbidding set of exams in the austere hall of Keble College followed by interviews with Christopher Hill and John Prest, I was successful. A scholarship brought with it a useful extra income of £80 a year, equivalent to a 20% uplift in the very adequate full maintenance grant to which, in those balmy days, my admission entitled to me. I had no need to go for the oral examination in Welsh required for my second choice, Jesus College, where I had been tempted by the idea of winning a scholarship endowed for people who were either Welsh or could speak the language. The list of Balliol scholarships even appeared in *The Times*. That was it. I was in. And I had the rest of the school year to spare.

So what should I do with two terms? Today I might have taken the chance to work abroad. As it was, I opted for the security of staying on to take another A-level, in economics and government, to give me a start for the Philosophy, Politics and Economics I had decided to read at Oxford. It gave me time to spend in two magnificent libraries: the round reading room of Manchester City Library and the wonderful Gothic spaces of John Rylands Library, Basil Champneys' masterpiece which has recently been superbly restored. It is a treasury, amongst other things, of nonconformist history. Then it was a haven of peace, relatively little used, where I could follow ideas along whatever route I chanced to find among its books and journals. The truth is that I had already got to know these libraries on unauthorised absences from school prior to O-level, when I would occasionally get the train in the wrong direction in order to spend a day in the city's libraries and bookshops: it was known as 'skiving', but nowadays you could call it self-directed study.

This period also gave me the chance to develop a sideline I had begun when an advertising salesman in our village decided to set up a free newspaper. I had gone in with him to be its sole reporter. It was a golden opportunity for both of us: the village was expanding rapidly and small businesses were looking to advertise, particularly home and garden materials. Free newspapers had scarcely been seen at that time, and the newspapers in the nearby towns were fairly complacent about covering the village. I wrote reports of parish council meetings and church events and wrote an anonymous comment column; all this was done for pocket money while I was still at school, with the added benefit that, with my modest post-scholarship timetable, I could slip out of school to report meetings of the Rural District Council and public inquiries which took place in the town. It was superb training – it taught me how to write press releases, it gave me a through grounding in local government, and it even gave me a subject for my B. Litt. thesis several years later. The paper is still going, 50 years on.

I left school with most of my friends bound for university. One, who was a very good violinist, was not: he left school at 18 and went straight into the bank, a fate which teachers warned would be ours if we did not work harder. While we became lecturers, vicars, museum curators and headmasters, he applied himself very effectively and ably and became the Chief Executive of Lloyds TSB. Peter Ellwood probably earned more than the rest of us put together.

— 3 —

BEING CHAPEL

Religion was not always a noticeable feature in my childhood home, but it became more so as I grew up. There was no sign at all in my father's family of association with the church or religion, except that, in the Glaswegian sense, they were Protestants rather than Catholics. When one of my father's brothers married a Polish Catholic they did not know quite what to make of her. She was a rather abrupt woman who believed that they should 'keep themselves to themselves', so we never learned much more about Catholicism. Curiously, when I later looked up the records in the Register Office in Edinburgh, all my father's ancestors were married in dissenting Presbyterian churches: the Reformed Presbyterians or the Associate Presbyterians rather than the established Church of Scotland, which suffered a serious split for nearly a century after 1843.[1]

My mother, in keeping with her frequent house moves, had in her youth gone sometimes to the Wesleyan Chapel and sometimes to the Church of England. Her sister, who had remained in Manchester, had stayed with the Wesleyans and met my uncle there.

Moving to our village had broken these ties, and I was christened in the Church of England along with many of the other babies of that year. The Parish Church did lively business in baptisms. But when it came to Sunday School, the Methodists had more to offer. There were two large

Methodist chapels in the village (previously Primitive and United Methodist Free Church, respectively, for Methodist historians to note) and there were two small chapels on the rural outskirts. Over half of the children in the village probably attended a Methodist Sunday School, with well over 100 children attending at each of the big chapels. Ours was an area of Sunday Schools: the nearby towns of Macclesfield, Bollington and Stockport had huge Sunday School buildings as big as their textile mills. Sunday School was how parents got peace and quiet on Sunday afternoons, and families who rarely if ever 'darkened the door' of the chapel packed their children off to Sunday School. There were classes for every age group from primary to seniors, and the year was punctuated by three major Sunday School events. These were the 'walks', the trip and the Anniversary. So engraved was the Anniversary on our consciousness that Barbara, who also went to a Methodist Sunday School, invented in her childhood an imaginary friend called Annie Versary. The walks were our imitation of the Manchester Whit Walks, when, on two different days, scores of Protestant and Catholic Sunday Schools would process through the city streets with banners and bands. So grand was the event that it had live coverage in the early years of Granada TV. Bearing in mind that we were only a village, our Sunday School procession was a pretty big affair, with all the chapels and churches supplying a banner, and contingents of children of all ages. Banners had cords attached to them – some held down the banner against the winds and, like the banner itself, were the preserve of young men; others were decorative ribbons, held by white-gloved girls. The youngest children were contained within decorative ropes, also held by white-gloved girls: in front of it all was the village band, which I was later to join. At designated points throughout the area the procession would stop for hymns to be sung. Parents crowded the pavements. After a long day's walking the reward was a spectacular tea, laid on in each of the chapels for its own contingent.

Then there was the Anniversary. For this, children learned songs and recitations, and these would feature in the morning and afternoon services. But it had not been forgotten that, on the posters of the more old fashioned chapels, these were 'the Anniversary SERMONS' (in very large type) which will be 'preached (D.V.) at 10.30 and 6'. A celebrated preacher would be booked several years ahead. Hymn sheets would replace the hymn books, because there would never be enough books to go around. Anthems would be rehearsed by an augmented choir. The twin objectives seemed to be to have an unforgettably inspiring service, and to raise as much money as possible for the activities of the Sunday School. This was achieved partly by attracting a packed congregation (extra chairs or benches brought into the aisles being an index of success), a published subscription list which would include donations from those from far and wide who had been to the Sunday School in their childhood, and the choice of an unusually large number of men to carry the collection boxes round the congregation (and they were always men). Being invited to 'take a box' at the Anniversary, even if you had only an occasional association with the chapel, carried with it an unstated but firm expectation that you would ensure that your box started its course around the pews with at least a £1 note and preferably a £5 note in it. The collection preceded the hymn before the sermon, and certain of the collectors would disappear with it into the Sunday School rooms. During the closing hymn one of them would excitedly hand up to the preacher in the pulpit a scrap of paper from which he would announce the grand sum achieved that day. To some this seemed a rather mercenary prelude to the benediction.

One of the things the money paid for was the annual Sunday School trip. At a time when many children had no chance of a holiday away, this meant the excitement of an outing to Blackpool, Southport or

25

St. Anne's with implausible cries of 'I can see the Tower' or 'I can see the sea' beginning at a fairly early stage on the bus journey. I later found that the Sunday School trip had a similar significance in the Scottish Border towns until relatively recently, where it took the form of a day at Berwick-upon-Tweed's promenade and beach at Spittal. The day began with a grand send-off from the market place of Kelso and others towns by the Provost and local ministers. I also remember one elderly Northumbrian who confessed that he had attended all three of the Sunday Schools in his village, C. of E., Presbyterian and Brethren, for the requisite number of Sundays to qualify for three separate Sunday School trips.

What was striking about Sunday Schools at that time was that they attracted large numbers of children from families who were not chapel- or churchgoers. Sunday School provided an understanding of what Christianity was about to people who had few other opportunities to learn Christian values, to understand the role Christianity played in society or to develop a spiritual life of their own. They provided valued community events, and they gave at least minimal contact with organised religion for parents who would not otherwise have it. I greatly respect the work of the countless men and women who gave up much of their time, especially their own precious Sunday afternoons, to Christian education of children and young people. They include many forgotten heroines and heroes of Christian service and example. The decline has been a loss.

The decline was partly, if unwittingly, encouraged by the churches themselves. The view developed that there was too much separation between Sunday School and the regular worship of the church, so it was argued that Sunday schools should happen at the same time as the main service: parents could bring their children and stay for the service; children would attend part of the service and leave for Sunday

School classes. The result was that in many places, only those parents who were regular churchgoers brought their children to the new style Sunday Schools, and the time limit set by involvement in the main service limited the scope of Sunday School activities. There were many other factors in the decline, particularly the massive expansion of other family, sporting, children's and commercial activity on Sundays (with greater financial means available to many families to take part in them), and the much wider availability of private cars for family trips. Latterly there has been the added problem of divided families in which the children may go away to stay with or be taken out by a separated parent at the weekend.

Not that Sunday School was always a great and life-enhancing experience. It cannot have been grabbing my attention when, at the age of nine, the words of a regularly broadcast song about 'cruising down the river on a Sunday afternoon' led me to think that there were limitless delights to be enjoyed outside Sunday School, so I stopped attending. We had no river: we had an attractive canal, but there were very few boats on it and none which would offer me a trip on the water. I had to content myself with riding my bike along the towpath. The only time I can remember any particular excitement from my new found Sabbath freedom was when a landslide caused the collapse of the platform at Middlewood Higher station, a remote outpost in the woods where stations were built on two lines, one of which passed over the other, thus enabling a change of trains to connect Buxton to Macclesfield. By taking messages from the repair gang to the next station on my bike I earned a brief spell on the footplate of the steam locomotive which stood there for most of that Sunday, and, with much excitement, I drank tea boiled over the firebox.

The alternative excitements proved few, and Sunday School came back into my life a few years later at the more ambitious Sunday School of the more popular chapel. They actually ran a taxi service loaded with children from our part of the village, although we went on our bikes. Out of the Sunday School grew a self-starting youth group – the adults held back and let a group of about 20 of us who had been drawn to Christian faith organise our own activities, which included worship, bible study, walking trips and music. Many of us were learning instruments, and we built up a small orchestra which occasionally played for services. Some became teachers in the Sunday School, and our focus was the Sunday evening service, where teenagers would take up the back pews, and we would have our own meetings afterwards, substituting evening walks in the summer months.

The minister, Rev. Arthur Noon, spent 11 years in the village, which was unusual in Methodism, and remained there in retirement. He was an ex-mineworker from D.H. Lawrence territory on the Nottinghamshire–Derbyshire border. He seemed to share with Lawrence, despite a sharply differing outlook on life, an extraordinarily vivid use of English which made him a much-loved preacher. He was not a great administrator, and brought despair to those who wanted immaculate order in both the business and the worship of the chapel, but congregations hung on his every word. He was not even an easy conversationalist; his manner and ways were quaint, and he had almost nothing in common with the interests and outlook of young people, yet they revered him as much as older people did. He had a capacity, based on his vivid language, to lift the curtain to reveal a spiritual world beyond everyday things. There is an Isaac Watts hymn which goes:

> Give me the wings of faith to rise
> Within the veil and see
> The saints above, how great their joys,
> How bright their glories be.

He gave people wings of faith. Bright glories were opened up. Something wonderfully worthwhile was brought into ordinary lives.

Under his encouragement four young men from the local chapel were to become Methodist ministers, and others became local (lay) preachers, as I did. Religion has played a major part in the life and careers of many other men and women who grew up in that environment. Prior to this, my mum had joined the chapel choir and my dad, for the first time in his life, became a regular chapelgoer and remained a committed Christian for the rest of his days.

Methodists like the idea of conversion experiences. John Wesley had one – he felt his 'heart strangely warmed' and was convinced that he was saved by Christ and must put his trust in Him. Many people have dramatic, life-changing experiences in which they adopt a faith they had not previously had. But John Wesley was a 'cradle Christian', brought up in a vicarage with a very devout mother, and he had been a clergyman in the Church of England for several years when he had this experience. It was not a new faith for him, it was a new experience of faith. Among those to whom he preached as he tirelessly toured Britain would be many who had a Christian belief and some who had none. What mattered was that his preaching awakened in them a sense of the significance of that belief for their lives. So did the preaching of the Primitive Methodists among the people of nearby North Staffordshire, among the miners of County Durham and among the fishermen of the Northumberland coast. For a group of young people in a Cheshire village in the 1960s, that is what preaching and the life of the chapel community did.

— 4 —

BEING LIBERAL

My first childhood encounter with politics was an odd one. At the end of our road was a grand house set back in its own grounds, owned by a businessman who kept horses for riding and had a carriage – probably an old Hansom cab. In the 1950s elections there were very tight rules on the number of cars the parties could use to get the voters to the polls. These rules did not cover horse-drawn carriages, and the businessman, a staunch Conservative, made his carriage available for the day. Since we knew the groom and I had a day off school for the election, I begged a ride on the box and spent an enjoyable day riding round the village and opening the carriage doors for voters assumed by the organisers to be Tory. Calls at the Committee Room, mainly to eat some of the hot pot which had been thoughtfully provided, introduced me to the marked register. This is a copy of the electors' list, set out on boards, marked up with the results of canvassing, from which names are given to those who are out knocking on doors to persuade known supporters to come and vote. Party tellers at the polling stations send in lists throughout the day so that those who have already voted can be ticked off. I was slightly surprised to find my parents on the list marked as Conservative voters. I had no recollection at all of any political discussion in our house, except general comment on what was happening in the country, and certainly none that revealed a party

31

allegiance. I knew that some of my friends' families were Labour, which seemed to be closely related to whether they worked for the Co-op or were active in the Union at the Avro aircraft factory in Woodford. Looking back on it, I guess that my dad's Glasgow origins, as they were nominally Protestant, might have been nominally Unionist. My mum's father had become an independent councillor just before his death, and he probably moved in predominantly Conservative circles at that stage. But it seemed unimportant, except when a canvasser returned to say that several people on whom she called were refusing to vote because there was no Liberal candidate. 'Tell them Sir Arthur[2] will be a Liberal for them' was the cynical retort of the fearsome woman in charge of the Conservative Committee rooms. The dishonesty stuck in my mind.

Quite a few years elapsed before, in the early years at King's School, I started to be more interested in politics. Political issues did feature in our Sunday School class discussions – particularly the Christian attitude to war. Three of the Sunday School teachers were pacifists and had served in ambulance units as conscientious objectors, while their own brothers, equally committed Christians, had been in fighting units. There is no doubt that I was also influenced by the three schoolmasters who taught me most and gave me most encouragement. Philosophically all three were liberal, and two were avowed (although inactive) Liberals in their politics. In the dark days of 1950s Liberal weakness, they wore this allegiance almost as a badge of eccentricity, along with their habit of riding old bicycles and liking the town's then unfashionable industrial buildings and streets. Those were the days when the election results on the wireless had a repeated chorus line 'And the Liberal candidate lost his deposit'.

The basis for a philosophical conversion to Liberalism was in my reading, historical, religious and political. Christian, and particularly Protestant, belief in free will and individual responsibility to God pointed to political freedom and the sacredness of the individual. The Whig interpretation of history, with Liberalism challenging the abuse and concentration of power, suffused school history. Reading Milton's prose works in English literature brought me into contact with the passionate commitment to free speech which made Milton's *Areopagitica* the volume that each Liberal Party President handed on to his successor. Reading French writings both about the persecution of the Huguenots and about the Revolution generated a conviction that societies need tolerance, and they need the capacity to achieve peaceful change. Violent revolution often merely transfers brutal authority from one group to another.

But could not Liberalism be pursued without attempting to revive a political party which at that time seemed in danger of becoming extinct? Why not join another party? The Conservatives, as well as seeming socially distant, a party led by those from the most privileged backgrounds, were pursuing a severely authoritarian colonial policy in Kenya and Malawi (then Nyasaland) and failing to challenge apartheid in South Africa. Week by week the *Observer* and the *Spectator* (then a relatively radical paper) would report on conditions in detention camps and repressive measures against opposition. The religious press reported the horrors of apartheid. So why not join the Labour Party? It was in opposition, and it had attacked some of these things; it had opposed the Suez invasion (which, at the age of 13, I had thought was justified until the truth emerged and I learned a lesson about the need for effective scrutiny of potentially dishonest government). Labour in the 1960s really held no appeal for a philosophical liberal except on the most cynically careerist grounds or on the basis of wholly naïve optimism about Labour's capacity to change. The redoubtable Lady Violet Bonham Carter, confronted by a Liberal who was joining Labour to change it from within, retorted 'My dear boy, the Labour Party is a veritable graveyard of Trojan horses'. Its dominant ideology appeared to be collectivist rather than Liberal, drawing as it did on trade union notions of 'one out, all out'. Labour conveyed a sense that it knew better than we did what was best for working-class people like us. Its leading figures, some of them from very privileged backgrounds like Tony (then Anthony Wedgwood) Benn, seemed to be telling us that in our own aspirations we should be content with a great deal less than they had enjoyed all their lives. Worst of all, Labour seemed to have unlimited and unjustified confidence in the capacity of the state to run everything. Experience of the railways at this time gave no support to this belief. And Labour seemed unconcerned about the dangers of concentrating more and more power in the hands of a controlling few. Soviet communism, about which some Labour figures seemed amazingly naïve, gave ample warning both of the inefficiency of concentrated power and of its dangers.

I write of the perception I had at the time, which clearly did not take account of the cross-current of opinion going on within both of the parties, which in the Conservatives led to Harold Macmillan's 'wind of change' speech in South Africa and, on the Labour side, to the massive upheavals and splits which eventually left the way open for Tony Blair and 'New Labour'. But it was how those parties appeared and, to a large extent, behaved. For a growing minority it was proof that an avowedly Liberal Party was still needed, perhaps more than ever.

Jo Grimond had sensed this and challenged the party to come alive around core Liberal principles. It was beginning to show results. Aided by the high-profile candidacy of Ludovic Kennedy in a seat with a Liberal tradition, the first extensively televised by-election campaign in Rochdale in 1958 showed what Liberals could achieve, winning 35% of the votes. Then Mark Bonham Carter won the Torrington by-election, the first Liberal by-election victory since before the war. There was a Liberal Party to join. I had to join it.

But where, and how? I looked up a guide in the Library and found that the local Liberal Party secretary was in fact the Sunday School Superintendent at the chapel. I suppose it was not such a surprise. When I asked him if I could join the Liberal Party he said 'Oh, nobody's done that for a long time ... I don't think I've got any forms'. He managed to find one, and he and I set about creating a branch, recruiting members, finding candidates for local elections, and winning some of them. We attended Executive meetings of the Macclesfield division, which was having some limited success in the town but it lay within a very safe Conservative seat. We got some advice from the more successful neighbouring constituency of Cheadle (now divided into the two Liberal Democrat-held seats of Cheadle and Hazel Grove), and I helped in that constituency in 1959, when Macclesfield did not even have a Liberal candidate. Cheadle was won at the subsequent election by Michael Winstanley, who was later to be my colleague at Westminster. The Cheadle team encouraged me to go to the party conference in Edinburgh, and with a lift in their car and a generous £7 donation for my subsistence from the Macclesfield chairman I was launched into political life.

— 5 —

BEING AT OXFORD

If secondary school was our own world, largely independent of parents, university was even more so. There were parental preparations: the college sent a set of precise requirements which every undergraduate had to have sent up in advance, including tablecloths, dusters and crockery for the college servants to set out, and my mum followed it to the letter. All was duly assembled, packed and despatched by my dad, whose working skills were satisfyingly relevant. The trunk containing clothes and books was duly despatched in advance on British Railways, and with a couple of my friends, I set off by train to a distant city and a different life.

Good friends who were a year ahead of me had invited me to Oxford for a weekend during the previous term to get the hang of the place, and that was invaluable. The buildings and gardens were entrancing. The range of activities available was mind-blowing. The changed routine of dinner at 7 and meetings and concerts starting at 8.30 or 9 was a bit puzzling at first to a Northern boy. The all-embracing provision of room, breakfast, lunch, dinner, bed-making and cleaning left ample time free for both work and leisure. It also created habits of dependence on the domestic skills of others which proved hard to shake off and fairly exasperating to those on whom I have since relied.

I was pretty quickly sold on the merits of the college system, and of Balliol as an example of it. Academic standards were high, and you were surrounded by people doing a wide range of subjects from whom you could learn a great deal. A huge range of lectures was available, and you could pick and choose, pursuing subjects beyond your own discipline and course. Philosophy quickly grabbed my attention as the most exciting of the components of the Politics, Philosophy and Economics (PPE) course, once I had struggled through the algebraic formal logic for which my past mathematical failures had left me ill-prepared. Politics should have been my preferred subject, and in political history, political philosophy and political theory the lectures and tutorials were good – we had Isaiah Berlin, John Plamenatz and Richard Hare among the stimulating array of lecturers. In political science itself, however, Oxford at the time was something of a backwater, with much of the interesting work going on at Manchester and L.S.E., while at Essex a fashionable trend was leading towards mathematical approaches to the subject both in theoretical concepts and in the enumeration of anything empirical which was capable of being counted. The full impact of this approach was yet to come, but you could get through PPE politics without being aware of it at all. Economics was potentially exciting and certainly entertaining with Thomas Balogh as tutor: the trouble was that he was forever disappearing to advise first the French government and then the Wilson government, upon whom he wished the unloved Selective Employment Tax. Even when present for tutorials he might lie on the floor or disappear behind the curtain; the undergraduate who paused in reading his essay, assuming Balogh was asleep or had left the room, was upbraided with 'Vy haff you stopped? Continue!' It was only in my final year, concentrating on public administration and local government under the guidance of Bryan Keith-Lucas of Nuffield College, that politics as a subject regained its excitement.

Politics as an activity took rather a back seat while I was at Balliol, except for vacation help in elections back home. I was a member of the Liberal Club, but not an active one, unlike my contemporary and long-time parliamentary colleague Paul Tyler. Things were to change later in my two years as a graduate student. In the meantime, I think I was also intimidated by the bluster and apparent self-confidence of the public school products who largely dominated Union Society politics. The Union was widely thought to be the natural training ground for politics as a career, which was not really part of my plan, and attendance at a couple of debates did nothing for my confidence. Union oratory, although occasionally very good and sometimes genuinely witty, shared with the House of Commons a preoccupation with entertainment and a desire to ridicule rather than a wish to reach solutions by discussion. It was a training for a House of Commons which was already in decline, in a style of rhetoric which would soon become outdated.

Religion, on the other hand, remained important to me at university. Oxford offered endless opportunities to listen to lectures on theology and religious history, to engage in argument and discussion about religion, to sample different kinds of worship, and to feel that religion and spirituality was an interest shared with many other people of differing backgrounds and lively minds. Whether in a small group in a weekday service in the college chapel or in a congregation of 500 in the Wesley Memorial Church, there was inspiration and exploration. Local preaching also took me out into the village chapels in the Oxfordshire countryside, which was a welcome reminder of real life outside a very cushioned Oxford environment. There was also welcome home cooking from hospitable members of the often very small congregations.

My religious experience was broadened in my third year when I took a room in a declining Unitarian theological college, Manchester College (since re-invented and thriving as the more broadly based Harris Manchester College). The room was available because there was only a handful of students for the Unitarian ministry, who, with a Buddhist and others of diverse views, constituted the student body. I knew the Unitarians, who were noticeable in Cheshire with three fascinating chapels built in the 1690s in Macclesfield, Dean Row and Knutsford. It was at Knutsford that Mrs Gaskell's husband was Unitarian minister and the town was the basis for 'Cranford'. Barbara, by then my fiancée, had attended a primary school originally set up by the Unitarians although run as a county school, and its ownership reverted to the Dean Row chapel when a new county school was built. Unitarianism is not, as is often supposed, defined by opposition to the doctrine of the Trinity, but much more by its rejection of any requirement to subscribe to a creed, which leaves the way open for a very wide range of views. Its role has been lessened by the greater breadth of beliefs now accepted within the Church of England and several of the Free Churches; a colleague of mine described it rather unfairly as 'a church for unbelievers who like religion'. A sixteenth-century room on Holywell and access to yet another delightful library combined with a lively intellectual and social environment to make Manchester College a very happy place for me. By a strange twist of fate I returned there 40 years later for the birthday party of my cousin's husband, who had been closely involved in the fund-raising which ensured the college's survival, although he was unaware at the time of a family link with the college.

A large part of my second year at university had been disrupted by my Dad's worsening illness and death. Bronchitis and emphysema had forced him to give up work and made him dependent on regular access to oxygen. My Mum had to give up the shop, and we had settled in a pleasant small terraced cottage, where Dad increasingly slept downstairs and was often unable to get up. He put up nobly with my bad piano playing and my even worse attempts to accompany myself singing in what had become his bedroom as well as our sitting room. My mother's sister, Auntie Doris, took three buses to visit him every week, and her irrepressible humour cheered him up and brought some brightness to an increasingly depressed household. Dad's transfer to hospital in Stockport brought me home for the whole term, as Mum coped with the increasing certainty of his death, and the ups and downs of his treatment and condition. There were numerous recalls to the hospital, involving a long bus journey. He seemed to be slipping away. The end came as an end to suffering, but it was still shattering, especially for Mum, who had not quite made it to a Silver Wedding in a devoted marriage. I should have been more understanding of the moods and tempers which the situation had caused to Mum, and should have been even more so as she tried to adjust to a life on her own, as I had to do myself many years later. When you find these things out for yourself it is too late, and often too late even to make amends to those you should have loved and understood so much better.

My final year demanded a lot more concentration on study, and getting a First became my target. Final examinations in Oxford are taken in *sub-fusc* – black suit, white shirt, white bow tie and gown – so it feels more like going out to a grand dinner than sealing your fate in a series of written papers. There was no element of continuous or coursework assessment in those days. What there was, however, if you were on a borderline between two classes, was a *viva voce* examination. In the same formal attire, you were confronted by 8 or 10 examiners and questioned. I was duly summoned and presented myself for what was clearly a review of my moral philosophy paper to see if it could be 'upgraded to first', as they say on airlines. After 10 minutes or so I left the room, waited a while and was summoned back to be told 'We have voted you an encore, Mr Beith', clearly indicating a division of view among the examiners. When I eventually got the result, with details of the papers, the First had eluded me – a fatal mixture of high and weaker grades had not, in the end, been rescued by the moral philosophy *viva*. It had not been my day.

It turned out not to be a problem. During the final year, I had been increasingly attracted by Nuffield College. Lord Nuffield, whose car factory had created industrial Oxford, had been prevailed upon to put his money into a graduate college specialising in economics, political and social sciences. With some uncertainty, and after rejecting one design for the college which he thought looked like a tropical hospital, he gave Oxford a college with an appearance of Cotswold cuddliness but with a fierce and generally productive competitiveness in academic fields in which the university had been underperforming. I applied for a studentship and got it, which meant rooms in college, freedom to pursue a higher degree, opportunities to teach, and unrivalled access to academic discussion among some of the most able men and women in Nuffield's areas of specialism. Bryan Keith-Lucas and David Butler were those with whom I worked most closely, Bryan on local government and David on the press coverage of election campaigns. I contributed a chapter to his 1964 election volume.[3] Then Bryan Keith-Lucas left to take up a Professorship at Canterbury, and I was left with the then Warden, D.N. Chester, as supervisor. Chester had worked for Beveridge on his Report in 1942, but by this time was largely interested in football (on which he chaired a Commission) and not much interested in students. We did not get on. Nuffield offered so much else in the way of academic encouragement that it scarcely mattered in the long term, but did cause complications in working on my thesis.

Between my first and second years, Barbara and I got married. We had agreed that, as teenage sweethearts, it would probably be quite a good thing for us not to try to be in the same university city: Barbara's passion was botany, and she was accepted at Birmingham where she found the course outstandingly good, under Professors Hawkes and Heslop-Harrison. The fact that we were both enjoying what we wanted to do eased the pain of separation, which was broken only by occasional weekends, or day train trips to meet in places in between like Leamington and Evesham. But our love remained strong, and we married and seized the chance of a college flat in North Oxford for my second Nuffield year. It was memorable for the fact that T.E. Lawrence had lived in a strange brick hut at the bottom of the garden, and for the day our ceiling fell in from the flooded bathroom of the Jaguar-driving junior research fellow who lived above. In later life I encountered him as the Foreign Office Legal Adviser. Barbara worked as a research assistant in the Department of Agriculture, and thoroughly enjoyed helping to develop knowledge of the polar transport of auxins.

There was also a political interlude. I agreed to be one of two council candidates for a ward in the city which we were unlikely at that time to win (although we have won it consistently in recent years). It is the literal truth to say that my election address was produced on the back of a fag packet. Wills Woodbine cigarettes used to be sold in paper packets of five; when this practice ceased, the Oxford Liberal agent acquired very cheaply a large stock of the green paper previously destined for the packets, green being then the Liberal colour in Oxford. The size and rather sickly colour of my first ever invitation to voters to support me were determined by this oddity.

To make matters worse, my fellow candidate in the two-member ward was one William Pinching, and from a distance the only words which stood out on our poster were 'BEITH PINCHING'. We lost. You live and learn.

They had been great days to be at university if you were from a family with no means. I had a full grant, a scholarship, no fees and no need of a student loan. Nuffield offered a privileged existence in the world of postgraduate studies. Equally, they were great days to look for a university job in politics, because universities were expanding, and the teaching of my subject was expanding. Early in my second year I received a visit in college from a head of department of a Scottish university, inviting me to apply for a prematurely vacant post. I declined it because I would have lost most of my second Nuffield year. Offers of tenured posts like that would be unthinkable today. I nearly secured a college fellowship, but was beaten by someone more senior, with at least a modest research record and teaching experience at LSE to his credit. It would probably have been very bad for me to settle into Oxford life, proceeding from undergraduate to don without any intervening experience of the real world outside – at least, that is what Barbara said, and she was usually right. I applied for a post at the then new Lancaster University for which I was second choice, staying the night for the interview at a hotel so old fashioned that its bills still had a line for 'servant's board'. Then I applied to Newcastle, was interviewed and got the job. It was one of the best decisions I made. Now I was really in the North.

— 6 —

HEADING BACK NORTH

Durham cathedral, magnificent in the early morning light, was Barbara's first impression of the North East, because it provided the breathtaking view from the window of the sleeping compartment as we arrived by overnight train. We had packed our belongings into the removal van from our temporary home in Oxford, and travelled up overnight by train, as you could in those days. The second impression was a different one: we boarded a wooden carriage of the ancient electric train which ran from Newcastle to the coast. The only other traveller to get in the carriage was obviously drunk, which at eight in the morning seemed surprising. He looked around before pronouncing 'Jesus Christ, it's nee smoking in here!' before politely moving on to the next carriage. With this interesting start we completed our journey to Tynemouth. I had rented a flat there which was our home until we put down the £200 deposit on a house in Corbridge. The house cost us £3,600. To buy it now you would need to multiply that figure by almost 100. My salary for the same period would only need to be multiplied by about 10 to reach today's university salary levels. That is the scale of house price inflation, which came late to the North East but soon made up for lost time.

Newcastle University was a good place to be. It was increasingly popular with student applicants, although the city had not yet gained the national reputation for city-centre social life which has made it an even more popular choice. The club scene then was working men's clubs, not city-centre dance clubs, and hard drinking nights out were thought to be largely the preserve of agriculture, engineering and medical students.

My own department, the Politics department, was built up almost from scratch by Professor Hugh Berrington, who, as well as being a deservedly popular lecturer had a consuming interest in the possibility of applying the concepts of psychology to the study of politics. His technique for building up the department was to make the courses so popular and so well taught that student demand generated increasingly unacceptable student/teacher ratios, leading in turn to faculty approval for additional posts in the department. The drawback of this strategy was, inevitably, very heavy teaching demands on the staff which did not allow for effective research programmes, and it was an emphasis which was eventually corrected. Despite the pressures, I was fortunate to have a group of extremely able colleagues, including the late Ben Pimlott, then working on Hugh Dalton but more recently better known for his biography of the Queen. Our neighbours in the Philosophy department (since sadly closed down) included Mike Brearley: I remember a lunch-time discussion in which he was weighing the advantages and disadvantages of switching to full-time cricket by taking on the Middlesex captaincy, and I was clear in my mind that, if he did, it would eventually be country as well as county he would lead at Lord's. In the History department, Norman McCord was my guide to much of the social and political history of the North East, while the region's strong links with Scandinavia were maintained by the Department of German and Scandinavian Studies, whose head, Professor Duncan Mennie, is affectionately portrayed in the autobiography of his best-known former student, Kate Adie.[4] For Newcastle University to have lost its Scandinavian specialism when it was so appropriately sited to be the main centre for Nordic Studies was deplorable, and the blame for it lies at the door of a later head of the department.

Newcastle University had not long since separated from Durham, of which it was originally a college. The child had outgrown its parent, and both universities have probably benefited from their independent status. Newcastle, previously dominated by medicine and applied sciences, was becoming a more broadly balanced university while seeking to maintain its traditional strengths. Our subjects were expanding, but some departments with high reputation were struggling to recruit students, mainly because of the neglect of science in schools and the tides of fashion. While we waded through piles of good applications, the Physics department was laying on tours and tea parties for anyone with the minimum A level qualifications to do the subject. Newcastle's current success in applied sciences, particularly but not only through the International Centre for Life Sciences, is a welcome and exciting development of traditional strengths.

Just across the road was Newcastle Polytechnic, the core of which became Northumbria University. So rigid was the binary divide that there seemed to be almost no contact or co-operation between the University and its higher education neighbour. In the Politics department we began to change that, making use of each other's resources in both examining and teaching, and working with each other in areas of common research interest.

Meanwhile, the city was changing visibly. Years of economic decline had saved many of its fine buildings and streets from destruction, because there was no money to replace them. However, this had left them vulnerable to decay and a late rush to redevelop. Labour had run the city in alternation with the Conservatives, a fact which seems astonishing given that, in more recent years, there have been no Conservative councillors at all in the city, and it was the Liberal Democrats who took over control from Labour. T. Dan Smith had become nationally known as Newcastle's high-profile Labour leader, with grand plans for the city and the then revolutionary concept of a city manager to be chief executive of the city administration rather than a solicitor Town Clerk. That the era of Dan Smith ended in a prison sentence is well known. What is less often discussed is the impact his administration had on the city. A lot of it was destructive, particularly in an inner-city motorway which destroyed historic buildings and streets. The magnificent Royal Arcade was demolished with a promise that it would be re-erected elsewhere: instead, a pathetic replica was built in the basement of a tower office block in the middle of a traffic roundabout. Even Dan Smith himself was later to ridicule the naming of John Dobson Street, attaching the name of the city's great architect to a highway rat-run of ghastly design which cuts off an area of attractive buildings from the city centre.

Thankfully, there was a conservation strategy of sorts in the plans of this era: it was based on the idea that the magnificent Grey Street, one of the finest nineteenth-century city streets anywhere in the world, must be preserved, along with at least some of the main shopping streets in what is now referred to as Grainger Town. These plans involved inserting incongruous canopies on the Grainger Street buildings to divide the shop front level from the more strictly preserved facades above. It would now be thought an inadequate approach, and the canopies have gone. This was a city still trying to recover its lost confidence, and needing to recognise the quality of the assets it possessed.

The pressure for redevelopment was also having its impact on the housing structure of the North East, in very much the way that it threatens to affect terraced housing in some urban areas today. Local authorities in Tyneside and Wearside were engaged in what they still thought of as 'slum clearance', although the areas they were seeking to clear for development often included large quantities of good or improvable housing, some privately rented and some owner-occupied. It involved the total destruction of neighbourhoods and communities, with local residents becoming dependent on council housing, much of which was inconveniently sited on the distant edge of the city or beyond its boundaries. Two of my colleagues in the University Social Sciences department, Jon Davies and Norman Dennis, were not only studying the impact of these demolitions on communities, but were actively involved in advising residents about how they could challenge the policies and their implementation. Clearance depended on declaring houses unfit, and council inspectors were using minor faults, such as not having enough electricity sockets in a room, as the basis for declaring the house unfit and listing it for a compulsory purchase. Davies and Dennis showed residents that by challenging the 'unfit' classification and challenging the compulsory purchase they could have a chance of saving their houses and their communities, although for many it was already too late.

It was the beginning of a change of attitude to traditional urban housing. A whole area of Georgian properties next to the university in St. Thomas's had been acquired by the city and was on short-life tenancies and student lets pending eventual demolition: it survived long enough to be restored, and is now a much loved part of the city's university area, along with the magnificent Leazes Terrace. Residents of Leazes Terrace lost their free grandstand view of

Newcastle United home games as the St. James' Park stadium grew to its present mighty proportions, needed in a city which supports its football club on a scale per head of population unmatched in any other English city.

Culturally, Newcastle proved a great place to be. The Laing Art Gallery and the University Museums had exciting collections and Newcastle University's Fine Art Department was a centre of creative activity, including the superb stained glass of Leonard Evetts. The Stone Gallery, a small commercial gallery, mounted exhibitions of Northern artists. L.S. Lowry was a friend of the owners, and I still have a catalogue of an exhibition of Lowry's at which I could have bought a picture for a few hundred pounds.

The Northern Sinfonia was developing its reputation as a world-class chamber orchestra, and a number of our friends were among its players; the Theatre Royal was a wonderful venue even before its superb restoration, and attracted Scottish Opera and the Royal Shakespeare Company; a theatre was built on the University Campus which has been through several of the changes and crises which are part and parcel of innovative drama venues; the museums and galleries of the university and the city had much to offer. At the same time, the region had maintained its lively traditional music scene, which had more of an outlet in the old format of regional radio than it generally gets from television or the DJs of local radio. The BBC studios in Newcastle, in a Dobson building which was the old 'lying-in' or maternity hospital, were a centre for this regional cultural tradition. Alex Glasgow, George House, Mike Neville, Tom Kilgour, the High Level Ranters, Jack Thackray and Wallsend shipyard humorist Leonard Barras were frequent contributors. Local comedians Bobby Thompson and Dick Irwin were continuing a tradition of entertainment which looked as if it would die with them, but later took on a new life with stand-up comedy finding a place in TV schedules. Beyond the urban area, in Tynedale and in the Cheviots, was a wonderful treasury of music-making by hill shepherds and farm workers like Will Atkinson, Will Taylor and Joe Hutton, which Alistair Anderson and Kathryn Tickell have recognised, supported and carried forward in their own music-making. Local bands like the Cheviot Ranters kept traditional dancing alive.

My involvement in the Methodist church drew me increasingly into the rural communities of Northumberland: the Hexham area had numerous village chapels which I visited as a local preacher, by motor bike before I managed to afford my first car. Amongst the very hospitable Methodist farming families of an area from Otterburn to Slaley I found a warm welcome and I learned a lot. At Slaley there was always a prayer meeting following the service, when members of the congregation would pray 'as the Spirit moved': with a disarming lack of confidence in my road skills one man prayed fervently 'that our young preacher may reach home safely on his motor bike'.

Politics was not far behind, but in the rather gentle form of Hexham Rural District Council. A vacancy arose, I was nominated, and for the only time in my life I was elected unopposed, probably because no one else had noticed the vacancy. It was a council on which many of the members were Conservative, although rarely declared as such, but its collective preoccupations and policies had little to do with those of the Conservative Party. Building more council houses so that local people could live in the villages, and retirement bungalows for farm workers and other local people, was far and away the most important issue for the council. At every meeting there would be discussion of plans for another development, and hopes from other villages to follow suit. Sale of council houses was not contemplated, and would have been opposed by even the most Tory of the councillors, on the grounds that these houses would be needed for local people in the future. The effect of right-to-buy and the removal from rural councils of their role as the engine of social housebuilding (begun by the Thatcher government and continued under Tony Blair) has been a social disaster for many villages. Its impact will be felt ever more keenly as house prices rise and many of the remaining council houses are sold. Rural housing problems, which are now acute, are quite different from those in urban areas and the policies required to deal with them are different, a fact to which governments pay no more than lip service.

I was re-elected as a councillor, and I was briefly a member of the new council which took over on reorganisation in 1974. More recent reorganisations have made people forget what the local government map was like before 1974. In what is now the City of Newcastle there was one county borough council, a county council with its headquarters in the city, two urban district councils and a substantial part of a rural district council's area. Eighteen councils governed the continuous urban area of Tyneside, where there are now four. In rural areas like Tynedale and North Northumberland, each town contained offices of both an urban and a rural district council, and there were rural district councils centred on smaller communities like Bellingham, Haltwhistle, Rothbury, Wooler and Belford. Some of these tiny councils had a local solicitor to act as part-time clerk, and would rely on one technical officer to cover housing, planning and sewage responsibilities, with a finance officer who might be the clerk's deputy, one or two clerical staff and a few skilled manual staff. Yet there is no evidence that people were more dissatisfied with the performance of these minuscule local councils than they are with the much larger local authorities of today, and in many matters the small local councils had more freedom to act than their much larger and more professionalised successors.

Northumberland County Council, on the other hand, was then bigger in area and vastly bigger in population, serving nearly a million people, instead of a quarter of a million as it does today. It included all the historic county of Northumberland, containing all of urban Tyneside north of the river, except the 'County of the City' of Newcastle and the County Borough of Tynemouth. At the time of the 1974 reorganisation the two County Councils, Northumberland and Durham, put in a bid to push their respective boundaries to the River Tyne, taking over Newcastle, Gateshead, Tynemouth and South Shields. Instead, both county councils had to make do with what was left when the major conurbations of Tyne, Wear and Tees had been carved out of them. Neither represents the real historic counties whose name they bear. Cricket and many other activities still use the historic county areas of Northumberland and Durham, but local government has long since ceased to do so.

Northumberland County Council, particularly in its pre-1974 form, is an interesting subject for the political historian, and I did some research into the operation of its then controlling political group, which went by the confusing name of the Northumberland Voters' Association (NVA). This was in fact a device by which the Conservatives and independents (who alternated with Labour in controlling the council) sought to recruit to their support anyone elected to the Council who was not Labour. The only qualification for being a member of the NVA was to have been elected to the council and to be willing to join it rather than the Labour group. To have defeated either a Conservative councillor or any other councillor who belonged to the NVA was not a disqualification. The NVA had no election machine of its own, and although there was an occasional attempt to agree elements of a programme, there were no policy commitments involved in being a member of it. Although there were some similar forms of local politics elsewhere, in some respects it was probably unique, and very different from models of local government political organisation to be found today. Throughout three decades Northumberland was led by the NVA, in which case the chairman was a Lord Ridley (father or son) or by Labour, in which case the chairman was Sir Nicholas Garrow, or his sister Mrs Mitchell. There was a relatively high degree of consensus, despite the political rhetoric, and therefore no dramatic policy changes between administrations. It was under NVA/Conservative administration that selective education was replaced by a comprehensive system, although the three-tier model, chosen at the time mainly because it could make use of some of the county's recently built secondary modern schools as middle schools, has become an issue again 40 years on.[5]

As the fairly small group of activists who made up the Hexham constituency Liberal Association we continued to do our best to build up the party locally. In the past the Hexham Liberal Association had an impressively large membership of around 2000, but this had been almost entirely due to the retired station master of Newcastle Central station, who lived in Hexham and spent his retirement walking around every village in the very large constituency, knocking on doors and collecting small subscriptions. When he died, he was irreplaceable. The seat had been held by the Conservatives since the retirement of Speaker Clifton Brown, and was by then the seat of Geoffrey Rippon, who played a key role in the Heath government's accession to the European Community but was not very popular in the constituency. All Hexham MPs tended to be compared unfavourably by the local Conservatives to the former MP, Sir Rupert Speir, who lived in retirement in the constituency.

During our time at Corbridge, Barbara was developing a teaching career, first at Westfield School and then at what was still Hexham Grammar School. It was a career she had never intended and to which she did not imagine she was suited. In fact she was a born teacher, with a natural ability to pass her irrepressible enthusiasm for biology on to her pupils, and an equally natural ability to relate to and win the confidence of children and young people.

My career plan was still focused on the university. When I was approached about becoming prospective Liberal candidate for the constituency, it was something I was willing to take on in order to carry the flag for the party and present its case locally, with no immediate thoughts of a career change to becoming an MP, and very little prospect of doing so in the short term. At the same time a university colleague in the Architecture Department, Derek Wilbie-Chalk, set about persuading me that it was the Berwick Constituency, not Hexham, for which I should stand. He was very persuasive, and I agreed. Life was to change, but not yet.

A VIEW FROM THE NORTH

— 7 —

BEING ELECTED

Berwick-upon-Tweed is the northernmost constituency in England and, like Hexham, one of the largest. It is bounded by the Scottish Border, the Cheviot Hills and the sea, with only its southern boundary ever subject to change. The constituency now extends 60 miles from Berwick to Belsay, from the Scottish Border to within 15 miles of the Newcastle City boundary: it includes Alnwick, Wooler, Belford, Seahouses, Amble, Rothbury and the former mining area around Lynemouth, Ellington and Widdrington. The Scottish border confuses outsiders because it runs almost North–South rather than East–West. Many neighbouring parts of Scotland lie south-west of Berwick town, which is on almost the same latitude as Edinburgh. The town of Berwick changed hands numerous times between Scotland and England and was represented in the Scottish Parliament at various times in the fourteenth and fifteenth centuries. It is believed to have sent its first representatives to Westminster in 1491, but its status remained distinct until it was resolved by the Wales and Berwick Act of 1746 and the Municipal Corporations Act of 1836. Prior to then, Acts of Parliament would refer to England, Wales and 'the town of Berwick-upon-Tweed'. But, for over 500 years, there has been a constituency called Berwick-upon-Tweed in the House of Commons. Since 1885 the constituency has combined Berwick itself, which had a long history as a two-member seat, and the Northern third of Northumberland, also formerly represented by two members. Both constituencies had a colourful political history with a considerable amount of corruption. W.E. Gladstone's father had won one of Berwick's seats in 1826 as a Conservative, but was unseated on a petition nine months later. A Beaumont and a Lambton fought a duel on the sands at Bamburgh during their rivalry in the Northumberland election of the same year.

The modern constituency was held for the Liberals by Sir Edward Grey from its creation until he retired in 1916. From then on it was hotly contested between Liberals and Conservatives. When Col. Hilton Philipson was unseated for expenses violations on a petition by the Liberals in 1923, the Conservatives successfully fielded his wife, who had starred in the original production of *The Merry Widow* at the Gaiety Theatre in London, and was something of a celebrity. Old people remembered her standing on the Town Hall steps blowing kisses and saying 'I love you all'. The Liberals recovered the seat on a recount in 1935; during the war the Liberal MP was George Grey (only distantly related to Sir Edward), who made a significant impact in the House and the constituency and had strong convictions about the need for social justice and 'winning the peace'. He never had the opportunity to do so, because he was killed in action in France in 1944. It was at this point that Sir William Beveridge became Berwick's Liberal MP, in a by-election which the main parties did not fight because of the war-time political truce. His 1942 Report on Social Insurance was the talking point of the 1945 election, but he lost in Berwick because the third-place Labour vote rose, no doubt swelled by people who supported his plans, depriving the Liberals of votes they needed to maintain a majority. The art of squeezing the third-party vote had not been developed, and Beveridge was no campaigner – his former agent used to say that when urged to address more meetings, Sir William would reply 'If they want to know what I think they should read my Report!'

From 1945 onwards the seat had been safely held by the Conservatives, latterly by Lord Lambton, but the combined Liberal and Labour vote generally approached or exceeded 50%. It was clearly a seat with potential.

I set about getting to know the constituency. It had a relatively well-organised Liberal Association, which had been revived by a farmer (Geoff France), my university colleague (Derek Wilbie-Chalk), an organiser from the Workers' Educational Association (Allan Morton) and a young architect (Allan Robson), and they had a professional approach to how it should be developed. Unheard of in those days, they required a legal contract setting out the respective duties of the prospective candidate and the constituency association. As well as new recruits, the Association included redoubtable figures who had worked for it all their lives, most notably Miss Gregson, who had been appointed agent while Sir Edward Grey was still MP with the intention that she would recruit the newly enfranchised women voters. She was fond of saying 'Now that we women have the vote we should not rely on husbands to tell us how to use it'. Liberal activity in the Berwick constituency was a fascinating mix of bygone days and new approaches. The Association's then healthy fund-raising owed much to its Saturday night beat dances in Alnwick's Northumberland Hall, which were the main social activity for young people from miles around. Local bands played for a packed dance floor, while burly Liberal fishermen from Boulmer acted as 'bouncers' and quickly removed anyone who looked like causing trouble. Years later I would meet people on the doorstep who, when asked for their support, would say 'oh yes, I'm Liberal – I met my wife at the Liberal dances'. The party eventually lost this financially valuable and socially significant role when a new dance venue opened in Seahouses – and now that has been demolished in its turn.

I set about pursuing issues of concern in the area, many of which were the same issues I was pursuing in the Tynedale area as a councillor. Many were rural policy issues, particularly those affecting the farming and fishing industries, and there were issues such as radio and TV reception in the rural area and the condition of the A1 road – partly improved over the years but still not dualled throughout. The town of Berwick has a constant battle to avoid being ignored when policies are devised and administered – it is the furthest town in England from London, and most of its commerce is with neighbouring areas of Scotland, from which it is administratively divided by the Border. Plumbers do not ask which side of the border you are on before telling you whether they can provide you with the service you need, but schools do, and now hospitals and dentists are beginning to do so. I was helped in demonstrating that a Liberal MP would be different by Lord Lambton's view – of which he made no secret at Westminster – that he did not need to concern himself with everyday issues in the constituency.

I thought I was making reasonable progress towards the long-term aim of winning the constituency over two elections. The plan was first to displace Labour who, during the period of Liberal decline, had taken over second place. Then came the General Election of 1970. It could hardly have been a worse election for the Liberals. The tide of revival had receded nationally; David Steel, my neighbour across the border, came very close to losing his seat, and Jeremy Thorpe and John Pardoe had very close shaves. The party was down to six seats. My hopes of gaining second place were dashed: Labour came second with a candidate sent up from Liverpool at the last minute.[6] The only silver lining in the cloud, not immediately

It was a war-time wedding for my parents, James Beith and Joan Harty.

Cottages
Poynton Green.
The date 1845 is on the window head
of the cottage next to Park Lane, - for
many years a sweet shop -

I was born in the upstairs room of one of the middle cottages, rented for
five shillings (25p) a week.

War babies celebrate victory with jelly and cake – I am the second child from the right, with my mother standing behind the neighbour who is holding me.

At the age when Jack had joined the Navy, I was getting involved in politics at Liberal conferences.

My cousin Jack never came back – he was one of 1,415 who were lost when *HMS Hood* was sunk in 1942.

An unforgettably happy day – getting married to Barbara.

More happiness with the adoption of Chris.

Copying Dad, who was too often on the phone!

Yet more happiness had come with the adoption of Caroline.

I make no claim to sporting prowess – it was just family fun.

Northumberland and Durham provided wonderful walking country whenever we could find time to enjoy it.

Barbara was popular with everyone, and especially so among those she taught.

Newcastle University gave me my first job.

Corbridge was where we took out our first mortgage, and we spent seven happy years there.

apparent in the disappointment of the count, was that Berwick was the only seat in the entire country in which the Liberal share of the vote increased in that election.

Lord Lambton resumed his seat. He was actually Mr Lambton at this point, because he had renounced the Earldom of Durham in order to remain in the Commons, and he was very annoyed by the Returning Officer's insistence on referring to him as Mr Lambton. As we went out onto the school balcony for the results to be declared, his wife Belinda got her shoes stuck in the felt flooring which was melting in the hot sun, but he was preoccupied with the argument about how his name should be read out. The Returning Officer, a solemn solicitor, stuck to his guns.

The ensuing Parliament with a Conservative majority looked as if it would run its term. I settled down to my university career, while continuing as prospective candidate for Berwick but pacing myself for a campaign which would reach its climax some time ahead. I had the opportunity of a six-month study sabbatical from the university and arranged to spend it at Oslo University, where I could develop a specialism in Scandinavian politics which could be used in combined courses with our Scandinavian Studies department. I was looking up arrangements and ferry timetables when the 'phone rang. Would I care to comment for the *News of the World* on the story the paper was running about the association of Lord Lambton and two prostitutes? No I would not, but as soon as I put the 'phone down I forgot about ferry times and started to think about what would probably happen next. Lord Lambton resigned. David Steel rang up to discuss whether I was prepared to stand, since he knew I was due to leave for Norway. We arranged to meet in a café near the Border, so that he could be near home while the imminent arrival of his son, Rory, was anticipated. There was really no question about what my answer would be. So began the longest by-election campaign in modern politics.

There had been a significant Liberal revival during the Heath government, with by-election wins at Sutton and Cheam and at Rochdale, where Cyril Smith had been elected. During the campaign we won two by-elections on one day at Ripon and in the Isle of Ely, where Clement Freud was elected. The Conservative high command sensed danger, and concluded, rightly as it turned out, that the longer they could delay the by-election the better their chances would be; so a by-election which became necessary in June did not take place until November. It was such an abuse of the system that it led to an agreement between the parties that all by-elections should take place within three months of the vacancy arising. The Conservatives chose a strongly pro-European Scottish business leader, Donald Hardie, and Labour fielded Gordon Adam, later to be Euro MP for the area, who had worked in one of the pits in the constituency during his training as a mining engineer. There was no Monster Raving Loony Party in those days, but there were two independent candidates, neither of them local: Robert Goodall carried the label 'English Resurgence', and Tim Symonds stood as 'New Independent': Tim and his partner Lesley Abdela were later to become active in the Liberal Party, and Lesley established the 300 group to promote women in Parliament.

Liberals and Conservatives immediately established headquarters and drafted in senior staff. My agent was John Spiller, previously agent to John Pardoe and architect of the successful Rochdale campaign. His first comment was 'This is going to be much tougher'. An American network filmed the entire campaign and it was obvious that they had put the final film together in the expectation of a Tory victory. We started from third place, with 22%. Early private polling brought a harsh dose of reality by revealing that all my previous efforts as candidate had given me no greater name recognition than the newly chosen Tory.

In many rural parts of the constituency, voters were unwilling to diverge publicly from their landlord's political affiliation, whether as farm tenants on the large estates or cottage tenants of a Tory farmer. In 1970 I had canvassed a line of farm workers who were singling turnips in a field: one of them said, jerking a thumb towards the big house, 'How is it that his man aalways gets in, when there's ten of wor doon here i' the cottages?' 'It's the wives', retorted another, although that was only partly true. Meanwhile, in the mining areas of the constituency where over a thousand men worked at two pits and many retired miners lived, Labour allegiance was deep-rooted and strong. We had long-established strength in the small fishing communities, and they had seen the Conservative government fail to secure their interests over the Common Fisheries Policy in its negotiation for entry to the EU. We had pockets of strength in the Berwick, Alnwick and Rothbury areas. We had keen local activists, but we depended on the massive voluntary effort of Liberals who came in from elsewhere. Many gave their summer holiday to the campaign, staying in beautiful countryside and tramping round the villages to canvass. Between us we determined to visit every house, however remote – and the constituency has some of the remotest inhabited places in England. In the four final weeks of the campaign we had three or four village meetings every night, with audiences varying unpredictably from, quite literally, two men and a dog, to a packed village hall in quite a small community. Just about every presentable Conservative cabinet minister visited the constituency during the campaign, and we had regular visits from Jeremy Thorpe, John Pardoe, Cyril Smith and Clement Freud, with

David Steel, who was the Party's Chief Whip at the time, present at least once every week. A key link man was David Steel's assistant, Archy Kirkwood, who was later to become my neighbour as MP for Berwickshire and Roxburghshire. Cyril Smith looked in amazement at the crowd assembled in a former Presbyterian church in Wooler which had become a public hall: all down one side were retired shepherds and farm workers, several with their dogs – he said he had never seen such a predominance of men at a big political meeting. Needless to say, his wit and storming speech delighted them.

On my way in to the packed eve-of-poll meeting in Berwick, I was handed the last-minute Conservative leaflet. It was bizarre, with a message from Donald Hardie in which he said that at this momentous hour 'Mr Heath is our Nelson, and we Conservative candidates are his captains'. It was a gift. I asked the audience: 'As this government breathes its last, what will Mr Heath, their Nelson, say to his loyal captain?' Unprompted, the audience roared 'Kiss me, Hardie!' It was another era, when election meetings were still entertainment, and there was a shared knowledge of stories from British history.

The count was an altogether more serious matter. It took place, as it still does, the day after polling day, because so many boxes have to be brought long distances, and the arrival of the Holy Island box depended on the tides. It was clearly very close. A massive camera and press corps was gathered outside the Alnwick Duchess' school hall where it was held, and glimpses through the windows were the basis of speculation outside. At several points we thought we had lost, and long Liberal faces must have led to the lunchtime TV news claiming that a Conservative victory was on the cards. A whole bundle of our votes went astray at one point, and there were two full recounts. It was not until four o'clock that we emerged.

The tradition in the constituency is that, for the declaration, the candidates follow the returning officer onto the balcony in the order of the result, and this we did, but the crowd outside were not sure, and our own supporters did not dare assume anything. We had won by 57 votes, and the place erupted.

It was the front-page lead in most national newspapers next day. There had been three other by-elections on the same day, with the Tories holding Hove and Edinburgh North, and Labour losing Glasgow Govan to Margo Macdonald of the SNP. *The Telegraph*'s headline was 'Crisis for Wilson after Berwick'. *The Times* took a similar line with 'Labour's failure to gain from Government's unpopularity in by-election phenomenon' (*The Times* had not yet cultivated populist brevity in its headline style). In reality, it was the Conservatives who had the bigger problem.

As I stood waiting at the bar of the House to take my seat, the Government declared a state of emergency because of the energy crisis. This involved Sir Keith Joseph presenting a message from the Queen, and it all added further drama to the occasion. A couple of weeks later I made a maiden speech in which I concentrated on the threat to local hospitals from health service centralisation and the need to maintain adequate health services to people who live 50 miles or more from main hospitals. It was to be a recurrent issue. Meanwhile, the Government's battle with the miners was building up, and I worked with colleagues to put forward ideas for resolving the dispute.

In the constituency I had rushed to order wreaths for Remembrance Sunday services two days after the count, and found that my predecessor had never attended these important occasions. I set about organising surgeries, which had never been the practice under Conservative representation, and which we had started during the six months in which the constituency had no MP. Almost everything I did was new to the constituency, and not a single item of correspondence, file or record was passed on to me from my predecessor. I thought I might have a year in which to get established and show that Liberal representation made a difference. Then Mr Heath dropped his bombshell with the February election. 'Who governs' was intended to be the issue – the Prime Minister or the miners? I represented over a thousand miners. It was not going to be easy to fight another election when I had barely had time to get my office organised, and it was clear that the election would not stick to the one issue the Prime Minister had posed. It was as much an election about the competence of the Government as it was about the miners.

After the by-election I had signed over 900 letters of thanks to voluntary helpers, many local, but many more from all over the country. Those who had come in to help would now be fighting in their own constituencies in the General Election. It takes at least 600 people to provide tellers and committee room workers to cover even the majority of the 120 polling districts of my scattered constituency. We had to find almost all of them locally. When the February election was over, I signed over 700 thank you letters. Somehow we had managed it.

Nationally, the Liberal campaign went reasonably well. Jeremy Thorpe, having had a close shave in 1970, did not risk being trapped in London for press conferences, and conducted the daily conference and interviews by a TV link from Devon. It worked surprisingly well, and Jeremy was a brilliant advocate for a party which presented itself as distinct from the dogfight at Westminster. In terms of votes nationally, it was a brilliantly successful campaign, raising the Liberal share of the vote from 7.5% to 19.3%. In a proportional system that would have given us well over a hundred seats. In the first past the post system it gave us a meagre 14, although Berwick was thankfully one of them, by 443 votes. No party had a majority of either votes or seats, with the Conservatives on 297 seats with 37.8% of the votes, and Labour on 301 seats despite a slightly smaller vote (37.1%). As Jeremy Thorpe put it, 'We are all minorities now'.

Mr Heath made an immediate approach to Jeremy Thorpe about the possibility of a coalition. It was a possibility for which neither party had effectively prepared itself or its members, and it was in any case doomed by the fact that a largely new Ulster Unionist parliamentary party, with no love for the Conservatives, had been elected and could have voted with Labour to overthrow such a coalition at any time. Heath's offer of a Speaker's Conference on electoral reform was clearly far short of a worthwhile commitment on a central Liberal policy, and electoral reform is essential to successful coalition governments. Even more important, Mr Heath had called the election specifically and solely to determine whether he had the authority to govern the country: instead of securing a clear mandate, he had lost, because he now had no majority either in Parliament or in the country. There was no way the Liberal MPs would have agreed to join a coalition in those circumstances, let alone on those terms. Jeremy Thorpe could not have persuaded us, however tempted he was by the possibility of getting the party to the Cabinet table (which was a perfectly proper ambition for a party leader to have). He did not seriously try to do so. The weekend's speculation around the meeting between Heath and Thorpe was extremely unsettling for Liberals across the country, and at our own victory celebrations in Berwick on Saturday night quite a few people came up to me to raise their concern. It showed me how important it is for the party to prepare for the possible outcomes of an election, and for party leaders not to appear to be rushing off on their own to do deals. In a country where the press demands instant decisions, a party involved in potential negotiations has to be prepared to sit tight, and reach considered decisions. To do otherwise is to hand a weapon to the other side when you need all the weapons you have so that you can achieve as many as possible of the policies which led people to vote for you.

Harold Wilson took office, and his game plan was obvious. The British system effectively allows a Prime Minister who has not won a majority to have a re-run of the election, at a date of his choosing, and after a period in which he will have done his best to please as many people as possible and offend as few as possible. A dissolution will only be refused by the sovereign – and should be refused – if it appears that someone else can command a majority in the existing House of Commons. In 1974 this had been shown not to be the case by the breakdown of talks between Heath and Thorpe. Accordingly Harold Wilson set his course. The miners' dispute was settled. A rent freeze was imposed. The Queen's Speech held out the prospect of pension increases and price controls, and the controversial plan for a third London Airport at Maplin was dropped. Two budgets brought food subsidies and a cut in VAT from 10% to 8%. Later in the year, plans for devolution in Scotland were announced. Not all was sweetness and light – there were strikes on the railways and in the health service, and in the North East two prominent Labour figures, Andrew Cunningham and T. Dan Smith, went to prison for corruption. A Labour MP and ex-minister, Christopher Mayhew, left Labour for the Liberals. In the Commons, Labour won the votes on the Queen's Speech because, if there was any danger of defeat, about 20 Conservatives were always mysteriously absent. Jokes abounded about them being locked in the lavatories by their whips.

The Conservatives were not ready for another election, and therefore did nothing to precipitate one. We made as much as we could of Conservative hesitancy, taking over the Opposition front bench on a couple of occasions to demonstrate that Liberals were providing the real opposition. However, the Conservatives tired of taking the blame for failing to carry their opposition into the voting lobbies, and we combined to defeat the government on more occasions as the session went on.

During the summer Jeremy Thorpe invented a new form of campaigning by touring the West Country holiday resorts by hovercraft, and getting a warm reception from big crowds. It ended rather ingloriously when the hovercraft broke down. At the party's September conference, time and valuable publicity was wasted on a fairly pointless but, for some, impassioned argument about whether the party was willing to enter a coalition after the next election, a situation which was not very likely to arise. At least it led to agreement on a process for making decisions in those circumstances, ensuring that the party in the country as well as the MPs were involved.

An early election was clearly inevitable. It would be the third election I had fought in a year, with a majority which was still less than 500. Enough of my voters could have moved or died to lose us the seat. Newcastle University had helpfully given me five years' unpaid leave of absence, which could cushion the precariousness of my political career. Parliament was more than a full-time job. In the summer I took a mobile surgery to 120 villages and hamlets in my constituency, a practice I have continued every year since. It generates a lot of work, but it keeps you in touch with every community, and it is time spent in beautiful surroundings. We had, in effect continuous election campaigning for a year, interspersed with relatively brief periods of sitting in Parliament (and in February, under old rules, I had no salary for the month that Parliament was dissolved). The election was announced with almost the shortest possible period for the formal campaign, 22 days. Nationally, the party fought another intensive campaign, this time fighting virtually every seat. Locally we threw in everything we could, resuming the roles everyone had carried out in February. We sensed that, because of the Heath–Thorpe discussions of February, we were having greater difficulty in holding on to some of the tactical votes we had gained from Labour. The total poll was lower on an older register – but still 81.4% as against 85.1% in February. Labour's share went up by a couple of points to 14%, which could have been fatal, but still we made it, this time by only 73 votes. The Wilson government got its majority. I could settle down to being an MP and to persuading people that I was worth keeping and that Liberalism had a future in British politics.

— 8 —

BEING AN MP

Being a Member of Parliament is a job with no contract, no job specification, no qualification, no training (at least, not in my early days) and no boss except the voters who can throw you out and the party members who choose you to be their candidate. Modern changes have brought some training, and modern electoral law has created an ability for party leaders, in parties which will put up with it, to withdraw both the Whip and the use of the party name in the election from an MP. Michael Howard notably did so when he forced the deselection of Howard Flight in a safe Tory constituency at the beginning of 2005 election campaign.

In practice you work out your own way of doing the job. I was helped in my first year by sharing a very small Westminster office with Cyril Smith, Clement Freud and Dr Michael Winstanley, all of whom were very effective constituency MPs with quite different styles. In the days when letters were dictated and 'phone calls rather than e-mails were the means of immediate contact, I learned a great deal from my colleagues. Staff resources were meagre – the allowance was only sufficient for one part-time secretary, whether at Westminster or in the constituency, compared to the equivalent of two or three full-time posts which more recent allowances have permitted. The part-time or shared secretaries usually had desks in other buildings, so you had to meet once or twice a day to deal with and sign correspondence wherever you could find a space to do so.

There are no rules about whether MPs should live in their constituencies. Now that there are allowances to enable them to keep a second house or flat in either London or the constituency, most will have a home in or close by their constituency, but many live in London, bringing up their families in London and using the constituency home as a base for regular visits to the constituency. I never felt I could do the job in that way and, following the example of my Liberal neighbour David Steel, I made my home in the constituency. It was also Barbara's choice: she had no wish to live in London or to bring up our children there, and she was happiest teaching in Northumberland, where our children went to school. In my early days my London home was the National Liberal Club; when the allowances improved I rented a flat, as I still do, which is a comfortable London base but never really feels like home.

There has been much media frenzy about the expenses MPs can claim. It is entirely proper that there should be transparency about such things, and it has helped to identify a few MPs who blatantly abused the system. Auditing procedures were inadequate for many years, and dated back to a time when allowances were very limited, as they were when I was first elected. But unless we are to return to a system in which you could only afford to be an MP if you were very rich or had a wealthy patron, there has to be a system, as there is in most other jobs, of reimbursing many of the costs you incur from doing the job. It is very frustrating for MPs when newspapers talk about them 'pocketing' secretarial allowances, when these sums are actually the salaries of the staff employed to help MPs serve their constituents, and the rents and rates on their constituency offices. When I was first elected, I could only run an office to serve my constituents by relying on jumble sales and voluntary contributions, so the improvement in allowances was very necessary. Similarly, if you represent and live in a constituency 300 miles from London, you physically cannot get home after a 10pm vote, let alone get back to London for a meeting at 9am the next day. You have to have a London base, for which you have to pay London prices, and I have always used the allowance to rent accommodation which I had to have to do the job. I sometimes think it would be helpful if the newspaper editors who condemn these allowances published, alongside their comments, details of their own salaries and expense allowances so that the public could put the issue in context.

The job of a Member of Parliament has many different aspects to it. First and foremost, you are the representative of your constituency, representing both its collective interests and the individual concerns of constituents, whether or not they are your supporters. It is a historic function of Parliament: the redress of grievances before the grant of supply. The Berwick constituency has a very wide range of general interests, such as those of the farming and fishing communities, coal mining, the textile industry before Pringle closed their knitwear factory, food processing and defence issues (the constituency having RAF Boulmer and much of the Otterburn army training area within its boundaries). It has issues related to the countryside – especially housing and rural poverty – as well as the general problems of remoteness, and part of it is in a National Park. The Berwick area relates closely to Berwickshire, on the other side of the Border, but is often the poor relation when more favourable provision or more sensible rules are applied to the same problems on the Scottish side. In education the Border is a barrier, and choice of secondary schools is simply not available. Such is the diversity of problems in Berwick that I used occasionally to envy a member who only had to concern himself with the steel industry, which employed almost all his constituents of working age. Then one day the steel industry packed up and left town, and the advantages of our economic diversity came into relief.

On some issues my constituency's position is unique, and on others unusual, which means that if the local MP does not pursue the issue there is no one else to do so. Salmon fishing is very significant to the economy, but it is also deeply divisive between the angling interests, with the considerable spin-off they provide for income in the tourism sector, and those who traditionally got part of their living as net fishermen in the Tweed or licensed salmon fishermen, fishing from cobles off the North East coast. Over the years I have had many hours of meetings with ministers and fishermen's organisations and have taken part in debates in which almost the only other MPs taking an interest were those who liked to come to Northumberland's rivers for the superb fishing they offer. The tensions were serious, and ministers would mysteriously hint that representations from 'the very highest level' (which I suspect meant the Queen Mother) had to be taken into account. In the end, the angling interests have come out on top, mainly because buy-out schemes led by a wealthy Icelandic angler have extinguished most netting rights in the River Tweed and many of the sea net licences.[7] We now have the extraordinary situation in which the Scottish Parliament can legislate for rivers in England, the Tweed and the Till, without the UK Parliament having any right to consider the laws, which could include confiscation of property or vehicles. I was almost alone in voting against the order which brought about this anomaly.

A constituency will have many other collective interests and aspirations which the MP will try to advance, with necessarily limited chances of success particularly when it is part of the competition for resources between different areas of the country and different areas of public spending. American politicians are, to a large extent, judged by their success in scooping as much as possible out of the pork barrel. They have powers which UK MPs do not have to insert appropriations for specific purposes in legislation, and their individual vote can be vital when the administration is in trouble. This opens up huge possibilities in areas like defence procurement or federally funded transport projects. Taken to that extent, it is a system which undermines value for the taxpayer and distorts decision-making. It is not absent from British politics: the Humber Bridge is attributed by some to a tight by-election in Hull, and gas for Northern Ireland became a key issue in seeking Ulster Unionist votes at Westminster. Parties in power usually do some favours for areas in which their support needs bolstering: when the mid-Wales railway line was threatened with closure, the late George Thomas is said to have pointed out that it ran through seven marginal constituencies. But in my experience it is, fortunately, not the case you can only do good for your constituents if you belong to the party in power. You can win some battles. You may be able to exploit an opportunity, to present a case which has not been effectively presented within the governmental system, and to get the ear of a sympathetic or fair-minded minister. I was able to persuade Shirley Williams, when she was Labour education secretary, to commit funds to building a further education annexe at Berwick's High School. I was able to persuade the then Chief Executive of Virgin Trains, Chris Green, to allow cross-country trains which passed through Alnmouth Station to stop there, creating good business for his company and a vital improvement in the service available at Alnmouth. By commissioning work from the National Audit Office – an immensely valuable parliamentary resource – I was able to show that the plan announced in 2004 to close RAF Boulmer and replace it with new facilities in Lincolnshire was fundamentally flawed and should not go ahead. The A1, perhaps our most celebrated constituency issue, has been a tougher proposition. Although I have played a part in securing the dualling of sections of the road, big gaps of inadequate single carriageway remain in the only all-weather route between England and Scotland. We made enough of a fuss for the Conservative Secretary of State for Transport to hold a press conference in Berwick prior to the 1992 Election promising to dual the whole of the A1, a promise which was promptly ignored when they returned to office.[8] Now it competes unsuccessfully for a limited roads budget with projects for crowded sections of urban motorway elsewhere in the region, and an unelected regional board makes the decisions.

On one occasion I needed to help resolve the work permit status of a New Zealand rider in the Berwick speedway team. Speedway is still popular in Berwick, and attracted bigger crowds then. The sport has always brought in overseas riders from New Zealand, Australia, Scandinavia, Poland and what is now the Czech Republic. Berwick was ruled to be competing in the wrong league to qualify for a permit for one of its overseas riders. I asked for a ministerial meeting, and the issue was resolved in our favour at a meeting attended, incredibly, by two ministers and eleven civil servants. Such are the ways of Whitehall. For those of us who deal with government, the TV series *Yes Minister* was so hilariously funny because it was so true – we had seen it all happen.

Similar demands for work permits for foreign players have not yet arisen for Berwick Rangers, the town's semi-professional football club, most of whose players come from Scotland with a few from the North East. In darker days, however, I did have to spend time with the club's bank manager, persuading him to keep things afloat until a new chairman could be found with money to put in. Playing in the

Scottish League brings publicity and visitors to the town, as well as adding to the confusion about whether Berwick is in Scotland. Being Honorary President of the club is a particular pleasure, especially when the Scottish Cup gives opportunities to try to re-enact the team's famous 1960s defeat of Glasgow Rangers. For the time being, I have had to be content with a rare but welcome defeat of Gordon Brown's team, Raith Rovers, and that was avenged later in the season.

The North-East has a very strong tradition of Working Men's Clubs and Social Clubs, run by their own members on a non-profit making basis, and there were many in my constituency. In my own constituency in Alnwick, Amble and some of the mining villages they were the social centre for large numbers of people and promoted many events for children and the elderly. I therefore served for many years as a Vice-Chairman of the All-Party Parliamentary Group of Non-Profit Making Members' Clubs, helping to ensure that the clubs' interests and their community role was understood at Westminster and recognised in legislation. Even in the club heartlands like Ashington they are no longer as numerous, as large or as prosperous as they were twenty years ago, but they remain an important social institution, democratically run by local people.

The other part of an MP's constituency role is as a representative of the individual concerns of constituents. It has expanded hugely, mainly because the activity and remit of government has expanded so much, and perhaps partly because MPs increasingly see that it wins them support from those they have helped. Some MPs delegate this work almost completely to paid staff, and there have always been a few MPs who acquire such a reputation for not dealing with casework that most constituents do not bother to approach them at all. In this part of the job the more work you do, the more work you attract. I have always insisted on seeing and signing all correspondence with constituents, although it can be difficult to remember it all when a constituent stops you in the street and begins 'About that letter you sent me …'.

Some cases will call for close personal involvement and the use of parliamentary mechanisms such as questions or adjournment debates. I had a battle lasting four years on behalf of an ex-miner constituent who, like many, had lost a lot of money by accepting advice to leave the mineworkers' pension scheme. His chances of compensation had been fatally undermined by delay and incompetence on the part of his solicitors. In the end a ministerial intervention was needed, and it took an adjournment debate to get it. As I left the debate I went to the nearest phone to bring the good news to my constituent. To my surprise he was already over the moon – 'I was watching it all on Sky' he said. Another case involving not just one but two incompetent solicitors concerned a young man badly injured in a car crash: following an operation he had not been given sufficient attention in the recovery stage and sustained such serious brain damage that he would need lifetime care. Both solicitors had missed crucial deadlines, and the case was long out of time. Proving that he would have had a strong case for compensation, and that the solicitors were therefore liable, involved getting documents out of the health authority before the days of freedom of information. I got the documents, and with the help of a Channel 4 programme the case was pursued. A large enough sum was awarded to provide for his lifetime needs in a bungalow with 24-hour nursing.

In some cases what an MP can do is to demonstrate that there is an injustice and get it put right. In others, even for a constituent to get a coherent answer explaining a decision is important. It is more than the bureaucracy has ever provided and gives some satisfaction. There are other areas in which an MP finds that the task is one of pressing an individual case in a situation of scarcity. It is hard to believe, with modern telecommunications, that in many areas in the 1970s it was virtually impossible to get a telephone line. Applications hugely exceeded supply and I wrote many letters and made quite a few calls on behalf of constituents whose circumstances made access to a 'phone urgent. One summer some years ago, the passport offices were in chaos. I was astonished by the number of very elderly constituents who had never previously travelled abroad but now needed a passport because their sons or daughters had booked and paid for a flight to Canada so they had at least one chance to see their grandchildren. A large part of my constituency population seemed to have emigrated to Canada after the war. Often, the only course was to get the Foreign Office to issue temporary travel documents, in some cases rushed to Newcastle Airport by motorcycle courier. Another constituent with a passport problem was a Ukrainian who had landed in Britain as a teenager during the war with no birth certificate or papers of any kind and had lived in the area ever since as a much respected member of the community. It took a long time to get him the passport he needed to get to Toronto, where his only relatives lived, and where he was delighted to find he could go into shops and be understood in Ukrainian for the first time in 50 years.

Now, the big scarcity issue is housing, as it was in my first few years. I can and do press for national policy changes to get more rented social housing in areas like ours where it is desperately needed because of massive rises in house prices and the sale of council houses. But the MP has no role at all in the allocation of houses. It is a local council or housing association decision, and all the MP can do is to draw to the council's attention all the circumstances of the case, particularly any relevant consideration which may have been missed. How appalling it is that in modern Britain people should have to go as supplicants to an arm of the state pleading for a house for their family, much as people had to do in the Soviet system. You do not have to plead for groceries or a car, but in many parts of Britain, when it comes to housing, many families on low or uncertain incomes are beggars in the land of their birth.

As well as representing constituents in Parliament, there is a sense in which MPs represent Parliament and the democratic system itself to their constituents. When you visit a school or take a party of school children around the Houses of Parliament, you are conveying to them what Parliament is for. At many public and social functions the MP's presence is welcomed. It provides a public recognition by the nation of the good work done by the voluntary organisations involved. The MP also represents the nation in sadder circumstances, most memorably when visiting the families of people who have lost their relatives in the service of the country. When the RFA ship *Sir Galahad* was hit so disastrously in the Falklands campaign in June 1982 one of my constituents serving on board, Second Engineer Officer Paul Henry, gave his breathing apparatus to a man he knew had a family. He was awarded the George Medal posthumously. When I visited and got to know his mother, I found a woman of great bravery and dignity, whose qualities had been passed on to the son who never returned.

A third role of the MP is to take up issues wider than those of the constituency alone. Here you have to be selective: it is impossible to be involved in every issue, or to be involved effectively and in depth in more than a limited number of issues. You have to rely on others, whether in your own party or across the House, to pursue issues on which you can give occasional but limited support. The issues in which MPs specialise will often arise form their own career background, their family experience or the topics which fascinate them. Having a son who was diabetic from the age of two made me realise the extraordinary problems that were faced by diabetics, and the parents of child diabetics, giving insulin injections with the old glass syringes. If you have tried holding a squirming child in one hand while trying to manipulate a glass syringe with the other you will understand the near impossibility of the task. I had been campaigning for many months to get plastic syringes prescribed for diabetics, against strong resistance in the Department of Health, when the Government indicated that it was planning to give disposable syringes free to drug addicts on hygiene grounds. I had come up in the ballot for Prime Minister's Questions, and it was one of those occasions when it was a good idea to alert the Prime Minister's advisers to the question, so that the process of preparing an answer gets things moving. It was in Mrs Thatcher's time, and I was sure she would not be willing to stand up and defend giving free syringes to drug users while denying them to diabetics, who have no choice but to have insulin injections several times a day. I could imagine what her response would have been if a draft answer defending such a policy had been put in front of her for approval. I was right; she took control of the matter, I got the answer I wanted and diabetics got their plastic syringes. Many more battles still have to be fought over medical facilities and treatments whose costs are far less than the longer-term costs to the NHS if a condition is allowed to deteriorate.

One unusual subject into which I was drawn was the refusal of the Ministry of Defence to accept that there were serious flaws in the official account of the loss of HMS *Glorious*, *Ardent* and *Acasta* off Norway in June 1940 with the loss of over 1,500 lives. Even a debate which I introduced in 1999 secured only a minimal change in the official view, which glossed over the mistakes and failed adequately to recognise the remarkable bravery of the destroyer crews who paid with their lives in a sacrificial effort to save an aircraft carrier doomed by errors. Families of the lost attended the debate: the story is told by Tim Slessor in his book, *Ministries of Deception*.

Many issues of wider interest are pursued by MPs in all-party groups in which co-operation across the party lines is the norm. Although there have been questions about some groups receiving sponsorship from industries which have a financial interest in gaining the support of Members, the wide range of cross-party activity in support of good causes is a valuable feature of a system. Parliament is not completely dominated by party conflict.

Parties are, however, a proper and necessary part of the parliamentary process, and another key component of an MP's role is as a member of a party. With very few exceptions, MPs are elected to Parliament on the basis of the support their party receives. They would not have been elected without that support. A Prime Minister takes office because he is known to have, on a vote of confidence, the support of a majority of Members of Parliament. Defeating the Government, for opposition parties, requires recognition from their MPs that only by acting together, and persuading some members of the governing party to join them, can they defeat or change legislation. The party aspect of Parliament attracts much public disapproval, and rightly so when it takes the form of an absurd shouting match or a puerile level of argument. It is equally discredited when governments with large majorities are able to force through measures which do not command support in the country without any concession to their critics. Constituents often used to ask how Mrs Thatcher could introduce the poll tax when it was so massively opposed; the answer, of course, was that the bizarre electoral system had given her a majority so large that she could defeat the combined forces of all opposition parties and the rebels in her own ranks, although she had no majority among the voters.

As a Liberal and later a Liberal Democrat my political career has been spent on the opposition benches. It is frustrating that we have been denied the opportunity to carry out our own policies, and would be even more frustrating if my only role or my overriding objective in politics was to be a minister in a government. It was not my only objective, because many of the roles of an MP do not depend on being part of a government. Indeed, some of them are difficult to carry out while serving in a government. Ministers may exercise some influence over limited areas of policy for which they are responsible, but they are largely precluded by the structure of government and by the pressures of their job from influencing much else. It is not only the representative roles of an MP which exist independently of ministerial office: in my time in Parliament, there has been a welcome reassertion of the responsibility of parliament to hold the Government to account. The executive is seen as over-mighty, and needing a challenge which is quite distinct from the party political role of supporting or opposing the continued existence of the Government, defending its general policy or advocating another party's alternative view. It is through the system of Select Committees that this role has been developed.

The essence of Select Committee work is to achieve cross-party agreement among the members, which is often possible even in reports which are strongly critical of the effectiveness of policy or administration. Being active in Select Committee work is now a key part of the activity of most MPs who are not ministers or members of their party's front-bench team, and Committee Chairmanship is recognised and salaried as an important role. I had my apprenticeship serving on the Treasury Select Committee. I have been the Chairman of the committee which, for the first time, scrutinised what was the Lord Chancellor's Department, and evolved first into the Department for Constitutional Affairs and then into Department of Justice. One of our first reports was so critical of the Children and Family Courts Advisory and Support Service, CAFCASS – a very necessary body, but very inadequately set up – that its entire board was replaced and a fresh start made.

Select Committees have important powers to summon witnesses, who are in turn protected by parliamentary privilege, so that they can give evidence without fear of penalty or punishment. I had to seek the support of the House to assert this privilege when a witness before the Constitutional affairs Committee, Miss Judy Weleminsky, was dismissed from the board of CAFCASS Advisory Service by the then Lord Chancellor, Lord Falconer, one of the several grounds of dismissal being that she had given evidence that "undermined the organisation" and was "in conflict with the evidence which CAFCASS itself had previously submitted to the Committee". The Privilege Committee agreed that there had been a breach, which it attributes to incorrect advice from a senior civil servant, and the Government had to apologise and issue new guidance to departments.[9]

The value of committee processes was demonstrated when Tony Blair decided that he wanted to abolish the office of Lord Chancellor. It was Thursday evening, and I got on the six o'clock train at Kings Cross to head for Berwick. As the train pulled out of the station, details of a Cabinet reshuffle were being announced. I was 'phoned with the details, but when I asked who was to be Lord Chancellor in place of Lord Irvine, I was told 'There isn't one'. 'Nonsense',

I replied: 'He is named in hundreds of statutes – he appoints judges and clergy – they can't just abolish him'. 'No. 10 are saying the Lord Chancellor's been abolished' was still the reply. By the 10pm news, which I picked up as I got home, the Lord Chancellor was back. Someone had pointed out that if he did not appear in wig and gown by 11 o'clock on Friday morning, the House of Lords could not sit. It was an incredible attempt to change the constitution on the back of an envelope, which would have been inconceivable in any other democracy, where there would be a written constitution. Because Tony Blair was reshuffling his ministers, he had not wanted to discuss his plans with anyone. Without such discussion, he had no understanding at all of the complexities involved in what was, in principle, a justifiable plan to separate the highest court of appeal, the legislature and the minister responsible for justice. This is a mixture of functions which we would never advocate for any new democracy. Good ideas can be ruined by hasty, incompetent or non-existent planning, and this was clearly happening.

Our committee began a series of detailed evidence sessions, questioning senior judges, experts, ministers and civil servants on the plans. Our Report was used to justify and inform longer and more detailed consideration in the House of Lords, and the process gave the Lord Chief Justice time to negotiate a concordat with the new Lord Chancellor (whose title survived in the end) in order to safeguard judicial independence. That in turn has led to the Lord Chief Justice and judges from all levels of the judiciary appearing before the Committee where they can set out, in a non-partisan environment, the concerns they may have about the functioning of the system. I am in absolutely no doubt that committee processes such as these are a major benefit in securing better government.

When I was elected, Parliament did not equip members for the range of roles I have outlined, either as individual MPs or as parties. Government has massive resources, but MPs had only their Library, which does provide excellent research information but cannot meet all the needs these functions create. The largest opposition party had publicly funded administrative support as well as additional salaries for several Whips and a car and driver for its Leader, but no research support; Liberals and other parties had nothing. It was Newcastle MP and Northumbria University Chancellor, Ted Short, later Lord Glenamara, who as Leader of the House introduced public funding for opposition parties in parliament, and it is greatly to his credit. It is still known as 'Short' money. When I was elected, individual MPs had just gained free postage for constituency correspondence and a small allowance from which a part-time secretary could be paid. One of the first things I was able to do was to remedy an injustice under which staff working for individual Members usually had no pension provision at all, unlike the staff of the House itself. When a motion was put forward to increase allowances for Members' staff, I moved an amendment, which was carried, reserving an extra 10% of secretarial allowance for the payment of employers' pension contributions. It was a direct incentive to ensure that secretaries and researchers took out pension schemes, and received an employer's contribution. I gather that several brokers built up their businesses out of the hundreds of new clients setting up pensions.

Although 'House' issues like these are supposedly decided on free votes, the Government had and still has too much day-to-day control of Parliament, given that Parliament's job is to hold government to account. There was a long and eventually successful campaign to get the budget and management of the House out of the Government's hands: this culminated in the setting up of the House of Commons Commission, on which I served throughout its early years, and for which it was my job to answer Parliamentary Questions on funding and staff issues. It took the Commission, under the usually very traditionalist influence of the Speaker and other senior members, many years to begin to modernise the way the Commons is administered, and the task is unfinished. I also served on the Liaison Committee, which brings Committee Chairmen together in a body which is really too large for decision-making, but which has developed regular two-hour questions sessions with the Prime Minister. This is a far more effective process for scrutinising government than the theatre of Wednesday Prime Minister's Questions.

The Commons will remain hamstrung, however, until it wrests control of the arrangement and timings of Commons business from Government control, which has become even stronger with the automatic timetabling of bills. Not many members would want to go back to the days when unlimited time was spun out in fruitless debates until a guillotine was imposed, but it is indefensible that huge chunks of new law would, but for the Lords, be completely unexamined because of the effect of the timetable.

So the functions of an MP as I see them are to represent constituents' interests, both collectively and individually; to pursue wider policy issues through the parliamentary process; to represent the democratic system to the people of the country; to be part of a party system on which governments and alternative governments depend if they are to function; and to make Parliament effective in its scrutiny of the Executive. It is a privilege to be able to do these things, but you need to enjoy hard work.

It may be hard work, but the people you meet and the places you see as an MP provide many more compensations than other jobs offer, and so much interest that it is never confined to a routine. Many of the places you visit are not at all glamorous or exotic: as a constituency MP with a prison and a young offenders institution in my constituency, and as Home Affairs spokesman and more recently as Justice Committee Chairman, I have made a lot of prison visits. With a mining constituency I made regular underground visits: in the old Shilbottle pit, face workers crawled along 18-inch seams and hand-filled the coal from a lying-down position because it was not high enough to kneel. Men did it every working day, while for me it was only a one-day visit. Conditions at Ellington pit were much better, but it was still hard and dangerous work. So is fishing in the North Sea, and so is the work on the oil rigs which I have visited in both Scottish and Norwegian oilfields.

As an MP, you are invited into workplaces, hospitals, organisations, and homes, often when there are serious problems – threats of job losses, floods, the impact of foot-and-mouth on the farming industry, problems of resources, bereavements and all kinds of situations. When I spoke in a debate about *in vitro* fertilisation, the leading surgeon in the field, Lord Winston, insisted that I should witness the whole procedure in the operating theatre. When the Committee which I chair was preparing a report on the operation of the small claims division of the county court, I sat through court hearings and discussed with the judge and the parties the strengths and weaknesses of the system. MPs get opportunities to visit our armed forces on duty, and my first experiences of this were with the Army on the streets of Belfast in the early days of the troubles, when children in the Divis Flats were throwing stones at us. Spending time as Northern Ireland spokesman took me into the Maze prison, meeting violent men from the Republican and Loyalist paramilitaries who, at that stage, were organised within the prison as if they were in a prisoner of war camp.

Not long before she died, I had the opportunity to meet Mother Teresa of Calcutta during her visit to London. Even in a short meeting the force of personality within the tiny frame of this remarkable woman shone out unmistakeably, as did the depth of her commitment to the homeless and dispossessed.

One of the most interesting and absorbing visits I have ever undertaken occurred when Mikhail Gorbachev had first convinced Mrs Thatcher that he was a man 'we could do business with'. He had visited London, and a return visit was planned under the auspices of the Inter-Parliamentary Union. Willie Whitelaw, Denis Healey and I represented the three parties, with a group of MP and peers. Willie was Mrs Thatcher's deputy, and the visit was meant to convey serious intent on Britain's part, without going overboard in dealing with a regime in which Gromyko, steeped in the cold war, was still president. There was no political freedom in the Soviet bloc, and the Russians were effectively occupying much of Europe and Asia through puppet regimes, but Gorbachev was clearly intent on change.

We were received with much grandeur, very comfortably accommodated and watched day and night. We knew that any discussion we had would be listened to, and we occasionally staged discussions with precisely that purpose. Our official host was the alarmingly named head of the Soviet Supreme Court, Mr Terebilov. Both Gromyko and Gorbachev held very long discussion meetings with us, each of them accompanied by a line of party dignitaries. With Gromyko it was a formality, but with Gorbachev it was more genuine, although stilted by the presence of the other politburo members. He was well-briefed: when I asked him a question about human rights he pointedly tried to deflect the question by noting that, back in England, the Liberals had just had a by-election success. What was clear, though, was that his loosening of the restraints on challenging incompetence and corruption in the factories would inevitably lead to pressure for similar freedom to speak out about government and officialdom.

Many dissidents, including Christians, were still serving hard labour in prison camps or confined to mental hospitals, so it was amazing to attend the packed Moscow Baptist Church and to visit the Orthodox Seminary at Zagorsk. Church activities were tolerated on a limited basis, with systematic party control to ensure that outspoken leaders and critics were not appointed to key positions in the 'tolerated' churches.

It was intriguing as a Methodist to find that Gorbachev was in the midst of a campaign against alcohol, which was and is a serious problem for many Russians, and alcohol was banned at all government functions, including those laid on for us. This was not very welcome to some of my colleagues, who were relieved when we got to Georgia: in that wine-growing country the doctrine was unenforceable. The wine flowed freely at dinners and numerous toasts would be drunk. We were accommodated on a country estate which had been used by Stalin (himself a Georgian). Stalin was still remembered, incredibly, with affection by Georgians: when I raised the fact that he killed millions of innocent people, the only response I could get was 'Stalin made some mistakes' or 'he became ill'. The staff who looked after us on the estate were astonished by the pictures in the British newspapers which were sent out to us, especially an advertisement showing someone tied to a chair, which they assumed must be the work of a British equivalent of the KGB.

St. Petersburg – then Leningrad – was memorable not just for its beauty but also for the way in which everyone was taught about the horrors of the Second World War siege, in which so many starved while the Nazis reached the very outskirts of Moscow. We also saw the headquarters of the Russian space programme and I got away with photographing the inside of the Mir space station before it was sent into orbit. One of the more unexpected sights of the visit was a park filled with young people, the girls in long dresses and the boys in white tie and tails, for a ballroom dancing competition.

The visit was a moment of history, followed as it was by the ending of the cold war, the removal of the 'iron curtain' and the Berlin Wall, the end of Soviet control of most of the satellite states, and the transformation from a state-run economy to a capitalist economy. Ironically I found myself on holiday with my family in the former East Germany, opened up to visitors after the wall came down, when the attempted coup against Gorbachev took place. There was a weekend of real uncertainty, and of real anxiety where we were in Germany. Tens of thousands of Russian troops were still stationed there, and no-one knew what they would be ordered to do if Gorbachev was overthrown.

On another occasion I was invited to give a lecture for the British Council in the Northern Greek city of Thessalonika, on attitudes to Europe in British politics. It was an enjoyable experience, well attended, and followed by a convivial dinner in a local restaurant. The next morning I was driven to the airport for the return flight to London, and the excellent Greek hospitality continued with the airport manager waiting at the entrance to see me off. When the military band started playing I began to think the send-off was getting a little over the top. The airport manager beckoned me to follow him in the direction of a line of dignitaries including a very high-ranking officer from each of the three services in dress uniform, flanking a carpet stretching across the tarmac. At this point I realised that I was actually *joining* the line-up rather than inspecting it, and at the other end of the carpet was not a British Airways jet bound for London but, incredibly, a Dakota. Three black cars swept on to the tarmac, and out stepped black-robed orthodox priests and monks bearing an elaborate casket. 'What is this?' I whispered to the airport manager. 'It is the Virgin Mary's belt' he whispered back. Sure enough, the casket was opened to reveal a richly ornamented and bejewelled belt, which the military commanders each proceeded to kiss before it was carried aboard the Dakota. The engines started, and off flew this Second World War aircraft with its bizarre cargo of an item of clothing improbably claimed to be from the wardrobe of Jesus' mother, and its monastic escort. It was apparently being taken from one of the monasteries on Mount Athos to Athens to be exhibited; a sort of inter-library loan, but on a ceremonial scale which is normally reserved for a head of state. Maybe the Greeks had a better order of priority.

MPs who are so inclined can spend a great deal of their time travelling the world in various missions, conferences and meetings. I have turned down far more travel opportunities than I have accepted, because the demands of the job at home make too much travel impractical. I was once obliged to go to Australia twice in six weeks, each time for only four days, which is not how anyone would plan an enjoyable trip to the Southern Hemisphere. And, in the nature of what we do, a lot of my travel is to centres of government with no time to see the real country outside the capital. In Britain I also find myself doing frustratingly short evening trips to beautiful places where I make a speech or take part in a meeting and have to leave again without ever seeing the place in the daylight.

It is interesting work, with all sorts of opportunities and challenges, but all the time spent in London or travelling means that the breath of fresh air when I get off a homebound train at Alnmouth or Berwick is the best thing of all.

— 9 —

RUNNING A PARTY: THE LIBERALS

Towards the end of 2002 I stepped down from the position of Deputy Leader of the Liberal Democrats to become Chairman of the Select Committee on the Lord Chancellor's Department. Apart from a short break, it was the first time in 27 years that I had not been involved in the management of the Liberal or Liberal Democrat Party as Chief Whip or Deputy Leader. It was a very refreshing change, made much easier by the vastly increased size of the Parliamentary Party, which meant that there were so many more people to take on responsibility.

I became Chief Whip in circumstances I would not have chosen. Early in 1976 the Norman Scott allegations began the process which led to Jeremy Thorpe's resignation as leader. Cyril Smith was the Chief Whip, and he found himself under enormous pressure as he sought to defend the party leader, who totally denied all the allegations Scott had made; Jeremy was later to be acquitted of conspiracy and incitement to murder. Cyril describes in his book *Big Cyril* how he was pursued by the press about matters of which he knew nothing except the little that Jeremy had told him. As more stories appeared, and more journalists gathered outside Cyril's home in Rochdale, he became ill with gallstones and was rushed to hospital. Heavily sedated, he took a call on the payphone at his hospital bedside from the *Daily Mail*, by whom he was quoted as saying 'I am almost being made to carry the can for something that's nothing to do with me'. Jeremy rang Cyril after midnight and said that he would ask me to take over, at least for the time being. I was in the City Hall, Liverpool, meeting Liberal councillors prior to a visit to the Wirral by-election, when Jeremy rang and asked me to take over temporarily as Chief Whip. I was keen to do so in order to re-establish order in the Parliamentary Party, but it had to be on my terms. I had seen my friend Cyril Smith shattered by his valiant attempts to handle a situation of whose truth or untruth he knew nothing. I was not prepared to play any role at all in defending Jeremy against these allegations. That was his business, and looking after the Parliamentary Party would be mine. On that basis we agreed, and one of my first tasks was to test the views of MPs on whether Jeremy should be asked to resign. Although 9 of the 12 thought he should resign because of the considerable damage the process was doing to the party, there was no majority to require him to do so. Liberals are not traditionally ruthless. When their leader protested his innocence, even of misleading them, particularly when that leader had at an earlier stage done so much for the party's success, most were reluctant to move against him. Clement Freud was particularly loyal to Jeremy, while Emlyn Hooson and Richard Wainwright, a good friend and fellow Methodist, were equally forthright in their opposition, which was in any case long-held. The following weekend I was on an official visit to Sweden, and returned hastily as Richard Wainwright made public his insistence that Jeremy should go. This finally tipped the scales for Jeremy, and by the time I got back he had notified David Steel of his resignation.

Liberals were the first party to hand over to their members in the country the right to elect their Leader. We had begun to devise the process, but it had not yet been approved and brought into the party's constitution. So we had an uncompleted new system for electing the Leader, and a vacancy for the post. The Parliamentary Party asked Jo Grimond to take over once again as Leader until the election process could be set in train, and we arranged a special conference to agree the new rules. Jo rather enjoyed his return to leadership. Some of the old flair was soon apparent, and the party conference was delighted to hear him again as a keynote speaker. The rules were put in place. John Pardoe and David Steel fought a lively campaign, and David won. Jeremy went on to be acquitted in a trial at the Old Bailey, but his problems were no longer centre stage for us. Some in the party found it very hard to believe that Jeremy had misled his colleagues in any way over the whole affair, and at the next conference there was some tension over his position and the possibility of his return, but we had moved on.

Being Chief Whip of the Liberal Party in those days seemed at times like trying to put on a performance of *Aida* with a very small opera company. A dozen MPs were attempting to represent the views of a fifth of the voters over the whole range of issues coming up in Parliament. Other parties had hundreds of MPs from whom to choose their front benches. I had to make use of everybody in several roles, just as the opera producer with the small company would send the same few soldiers back on stage in different helmets repeatedly to produce the effect of the Grand March. For most of the time my colleagues coped amazingly well, switching from transport to education to health at a moment's notice. But as in an opera company, I had prima donnas. To be elected as a Liberal MP in those days required a personality which stood out, and such personalities, like Clement Freud, Cyril Smith or Stephen Ross (the very hard-working MP who seized the Isle of Wight from the Tories) they had short fuses. With minimal staff and no deputy whips I spent a lot of time persuading, befriending and cajoling not only my small band of MPs, but also their wives or mothers, who were often the key influence on whether I could get them in for a crucial vote or persuade them to speak for us in a debate for which I had no one else available. To make matters more difficult, most of my colleagues represented and lived in constituencies which were hundreds of miles from London, so the travel burdens were severe, and the House sat enormously long hours, with crucial votes in the early hours of the morning, or through the night. Richard Wainwright was an early bird who was very uncomfortable with late votes, so if I could manage without him I would let him go at 11pm on condition that he returned at 5.30 in the morning to let someone else get some sleep. Jo Grimond, who was a wealthy man, was extremely frugal: one night we were persuading him to stay for a 1am vote and he complained that he would miss the last tube to Kew. 'Get a taxi', we said, and at David Penhaligon's suggestion we each jokingly put 50p on the table towards his fare. We were slightly taken aback when he agreed to stay but pocketed the money.

There is a general public assumption that Whips exist mainly to force MPs to vote against their beliefs. Sometimes that is what they do, and I have watched Whips in other parties threaten, browbeat or induce MPs to support the party line. A Labour Whip some years ago boasted to me of an exchange he had just had with a member who voted against the Whip. 'You enjoy the Select Committee, don't you' said the Whip. 'Yes', replied the member. 'Well, you're off it as from the end of the week'. But most of the time it is not like that at all, and Labour and Tory Whips have increasing difficulty in deploying such threats to useful effect. If you are running a party properly, most members most of the time want to vote together because they see

Starting my first (unsuccessful) General Election campaign in Spittal in 1970.

Finding out about the fishing industry from one of the Stephenson brothers in Boulmer – they also served as 'bouncers' at Liberal fund-raising dances.

Being taught about the finer points of sheep by farmer and voluntary agent Geoff France, M.C.

Village campaigning, seen here in Belford.

Deep mining was a major employer until a few years ago.

David Steel's constituency bordered the Berwick seat, and his help and example were very valuable to my campaigns.

'...Don't worry Alan – actually it's quite a canny turnout for these parts – the other lot made absolutly no impression at all...'

The late Henry Brewis was a brilliant portrayer of country life in Northumberland – including rural electioneering!

Victory by 57 votes!

THE TIMES

:ation

:e pact

Cairo, were accepted
le " by the Israelis.
irmed in London that
Meir will meet Mr
she visits London this

:eremony

officials do regard the agreement, worked out by Dr
Kissenger, the American Secre-
ary of State, as a breakthrough
n a situation which was beginning to look very ugly.
It appears to have cleared up
the two main points on which the
Middle East ceasefire was being
held up—the Egyptian demand
or supplies for Suez, and for the
Third Army on the east bank ;
nd the Israel demand for the
elease of prisoners of war.
The terms of the agreement
ere handed over to Dr Wald-
neim in a letter from Dr
Kissinger. Mr John Scali, the
American permanent representa-
ive, gave Dr Waldheim the
etter and stayed for a 45-minute
liscussion during which they
vent over what had been agreed,
nd how it should be carried out.
In a statement after the meet-
ng Dr Waldheim said that he
velcomed the agreement
Meanwhile, the diplomatic acti-
ity was punctuated by sporadic

Liberal jubilation at Berwick-upon-Tweed : Mr Alan Beith, who won the seat at his second attempt, with his wife after the result

Labour's failure to gain from Government's unpopularity is by-elections phenomenon

By David Wood
Political Editor
When the declaration of the
result at Berwick-upon-Tweed
yesterday gave the seat to the
Liberals by 57 votes, on a recount, only the Labour Party
came out of the four by-elections
on Thursday without a consolation prize.

Details of the voting at
Berwick-upon-Tweed are :
A. J. Beith (L)   12,489
D. Hardie (C)   12,432
G. Adam (Lab)   6,178
T. Symonds (New Ind)   126
R. Goodall (Eng Resurgence) 72
                    L maj 57
The swing was :

the failure of the Labour Opposition to benefit from the Government's electoral unpopularity.
At Westminster yesterday
Labour MPs made no attempt to
conceal how crestfallen they are.
When any Labour leader tried to
gloss over Thursday's setbacks
by suggesting that Labour's new
policies have not yet had time

where Labour could put up no
effectual challenge at all.
In any other party, Labour's
persistent failure to look like the
alternative government at a time
when the Government is in difficulties would lead directly either
to a leadership crisis or to a re-
orientation of tactics and policy.
Nothing is less likely than that

Allegations denied by the Attorney General

Sir Peter Rawlinson, QC, th
Attorney General, denied la:
night that he knowingly mad
false allegations in a majo
murder trial 20 years ago.
Mr Herbert Hannam, a forme
detective chief superintenden
in a letter published in Th
Times and The Daily Telegrap
yesterday, said defence counse
in the case had written him
letter admitting that he knev
that allegations that Mr Hannar
had forged the defendant's cor
fession and signature wer
untrue.
It was disclosed by Sir Peter'
office that the Attorney Genera
was the counsel involved in th
case. Mr Hannam's letter wa
written in support of claim
about a " small minority " of un
scrupulous criminal lawyer
made this week by Sir Rober
Mark, Metropolitan Police Com
missioner.
Mr Hannam said last nigh
that he had never suggested tha
Sir Peter was one of the " shad:
lawyers ".
Mr Hannam said in his letter
that counsel wrote to him admitt
ing that the allegations were un
true but saying he had beer
instructed by his client to mak
them. According to Mr Hannam
the letter ended : " We knev
they were all untrue but the:
were my instructions."
A spokesman for Sir Pete
said Mr Hannam now accepter
that the sentence did not appea
in the letter." Sir Peter did writ
to Mr Hannam after the case i

The Times still went in for long headlines – and failed to spot that the Tories were heading for defeat in a matter of months.

Elections may have brought out a "battlebus"...

...but a more basic camper van provided my mobile "surgery" for the scattered villages of the huge Berwick constituency.

A welcome to Westminster from Jeremy Thorpe and David Steel.

The conference platform at the 1974 Liberal Assembly, with Cyril Smith, Jo Grimond, Clement Freud, Emlyn Hooson and Jeremy Thorpe.

"Ah, Jeremy, would you close the door — on your way out!"

Things changed dramatically for Jeremy and the Party...

...and I found myself at the Chief Whip's desk.

that they are making progress towards agreed objectives. When the issue is one of priorities in spending commitments, most members recognise that a party has to agree a spending package which involves a compromise between competing demands in which no one can win all they want. In the Liberal Party and the Liberal Democrats we have a very consistent record of voting together, not because of brutal whipping techniques, still less because of hopes of ministerial office, but because as far as possible we sit down together and work out agreed positions. It is the nature of Liberals not to want to take orders, but to encourage processes by which people agree to accept the outcome of a democratic decision. Most Liberal Democrats would not accept being told how to vote on issues they had been given no opportunity to discuss.

There are issues on which parties recognise that members' individual convictions are too strong to enforce a party line, and 'free votes' take place, sometimes with no party guidance, sometimes with an indication of the front bench view but a recognition that there will be differences of view. The abortion issue is one on which no whip could persuade me against voting for more protection for the rights of the unborn child, and none has ever tried.

In fact, it is not on persuading MPs how to vote that Whips spend most of their time: it is on making sure that members are actually present to vote or speak when they are needed. When votes are tight, ministers who have just arrived for negotiations on the other side of the world are told to get the next flight back before they have even got out of the arrivals lounge. I have spent time, before the days of pagers, phoning round airport hotels until I could track down Russell Johnston, on his way to some European meeting, in order to bring him back. When things were really bad and sick members were not being 'paired' I have seen the disgraceful spectacle of seriously ill members being brought in ambulances so that their vote could be recorded. As long as the ambulance is in the precincts they can be 'nodded through'. I have even had the job, as Whip, of checking that they were actually there in the ambulance. Usually, seriously ill members are desperately keen not to let their colleagues down by causing a vote to be lost, but it is ridiculous and potentially dangerous that they should ever be expected to go to such lengths. With larger majorities it has not been happening lately, but unless the rules are changed it could arise again.

Close votes like this were an increasingly frequent problem for the Labour government of Harold Wilson, and continued when Jim Callaghan took over. When Labour lost a vote on a timetable for its first devolution bill for Scotland, and lost by-elections in the safe seats of Workington and Walsall, with a background of seriously rising inflation and mounting union disputes, they had to do something. They explored the possibility of a deal with the Ulster Unionists, who were of a new generation and no longer joined at the hip to the Tory Party as their predecessors had been. The Ulster Unionists had issues on which they were prepared to do business, including some devolved government and an increase in Northern Ireland seats at Westminster. But no deal emerged, and with a confidence motion coming up, Callaghan approached the Liberals. It was potentially an opportunity for us to demonstrate that we could make a difference to how the country was run. It would be a chance to show that things could be achieved by parties working together in government. Some political commentators find it difficult to accept such a concept, as proved to be the case in the early media hostility to coalition government when the Scottish Assembly was set up. Agreement was eventually reached which included anti-inflation policy, re-introducing a devolution bill for Scotland and Wales, carrying through the Homeless Persons' Bill which Liberal MP Stephen Ross had brought in as a private member's bill, appointing a minister for small business with genuine business experience, and direct elections to the European Parliament, although that commitment was fatally weakened by allowing only for a free vote rather than a whipped vote on whether the system should be proportional. Labour measures to which we were opposed were dropped, and a consultative structure was set up between ministers and their Liberal counterparts. It was not a coalition, and it was far from perfect, but the Lib–Lab pact worked in providing the stability for a big reduction in inflation, and it was a learning experience both for us and for the system.

However, the pact convinced me that if you are going to work with another party in government, you should do it through a coalition in which you hold key ministerial positions: without this, your input is severely limited and the government machinery is only working for the party which has ministerial office. It did have some particularly gratifying moments, not least when Tony Benn discovered to his surprise that he could not force through a massive centralisation of the electricity industry because we simply would not accept it. We forced the Chancellor to introduce a lower rate band on the lowest levels of income and to promote profit-sharing in industry. The pact started to come apart, as it was bound to do, when Jim Callaghan could not deliver enough of his party in the free vote to secure a fair system for the European elections. Dissatisfaction with the pact within the party and in the country was growing. It was a matter of choosing the time to end it, and the end became inevitable when the Government started to lose its grip on inflation policy and rejected Liberal proposals to strengthen it. In May 1978 we announced that we were withdrawing from the pact.

Callaghan found a temporary alternative with the Unionists, to whom he conceded the extra Northern Ireland seats (which were in fact justified by the population figures and the absence of devolved government). The Government limped along until its final crisis came in March 1979.

As a party we had not won a by-election for six years, and the short-term unpopularity and press criticism of the Lib–Lab pact were not good signs for a General Election which was clearly fast approaching. A by-election suddenly arose because of the death of the Labour MP Sir Arthur Irvine in Liverpool Edge Hill. It was a seat where a young candidate, David Alton, was already hard at work, but it was a by-election which Labour could easily have deferred until the anticipated General Election made it unnecessary. We had no means of forcing the by-election, so I had to persuade Labour's Chief Whip, Michael Cocks, to grant it. He and I had built up a good relationship while we worked together in the pact, and I also knew that he was bitterly opposed to the growing strength of the extreme left in the Liverpool Labour Party. So I installed a bottle of his favourite whisky in my office – whisky not being a normal part of my office equipment – and, in a series of discussions between late votes, convinced him that he owed us a favour; that it would be bad news for the Tories if we did well in the by-election; and that he would be better off with a Liberal MP than, as he put it, 'another head-banger from Merseyside'. It worked, and he got to his feet two days later to move, in the quaint language of the House, that 'Mr Speaker do issue his writ' for the election of a new member 'in the room of the late Sir Arthur Irvine', knowing full well that Labour might lose the seat to us. We threw everything into the by-election.

Meanwhile Labour was facing a vote of confidence on the eve of polling day. Their Whips were making frantic attempts to garner in votes, even contacting Clement Freud while he was campaigning in Liverpool to promise that if he 'missed the train' and failed to get back for the vote of confidence, the Government would withdraw its previous opposition to his Freedom of Information Private Member's Bill. It was a blandishment he rightly resisted since the Government had no real commitment to the Bill and could not have survived long enough to get it through. The Government lost the vote by one, so a dissolution became certain, with a temporary budget and Finance Bill. The by-election still went ahead, and we won. It was a marvellous boost for the General Election campaign, but I had to get David Alton into Westminster in double-quick time if he was to take his seat as an MP before Parliament was dissolved the following week. Urgent messages were sent to Liverpool, and the City Solicitor brought the writ down by train on Friday morning, enabling David Alton to take his seat and make his maiden speech on the Monday before heading straight back to Liverpool to start the campaigning all over again.

The General Election saw Labour defeated, divided, and out of power for the next 13 years. We did better than some had predicted, retaining 11 seats with 13.8% of the vote but losing Emlyn Hooson, John Pardoe and Jeremy Thorpe. The Thatcher years had begun.

It was to be a dramatic time in both government and opposition. In November 1979 Roy Jenkins delivered the Dimbleby lecture. It was the opening shot which led to the breakaway of the 'Gang of Four' from the Labour Party and the creation of the SDP. David Steel had been encouraging the process, first privately and then publicly, following a discussion he had with Jenkins, then President of the European Commission, shortly after the General Election. There was a key strategy decision for David Steel – whether to persuade Roy Jenkins to join the Liberal Party, or to encourage him to aim for what was potentially a much larger breakaway of Labour MPs by creating a new party. Many in the Liberals felt that the first option was the one he should have taken, and, if Jenkins and a few others had joined us, our prospects would undoubtedly have improved significantly. However, Jenkins and Steel both believed that a much larger number would leave Labour for a new party, with which Liberals could co-operate, and that the resulting shift would be much more likely to lead to fundamental change in the UK political map. So it was that Shirley Williams, Bill Rodgers and David Owen, the first two of whom had not contemplated joining the Liberals, and the third of whom would never do so, joined Jenkins to form the collective leadership of the SDP. They quickly attracted many recruits inside and outside parliament. The MPs and activists were mainly from Labour, but there were many supporters who had not previously been involved in politics, and there were a few Conservatives, including one MP. The Labour MPs who joined the new party were a diverse mixture, including philosophical Liberals like Bob Maclennan, Tom Ellis and John Roper, pro-Europeans of not particularly liberal hue like Mike Thomas, and members approaching retirement with a variety of reasons for discontent. When Islington MP Michael O'Halloran joined, temporarily as it turned out, I warned publicly about the new party becoming a refuge for political 'machine men whose machines have broken down' and 'refugees from re-selection'. But the SDP brought a new professionalism to its national presentation. It caught a popular mood of despair with Labour, now seen as irredeemably 'old left' under Michael Foot, and the increasingly harsh tone of the Thatcher government. Roy Jenkins and Shirley Williams went on to win spectacular by-elections at Glasgow Hillhead and Crosby, while we won by-elections at Croydon and at Bermondsey, where Simon Hughes established an unassailable stronghold by sheer hard work on behalf of deprived communities.

From the beginning of the SDP, the Liberal Party had a tactical challenge. Cyril Smith put it brutally by suggesting that we either had to take the new party over or 'strangle it at birth'. The second was not a real option, because the only way to do so was to fight in elections against each other. That was a policy of mutual destruction from which we would ourselves have been sufferers. Clearly we needed to work together, not simply for that negative reason (which would not have applied under a proportional voting system) but for the much more positive reason that we were both appealing to a growing section of the electorate who were attracted by things we both stood for and by the prospect of an electable alternative to the two parties who had run Britain for so long. We therefore had to co-operate at every level: leadership, parliamentary activity, policy-making and election-fighting. Leadership was in the end to prove the most difficult, when David Owen later took over from Roy Jenkins. Policy-making took the form of negotiating joint statements, programmes and election manifestos, a process in which I was closely involved. Parliamentary co-operation was much easier, smoothed as it was by my very good relations with the SDP's equivalent, John Roper, and the close co-operation between our key staff members, Andrea Hertz and Sue Robertson. The two parliamentary parties had joint weekly meetings, and we were able to deploy much larger numbers of spokesmen and women from our combined resources, some of them particularly articulate and expert.

The SDP members and David Steel faced visceral hostility from the Labour benches around us, and we had battles to be physically heard over the heckling and even to have space to sit on the benches. Roy Jenkins was never comfortable with having to battle for a hearing, but the sheer force of his intellect and his mastery of the language won through.

Co-operation over which seats each party should fight was inherently very difficult. For by-elections we took it in turns. The alternative, of leaving the two parties locally to choose from candidates drawn from both parties in joint local selection, fell foul of the Liberal Party's constitution and, later, of the SDP's anxiety to have 'parity of representation'. So, in preparation for the General Election, detailed seat negotiation had to take place in every region of the country. It was largely successful, but it did reveal the different outlooks of the two parties. The SDP was a much more 'top down' organisation, with nationally determined objectives for the negotiations, and a negotiating style learned in the tough world of trade union bargaining, which Liberals found it hard to get used to. The SDP recognised that Liberals had built up very good prospects of success in what they referred to as 50 'gold' seats, and should fight most of them, balancing this with the SDP having two thirds of 150 promising or 'silver' seats. This mechanistic approach seemed to Liberals to ignore the crucial dependence on established local campaigning to secure victory, and our supporters saw no benefit in reducing the chance of success by withdrawing an already established Liberal campaigner in favour of an SDP candidate without a local track record. There were plenty of seats where, given our limited resources, Liberals had no such claim, but the argument illustrated the SDP founders' tendency to believe that, if the national campaign went well enough, seats with the right characteristics would fall to us like apples from the tree. Years of third-party campaigning had taught us differently.

The amount of time and energy taken up with these processes, and the occasional burst of unhelpful publicity generated by disagreements, were a distraction from the effort needed to push the Alliance from good poll figures up to the 30%-plus vote which we needed to make a General Election breakthrough. No one had ever brought together two parties on such a scale before: there was no handbook and no experience to build on, but a large part of the electorate was behind us and wanted us to succeed.

Meanwhile, events on the other side of the world were moving in a direction which would dramatically change the political situation. We had taken part in exchanges in the Commons over the future of the Falkland Islands, expressing concern at the Government's apparent willingness to signal that it might be willing to go over the heads of the inhabitants and reach some sort of deal in defiance of their unanimous wish to remain under British rule. In a move which was clearly going to be seen by Argentina as a signal that Britain was not interested in the islands, Mrs Thatcher's government announced the future withdrawal of *HMS Endurance*, the survey ship which was part of the islands' nominal defence. The Commanding Officer of *HMS Endurance*, a courageous man who later became my constituent, was sending back signals about Argentine intentions, attitudes and military activity, but they were ignored. A group of Argentine 'scrap dealers' took over South Georgia, testing Britain's reactions, and got no clear answer. On 2 March 1982, General Galtieri launched an invasion of the Falklands. It was an invasion which could have been prevented had Mrs Thatcher made abundantly clear that we would fight to recover the islands, and if she had not given several apparent signals to the contrary. Decisive action would have saved thousands of British and Argentinian lives.

It was a grave misjudgement for which any government could have expected to pay a severe political price. British servicemen and women saved the islands, and in doing so they saved Mrs Thatcher. The decision to launch a naval task force, which we strongly supported, and the opportunity to appear as an effective and decisive war leader, saved her from the political consequences of her earlier lack of decisiveness. A month before the invasion, both we and Labour had been on 33% in the polls, a breakthrough situation for us; but as a worried nation rallied round its leaders in support of our servicemen and women, the political ground shifted back in favour of the Conservatives. Despite a 28% showing in the post-victory local elections, with the exception of Simon Hughes' Bermondsey victory we did badly in parliamentary by-elections. The 1983 General Election gave us a quarter of the votes but only 23 seats, all but one of the gains being Liberal rather than SDP. For only 2% more votes than the Liberal/SDP Alliance, Labour had nine times as many seats. The Conservatives were a minority in the votes, with 42.4%, but had a huge majority of seats – over 150 more than all other parties. The British electoral system had spectacularly demonstrated its ability to defy the wishes of the country's voters.

During the campaign there had been a significant indication that the balance of power on the SDP side of the Alliance was shifting. A strategy meeting had been fixed at David Steel's home in Ettrick Bridge. It was a Sunday: I had a long-standing commitment to preach at the morning service at Berwick parish church. I had offered to withdraw if they were concerned about having me as the preacher during the election campaign, but they were keen to go ahead. A helicopter was arranged to take me from Berwick to the meeting, but fog grounded it, so I arrived after the discussion was well under way. There was one issue: the leadership. Roy Jenkins, to whom David Steel deferred as the senior of the two leaders, was rather optimistically described as our 'Prime Minister-designate', but he had a bad press in much of the campaign and there was some particularly unhelpful TV footage featuring him during bleak canvassing on a wet day in the West of Scotland.

When I arrived at Ettrick Bridge, the case was being put for David
Steel to assume the leadership of the Alliance for the remainder of the
campaign, and it was being fiercely opposed by SDP peer Jack
Diamond, who had the advantage that he was not actually fighting
the election as a candidate, as most of the rest of us were. It must
have been fairly embarrassing for Roy Jenkins, but he was probably
as surprised as anyone by the way David Owen weighed in on his
behalf. Given that the two were as far apart politically as it was
possible to be within the SDP, it seemed obvious to me that Owen's
interest was in the future. He was preserving the position of SDP
leader within the Alliance in the belief that he would soon be
occupying it. Clearly we were not going to be able to agree on any
formal change. We trooped across the road to the village hall for a
very well-attended press conference, which I sat through in mounting
gloom. It was explained that there would be no change, although
David Steel did have a number of prominent appearances already
planned in the remaining days of the campaign. The assembled press
simply did not believe us: they thought we were glossing over a Steel
takeover to save Jenkins from embarrassment. So the story they all
wrote was pretty well the opposite of what had actually happened
and, unwittingly, they did us a favour. Behind the scenes, however,
Dr Owen was looking to his future.

I shall not forget that day, but equally I do not forget a delightful
Jenkins moment immediately before the election. Prior to elections
there was a meeting at which the Leaders and Chief Whips of each
party negotiated the distribution of party election broadcasts, which
is significant not only for the party broadcasts themselves – generally
thought to be very unpopular – but also because the ratio of party
broadcasts is used as a rough guide to how the news programmes
divide time in their coverage of the campaign. It is a meeting in which

arguments of spurious rationality are deployed to disguise a battle for party advantage. On this occasion the Tories wanted no ground given to the Alliance, seeing themselves as much safer with Labour as the opposition, and Labour saw any concession to the SDP as time stolen from them by turncoats; all this was in the face of the polling and by-election evidence that levels of support for the Alliance matched or exceeded Labour's.

The Labour Chief Whip wanted five broadcasts each for Labour and Conservatives, with only three for the Liberal/SDP Alliance, while the Conservatives thought we should have two but might concede three. We thought we should have parity, or at least four broadcasts. The broadcasters said that if the disagreement was not resolved they would impose a 5–5–4 ratio. After excluding the broadcasters, resuming, adjourning the whole meeting and resuming again, the other two parties concluded that it was better to agree 5–5–4 than allow the broadcasters to get away with imposing it. Roy had contributed little to these exchanges, leaving the task of negotiating to me. When silence marked another deadlock, Jenkins observed 'This is the first such meeting I have attended … that is to the good, since constant attendance at meetings like this would undoubtedly warp the personality'.

After the election, Roy Jenkins resigned the leadership of the SDP and David Owen took over. Just at the time that the members of the two parties at local level were becoming comfortable with working together, the leadership moved from a comfortable partnership to competitive and mistrustful power-sharing. Shots of two leaders relaxing in suspiciously matching pullovers soon gave way to the *Spitting Image* shot of a tiny David Steel in the pocket of a disdainful David Owen. It was a damaging portrayal but it was very misleading – David Steel was no pushover, as his determined pursuit of realignment had shown, but Owen saw a Liberal threat to his personal views and prejudices round every corner. Combat at the top was inevitable. Although Owen had ability and determination, his personality made him extremely difficult to work with, and his conviction that he was right meant that he could never voluntarily reach a compromise. This inability to work with others or to reach an accommodation meant that no party was small enough for David Owen's presence in it to be other than fatally divisive. He eventually led a party of four MPs until it, too, fell apart.

I make this criticism despite recognising the value of the stringent reappraisal of policy and manifesto commitments on which Owen rightly insisted, and in which he actively participated. His passion for detailed policy was the opposite of David Steel's impatience with it. To my surprise, Owen wanted me to draft the manifesto for the 1987 election, and we then took it through enormously detailed joint discussions, culminating in an all-night session at the printers to ensure that every dot and comma was as agreed.

Roy Jenkins was not the only Alliance leader to resign in the aftermath of the 1983 election. So did David Steel, who had actually become ill with post-viral depression and exhaustion. I still have his resignation letter, which I retrieved from the Party President, John Griffiths. Nearly all of us at the top of the party believed that neither the timing nor the reasoning for a change were right, and that David Steel was in no state to be taking the decision. We persuaded him to take a break until the new parliamentary session started later in the year, believing that he would return with renewed energy. We were right, and he did. I took over as acting leader, giving me opportunities which came my way quite often in later years to make use of the Leader's slot at Prime Minister Questions; it is something I have always perversely enjoyed, and managed to use reasonably effectively. But there was a far more challenging task: Mrs Thatcher sent Willie Whitelaw to be her Leader in the Lords, creating a by-election in the apparently very safe Conservative constituency of Penrith and the Border. It was, however, a seat with some Liberal tradition: it had returned a Liberal MP in the memory of older voters. I believed that we had a good chance, but the most difficult task was to get Liberal volunteers, exhausted by the General Election, on which many had used up their annual holidays, to get to Cumberland for a by-election which, from the South, did not look that promising. We fought an intense campaign in a very large constituency which is like a gramophone record with a hole in the middle, the hole being the separate constituency of Carlisle. David Steel broke his sabbatical to make several visits from his home nearby in the Scottish Borders – Carlisle was in fact his nearest railway station, and he knew the area well. The weather was scorching, the response on the doorstep was good, but still we struggled to bring in enough volunteers for so large an area. When the votes were counted, we were barely 500 short of victory. It was one of the most disappointing by-election moments I can recall, because a victory could have given us an enormous boost.

During the 1983 Parliament I gave up the post of Chief Whip, with David Alton as my successor, and became Deputy Leader and Foreign Affairs spokesman. It was an enjoyable period of partial release from some of the party management pressures, which are particularly heavy on the Chief Whip. When you are Chief Whip, if you take the job seriously, you go through life with a sense that if something goes wrong in the Parliamentary Party or the Party Conference it is your fault for not having taken effective action to prevent it.

The disappointment of Penrith was compensated by four by-election victories, two by the SDP and two by the Liberals. A fifth by-election early in 1987 was, sadly, in a seat of our own which we retained. My closest friend in the Parliamentary Party was David Penhaligon, a much loved and entertaining but also highly intelligent and shrewd Cornishman. He was an extremely hard-working constituency MP who had won his seat in the second general election of 1974, a feat in itself. Driving before seven o'clock on a dark December morning to visit the postmen as they sorted Christmas mail, he skidded on ice and did not survive the crash. It was a shattering blow for his young family and a terrible personal blow for many of us at Westminster. He and I had a meal together in the House of Commons virtually every day: what was lunch for me would be his breakfast, since he often worked on letters through the night and, unless he was on a committee, he would then sleep through the morning. We each knew that we would probably be candidates for the party leadership at some point, and would need to sort out whether we could avoid standing against each other, because we had great respect for each other's different qualities. David would have brought a huge capacity to win votes and a great deal of commitment and toughness to the leadership, but he would have needed support to cope with his tendency to be disorganised and his lack of thoroughness in preparation. Now we would never make that plan. Apart from the deaths I was to experience in my own family, no death has ever affected me as deeply or as grievously as David's did.

In the same year, 1986, we had one of those occasions when Liberals snatch defeat form the jaws of victory. Negotiating an agreed defence policy between the two parties was already proving difficult, not least because of the presence within the Liberal Party of a substantial minority of unilateralist views – the very issue which had motivated some of the SDP to leave the Labour Party. David Steel, David Owen, John Cartwright and I had been looking at European (i.e. Anglo-French) options for co-operation on nuclear deterrence, a concept which was attractive to those in both parties who were worried about Britain's dependence on the US for its deterrent. For years it had not been genuinely independent. In presenting a resolution to the party conference at Eastbourne we included that element in a wide-ranging resolution. We then faced an amendment, whose effect was simply to rule out any nuclear element in European defence co-operation, but which would be interpreted outside the party as a complete rejection of any British nuclear deterrent. By a combination of barnstorming speeches, ambiguous amendment drafting and the relatively open access to places at the Liberal Party conference, we ended up with a defeat by 652 votes to 625. We dropped to our lowest levels in the polls for two years.

One of the things that has always kept me going at difficult times is the way in which there is a funny side to most events, even the most trying. After the defence vote I had to do a live TV interview with Robin Day in the next morning's breakfast programme. It was staged in the Conference hotel, with large windows behind me revealing a glittering sea on a beautiful sunny morning. As I sought to explain that we had not gone completely unilateralist and would emerge with a continuing commitment to deter any nuclear aggressor from attacking Britain, the camera crew seemed to be having difficulty suppressing the giggles. The questioning went on longer than I thought we were allowed, until it was clear that we were off the air. I discovered that during my deeply serious presentation a ladder had appeared at the window behind me, followed by a wash leather, followed by the cheery face of the window cleaner. When he saw the camera, his face was a picture, and a much more memorable one than my presentation of Liberal defence policy.

Parties do have to be managed, so David Steel set about repairing the damage with a new statement on defence policy, agreed between the

parties and backed by key Eastbourne rebels including Simon
Hughes and Michael Meadowcroft. The statement recognised that
Britain would maintain a minimum nuclear deterrent unless it could
be negotiated away as part of global arms reduction, which could
remove the threat with which it was intended to deal. The
effectiveness of the party's damage repair and recovery was
demonstrated in the massive majority the 24-year-old Matthew
Taylor secured in retaining David Penhaligon's Truro seat, and in
the dramatic gain by the SDP's Rosie Barnes of the Labour seat of
Greenwich.

The Alliance had begun 1987 with a major relaunch, anticipating a
General Election, and despite the tensions and differences, Owen
and Steel worked hard and used their considerable skills effectively
in presenting their case that the Alliance was the way of achieving
fundamental political and social reform. It was the opportunity to
break with the stranglehold of the two parties and the highly
centralised, ineffective and divisive system of government which
between them they had created. Things looked good, and in one
sense they were: we were heading for 22.6% of the votes, closely
behind Labour's 24%, but the British electoral system cheated us on
an extraordinary scale. We gained only three more seats, while we
lost five and the SDP lost Roy Jenkins. Our gains included Menzies
Campbell in North East Fife, a welcome arrival and one well-
deserved at his fifth attempt.

Much of the blame for so frustrating a result, at least in Liberal
circles, was ascribed to having a dual leadership, an issue which was
frequently raised on the doorsteps. The election was scarcely over
when David Steel challenged the parties to join together. At the local
level in many places the parties were joining, but the barriers were
at the top. David Owen was bitterly and incurably opposed to

merger, while Charles Kennedy was known to want a merger (having been elected with a largely Liberal team locally), and Shirley Williams and Bill Rodgers were expected to come out in favour. A ballot of SDP members showed a majority for merger, whereupon Owen resigned as Leader. His successor, Bob Maclennan, was an awkward speaker, not an obvious leader, and a difficult and strangely emotional negotiator, but he was a natural Liberal. He later abundantly proved his worth to the new party in negotiating with Robin Cook an agreement on constitutional issues which, quite remarkably, determined the constitutional agenda for the first Blair government.

A tortuous and inevitably painful process of merger negotiation then began, and occupied a great deal of my time as well as that of the other participants from both sides. No two national parties of comparable size had ever attempted to negotiate a merger in this way before. At the end of the process I felt like discouraging any party in its right mind from ever doing so, because it proved increasingly difficult and, in the short term, so damaging. We had to pay a high political price at a time when we could least afford it, in order to create a viable third party with Liberal principles and the range of additional talented people brought to the party by the SDP. We had to agree on principles, structures and policies and – amazingly the most difficult thing of all – on our name.

Negotiating teams were set up with seventeen members from each party, and we worked from late September until Christmas 1987. From the beginning there was a difference in style and method between the two teams; the SDP members, as in the seat negotiations, came with agreed positions. Members on their side rarely departed from those positions in discussion, and, if agreement was not reached, their instinct was to withdraw and consider among themselves whether or not to vary their position, and preferably to hold out for what they wanted. The Liberal team, under David Steel's leadership, had sometimes not had prior opportunity to consider positions, and would sometimes find that its Leader was prepared to give ground in the full meeting without consulting his own team. The whole process was documented fairly accurately by two of the Liberal participants: Rachael Pitchford, who chaired the Young Liberals, and Tony (now Lord) Greaves.[10] A lengthy process produced a structure for the new party which contained both Liberal and SDP characteristics. To meet Liberal demands, autonomy within a Federal Party was secured for Scotland and Wales, regions in England retained a significant role, and the Conference remained the authority for policy and was to be democratically elected. The SDP secured a tightening of the numbers which each local association could send to conference and devised a much more deliberative process for policy-making by the Conference. They also secured postal ballots for the selection of local candidates. The end result was a party structure which, with a few exceptions, both sides could live with. There was a rather silly SDP insistence that NATO membership should appear in the preamble to the party's constitution – a wholly inappropriate place for what is a policy rather than a philosophical principle, and a distraction in a document which had been successfully negotiated up to that point. The issue's importance for the SDP was all about holding on to Owenite members, but it caused unhelpful friction between the negotiators.

The two things which caused the real problems were, in a sense, extraneous to the process of agreeing a party structure. One was the name; few Liberals would contemplate a name which did not include the word 'Liberal'. It is how our core voters identify themselves, and it directly states our central belief in the freedom of the individual. Unwillingness of the SDP team to agree on 'Liberal Democrat' meant that we were left with an inevitably temporary and cumbersome name, 'Social and Liberal Democrats' and with an unresolved problem which later came close to derailing the new party's leadership. Then, when the weary negotiating teams had virtually concluded (minus four Liberals and one SDP negotiator who did not accept the final agreement), they were left with one final and unmanageable problem created for them by their leaders. The two parties had established very extensive agreement on policies, mainly through their work together in Parliament but also because of the shared convictions about Britain's needs which had brought them together. We already had plenty of policy, and whatever new policy we needed would be for the new party's deliberative policy process to determine. This was not enough for David Steel and Bob Maclennan, who wanted an eye-catching policy statement to be presented as part of the merger agreement.

So they commissioned two journalists, Hugo Dixon and Andrew Gilmour, both of whom happened to be the sons of Tory MPs, to write a draft policy statement. The result was a document of distinctly Thatcherite rhetoric and woefully ill-considered and gimmicky policy proposals. It might have made an acceptable series of polemic articles for the *Economist* magazine, but it neither reflected the thinking of the new party nor had any parentage within it. I am not even convinced that David Steel had read it properly. Our party's policy committee rejected it, at least unless it was massively changed, and I kept pressing the negotiators, who were bogged down with the name issue, to have some serious discussion about it.

We ended up discussing the policy document through the night on the very last day allotted to negotiation. There were a lot of amendments agreed, but it remained a liability. At about four in the morning, when it was clear that the Leaders were insistent on going ahead, we broke up. I was deeply depressed, and knew that I could not support the document and would have to make my views public the next day. After a couple of hours' sleep I got up to phone David and let him know my position. Several of my colleagues, notably Alex Carlile, had already done the same. The planned Press Conference was postponed until later that day. The Parliamentary Party met with the SDP members. Not a single Liberal MP backed the policy document. When the negotiating teams met again, it became clear that there was a total impasse. Bob Maclennan appeared uncontrollably distraught, and Charles Kennedy took him aside in order to prevent him from abandoning the whole process. A grim press conference announced that negotiations had been 'paused', and both leaders found themselves under pressure from their own parties to abandon the 'dead parrot' policy document, as it quickly became known.

And abandoned it was, with a small group set up to write a new policy statement based on the many worthwhile policy statements we had already made. It was done quickly, easily, and well, and the merger was put back on track. It was announced with much excitement on the steps of Cowley Street (the fine headquarters building of the SDP, rented from the Church Commissioners, which became the new party's headquarters). To everyone's amazement, Bob Maclennan announced that he was off to Limehouse to invite Dr Owen to abandon his recusant position and join the new party: it was a futile move, and it revealed how much the SDP negotiators had been influenced by their fear of the short-term damage Owen and his few supporters could do to the new party.

Willie Goodhart, the SDP lawyer who became a huge asset to the new party, later said of the negotiations, in which he took part, that David Steel 'was not prepared to put up a stiff enough fight against us, with the result that on some issues we won when this was not in the long-term interest of the new party'. The refusal to accept the Liberal Democrat name (which we were later to adopt) was, he wrote, 'the prime example of the SDP team's more effective negotiating skill enabling us to win battles which it would have been better for us to have lost'.[11] He was right. He was right also in his overall assessment that the merger worked, drawing together so many of the good features of both parties. In a fairly short time the joining would become so close that past party allegiance became irrelevant. But the final stages of the process itself had done short-term damage, and would continue to do so until the outstanding issues were resolved.

At last we were able to take agreed merger proposals to a Special Liberal Party conference at Blackpool, which in terms of weather was not at its best in late January 1988. 'What am I doing on a Saturday in this wet and windy watering hole?' mused Ludovic Kennedy, whose excellent by-election performance in Rochdale in 1958 had been one of the spurs to my original decision to join the Liberal Party. Over a thousand of us were there to decide on, and in most cases to support, a merger with the SDP on the terms we had so painfully agreed. It was a good natured but intense all-day debate in which most of those of us who had been involved in the negotiations spoke, and many more of the party's best known figures. We comfortably secured the necessary two-thirds majority. Most of those who had been critical of the merger or its terms stayed in the party, although one who did not was my colleague and deputy Michael Meadowcroft, whose abilities I respected despite our disagreement on the merger and on defence. He recently rejoined.

We all knew that it would be different for the SDP's Council: although the majority for merger was comfortable, the Owenites, whose official line was to abstain rather than actually block the merger, were clearly set on staying out of the new party. A national ballot of the members of both parties produced a huge majority of support in the Liberal Party and just short of a two-thirds majority in the SDP. The new party, with exciting prospects but a ludicrously cumbersome name, was born on 3 March 1988. The name argument, which stood for a great deal more, was not over, but next came the leadership election.

There was no way David Steel could win Liberal support to lead the new party. He was entitled to be regarded as a Moses, who had laboured long to bring the people to the promised land but would never, as leader, see it himself. His speeches, his determination and his strategic vision had brought us to this point, but he had acquired far too much unwelcome baggage in the merger negotiations, and his mishandling over the policy document was the last straw, particularly for many of his parliamentary colleagues. David Steel and Bob Maclennan had been interim leaders of the new party, but neither sought the leadership, and an election contest therefore began in the early summer, culminating in a ballot of all the new party's members and the announcement of the result on 28 July.

It was quite clear, and had been since the day he arrived at the House of Commons in 1983, that Paddy Ashdown intended to be party leader. His winning of the Yeovil seat was a tremendous achievement, based on hard work and considerable sacrifice at a stage in life when he could have been continuing an international career. Ambition, determination, and a constant search for the next objective are Paddy's hallmarks. At times his obvious ambition irritated his colleagues, which is why he might not have won the leadership under the old system, in which only the MPs had votes. A classic memory is of a party conference in the Pavilion Theatre, Bournemouth, which was only the Conference venue by day, because – and you could hardly make this up – The Krankies were appearing in the evening variety show later in the week. The Krankies' dressing rooms were assigned as the Whip's Office base, from which we provided support to our MPs during the conference. When the Whip's Office staff arrived, the office had been occupied by Paddy's bulky computer equipment (he was a pioneer in applying IT to politics). A sign had been stuck on the door saying 'Paddy Ashdown's office'. Neither it nor the computer equipment were there an hour later: it is never wise to fall out with Whips' Office staff in any party.

Should I stand? Paddy had shrewdly kept his distance from the entire process of negotiating the merger: his hands, politically speaking, were not soiled by the attempts to resolve disagreements between the parties. He was particularly liked by the Social Democrats because he did not appear to carry what they would have regarded as Liberal baggage, and for the same reason he was viewed with anxiety by some Liberals who had not seen enough evidence of his commitment to the Liberal principles which were the party's fundamental reason for existence. I shared some of these anxieties. I certainly felt that there should be a contest, and that clear philosophical ground should be staked out so as to enable the party to establish its values from the very beginning. We had not gone through these painful processes simply to provide an alternative party at a particular juncture in twentieth century British politics, in response to a particular set of circumstances. We had not done this merely to seek an opportunity for some Liberals and some Social Democrats, excellent previous or potential ministers though they were, to get to the Cabinet table. We were in it for the long term, and we needed to be clear what those long-term purposes are. Standing in the leadership election, even when the prospects for success were not good, was a way of making those purposes clear.

A ballot of our party members can be a very good way of choosing our party leader, because it tests those qualities and skills which you need to win greater success for the party, and our full membership reflects a very broad swathe of society from which we seek political support. The leadership election process tests who can be most effective in raising funds for a campaign, planning that campaign, getting enough key people in place to support the campaign, and getting a compelling image across to those who have the votes. Paddy won the campaign on all those counts. The campaign also tests how well each candidate can inspire those members who come to hustings meetings: most observers thought the outcome on that was either a tie or in my favour, but most of the voting members do not attend hustings meetings, and some of those who do have already voted in the postal ballot. What matters, as in a General Election, is how effectively you come across to those who do not attend meetings and who get their picture of the election from the media. Paddy also had the added advantage that a very high proportion of our paid up membership was in his own region of the South West, in the South and in the Home Counties where he was best known. Although we held more parliamentary seats in Scotland, the North and Wales, where I was able to do well, membership there was much lower. A significant factor, much referred to in the press, was that Paddy was new, seemingly unconnected with the merger process or the leadership of David Steel, while I was seen as a continuation of what had gone before.

The campaign, in which I was greatly indebted to Monroe Palmer for his organising support, was exhausting but enjoyable. It involved much travel and the opportunity to see old friends and new. I started it with a packed meeting in my old primary school in Poynton, Cheshire, a location which enabled me to bring together Cyril Smith, Alex Carlile and Emlyn Hooson, stalwart supporters who got the campaign off to a fine start. The school was in the first ward in which I ever campaigned successfully in a local election, and it was still represented by a Liberal. From Edinburgh and Cardiff to Cornwall and Hampshire, I travelled the country in glorious summer weather. I teased the press for making the two of us seem like a contrast between Oliver North (President Reagan's buccaneering and law-breaking ex-marine supplier of arms to the Nicaragua contras) and John Wesley. It stuck, which taught me never to tease the press. Central to my case was that we had to establish the identity of the party in the minds of voters, while ensuring that we kept both Liberal and SDP support, as a party which offered a route to a society in which we have both freedom and fairness, in which we combine economic opportunity and a sense of community. We should define ourselves by the values for which we stand, not by reference to which of the other parties we wanted to replace or which might co-operate with us: we had a firm basis of belief in freedom, opportunity, resistance to uncontrolled power, internationalism and care for the environment. The other parties were in the process of discarding the ideologies of Socialism and old Conservatism without having anything to replace them, and events could carry them to unknown destinations. Just how far the other parties were to move in the ensuing years I could scarcely have imagined.

We knew what the result would be before the campaign was over: in reality, we knew before it officially started. Paddy won decisively. In his diaries, Paddy commented on my reaction when the result was declared. He wrote 'Alan was gracious in defeat but put down one or two markers which, I confess, worry me: he did not alter his "values" line from the campaign'. That was true, and Paddy's first two years as Leader amply demonstrated why I was right to be concerned about values and identity. He made precisely the mistakes

I had feared he would make, and it was those fears which had impelled me to stand and set out clearly what I thought we ought to be doing. Having, as he himself later realised, thrown away two years when he could have been getting off to a much better start, he went on to become an absolutely outstanding leader, doing enormous good for the party, earning wide respect, and demonstrating a much firmer commitment to the principles of Liberalism than seemed possible at the beginning. It was a privilege and a stimulating challenge to work closely with him, as I did through most of his leadership.

—10—

RUNNING A PARTY: THE LIBERAL DEMOCRATS

The new party assembled in Blackpool for a Conference in September 1988. Hanging over us, however, was the question of the name. What's in a name? Quite a lot, when you think about it. For party members, the name is a symbol, a shorthand, for beliefs and for the efforts which brought them political success. For voters more widely, a name is a brand. Owners of established commercial brands do not often throw away well-known brand names, and they pay a price if they do. The merger negotiations had left us with the cumbersome title of 'Social and Liberal Democrats'. Hardly anyone wanted to use it. It could not even be pronounceably abbreviated, except, ridiculously, as 'Salads'. It was clearly only a temporary label. The SDP had resisted the obvious title of Liberal Democrats for reasons of very short-term anxiety: they thought that David Owen would be able to use it to say 'Liberal Democrats can join the merged party, but Social Democrats should follow me'. There was still a lurking fear of Owen's destructive power in the SDP leadership. So Paddy took up the idea of calling the party 'Democrats', a term which conveys nothing in British politics, and only has meaning to those political enthusiasts who follow American politics. The US Democrats offer no reliable parallel to what our party stands for.

Most of us in the Parliamentary Party believed this was a serious error; some of us felt that it was so important for us to keep 'Liberal' as part of our designation that we were not prepared to change our description or, ultimately, to accept the whip of a party which had so lost sight of its core beliefs as to abandon its historic title in favour of something so vague and unrecognisable. With the help of Shirley Williams – always a superb speaker, and on almost every other occasion on the right side of the argument – the title of 'Democrats' got through the Conference by 650 votes to 500. To have divided the new party right down the middle, and with feelings running very high, was a crazy way to have begun a leadership. The issue was going to rumble on, and my old Welsh-speaking friend Geraint Howells, MP for Ceredigion, was quite public in his determination to see the 'Democrats' title consigned to the dustbin, insisting that it would never be used by the party in Wales.

It took until July the following year, after another late-night Parliamentary Party showdown, for Paddy to apply himself effectively to the name problem. The issue was undermining his position at a time when he needed to establish himself in the House, to sort out the party's finances, and to deal with the temporary problem posed by David Owen, which was mainly one of split votes. That problem was particularly evident in the by-election in Richmond, North Yorkshire, where it turned out that the Owenites, who were now fighting as a separate party, had the better known local candidate. Either party could have won if only one had stood, although the Owenite candidate was clearly the better supported of the two: between us we had enough votes to win. Had we done so the young William Hague would not have got started on his parliamentary career. More generally, we were getting poor by-election results, and we had appalling results in the European elections. Party morale, as Paddy admitted in his diaries, was 'rock bottom, with implications for membership, finance, the wretched name and everything else'. Something had to be done, and with encouragement from Roy Jenkins (who had long favoured calling the party 'Liberal Democrats'), it was finally resolved by a ballot of conference representatives. They voted overwhelmingly in favour of 'Liberal Democrats'. This diversion had taken until October 1989, nearly a year and a half after Paddy's election as leader.

It was a turning point in Paddy's leadership, and, having put right his mistake, he concentrated much more effectively on getting the party into shape for a general election. The Owenite breakaway party was closing itself down.[12] Paddy's sound judgement on the international issues, and his determination to stick to it, showed itself to advantage during the first Gulf War over Saddam Hussein's invasion of Kuwait. I found it increasingly easy to work with him once these initial difficulties were out of the way. This I did first as Treasury spokesman, and later in 1992 as Deputy Leader. On reflection, 'easy' is not the best word to describe working closely with Paddy. He is driven, determined, strategic in his thinking, genuinely keen to win his way by consultation but, paradoxically, sometimes inclined to play with his cards close to his chest, keeping everyone guessing about his next move. But we developed a healthy respect for each other and an ability to work together. Our first objective had to be to survive the next General Election and bring back enough MPs to have an impact in the next Parliament. We did not start from a very good position. Neil Kinnock was leading the Labour Party, and Mrs Thatcher was still in power. Mrs Thatcher's mounting problems culminated in her very reluctant resignation in November 1990, and she was replaced, to most people's surprise, by John Major. He would now have held three of the four principal offices of state in less time than the duration of a single parliament. In the 1992 General Election we managed to win 20 seats, two more than we had won in 1987: far fewer than our votes justified, but a viable base for a new Parliament in which Labour was going to start with turmoil and John Major had hung on with a party deeply divided over Europe.

In the new Parliament I was elected Deputy Leader, and so began a period of working more closely with Paddy, although I had already been working with him on detailed planning for what would happen in a 'hung' parliament, where no party had a majority and our votes could be crucial. His diaries reveal that, in the event of a coalition emerging from that election, he wanted me in the Cabinet as Chief Secretary to the Treasury.

At the heart of Paddy's strategy was a desire to change the whole shape of British politics, and to do so by making the Liberal Democrats an instrument in the creation of an alternative progressive government in Britain – an alternative, that is, to the Conservatives. There was nothing new about this. It was the motive for the creation of the SDP and the Alliance. Some of those most critical of this objective were inclined to forget that it had also been Jo Grimond's objective in the early 1960s, when he envisaged non-socialist Labour supporters and some progressive Conservatives joining with Liberals in a 'realignment of the Left' (a term I have always thought misleading and unhelpful). It lay behind David Steel's insistence that the Liberal Party must be prepared to share in government, as we had done in the Lib–Lab pact. There are some serious problems with such a strategy. In the first place, it presupposed that the Labour Party could be shorn of much of its active membership and pushed to the sidelines: the fact that Neil Kinnock had lost disastrously made this seem, to some at least, more plausible. My view, based on greater knowledge of the North, Scotland and Wales than Paddy had, was that Labour was never going to disappear, however ineffective it was and however incapable it proved to be of winning a General Election. Labour had heartlands: in some of those heartlands we had shown that Liberal Democrats could beat them, but only in the limited number of areas where we had people who were willing and able to sustain extremely hard work over a long period. Furthermore, if we looked as if we were closely associated with Labour, or used Grimond's easily misunderstood language about 'realignment of the left', we risked alienating former Conservative voters whose support we needed in most of the seats we had a chance of winning.

The logic of the Liberal Democrats' commitment to electoral reform is not that a party such as ours has to look for some restructuring of the party system, but that the different strands of opinion represented by the parties can remain independent, and can work together through the formation of post-election coalitions (unless one party actually commands a majority of the votes). Proportional representation prevents minorities from acquiring the powers of majorities: the majority needed to form a government has to be drawn from a genuine majority of the voters' representatives through the forming of coalitions. Because we do not operate under such a system, except in the Scottish Parliament and the Welsh and Northern Ireland Assemblies, taking part in a coalition or showing willingness to do so can be politically very risky, because it can lead to a disproportionate risk to the seats we hold or need to win. It gives the impression that the party's independence is being threatened or compromised. It makes MPs and candidates very nervous. Yet it is the logical conclusion of advocating proportional representation, and it is also clear that proportional representation will not be achieved unless Liberal Democrats are part of a coalition which brings it in. With the exception of Northern Ireland, every system of proportional representation currently operating in Britain is the result of Liberal Democrats being in a position to bargain to achieve it: that was true in the Scottish constitutional convention and the devolution bills, it was true for the introduction of STV in Scottish local government, and it was true for the European elections.

That being the case, and on the basis that government is better if it has broader support, I have always been prepared to consider potential Liberal or Liberal Democrat involvement in coalitions. Experience of the Lib–Lab pact strongly confirmed my view that offering support from the opposition benches on the basis of an agreement, without ministers in key positions in the government, is a very unsatisfactory alternative. It leaves the party with no continuing influence on a massive government machine which will work in support of the party whose ministers are directing it: the party in charge will take credit for all the achievements, and the minority party will get the blame for all the errors that it can do nothing to prevent.

It is also my view that creating a presumption that there is only one party with whom you are prepared to form a coalition is fundamentally mistaken. If everyone knows that you only have the authority or the will to go in one direction, your bargaining power on behalf of your voters starts to disappear, and the party's vote will itself be reduced because you are seen as the natural or inevitable ally of the party to which many of them are wholly opposed. We had, therefore, normally maintained a position in which nothing was ruled out and nothing was ruled in – there was no theoretical bar to coalition with either of the other parties, assuming that a programme for government could be agreed and the circumstances were such that such a government could succeed. It was sometimes misleadingly referred to as 'equidistance': misleading because a position cannot be defined from two moving points, and both the other parties have moved long distances politically in recent years. Our position is defined by what we believe, not by reference to the shifting beliefs of our opponents. There are, of course, circumstances in which it is pretty obvious that a coalition with one of the parties is not politically conceivable. If either Labour or the Conservatives had become the largest party on the basis that they would withdraw Britain from the European Union, for example (and Labour once tried to do so), it simply would not be possible for us to agree a programme in which that was included. Equally, if a Prime Minister has gone to the country explicitly in order to seek a new mandate, as Ted Heath did in 1974, and has clearly failed to get it, that is not a sound basis for joining a government.

However, my instinct is that it remains better to be free of prior obligation or prior commitments. Here lay a difference between Paddy's approach and mine. He was not only interested in exploring quite specifically the coalition possibilities with Labour – his view developed into a realignment approach which echoed Jo Grimond. The real value of his approach for us was that, once cast in the role of suitor, he was able to use it to exact commitments from Labour which he could not otherwise have obtained.

But other things happened first. One of them had the effect of accommodating my view that we should be prepared to work with either of the other parties, depending on programme and circumstances. John Major needed to get the Maastricht Treaty through Parliament, and his party was bitterly divided, with a band of determined Euro-sceptics. Labour's position was crudely and dishonestly opportunistic: they were in favour of the treaty, and would not vote against it but would vote against all the procedural motions that would be needed to prevent it being 'filibustered' or blocked by the 'Eurosceptics'. We were in favour of the Treaty but we also believed that there should be a referendum. Unlike Labour, we would vote for such a referendum, but wanted to ensure that the bill itself got through. So, night after night, we voted with the Conservative government against a combination of Labour opportunism and Conservative anti-Europeanism. When the Government won a key division by only two votes, Labour attacked us bitterly. In an orchestrated campaign they claimed that we had kept the Tories in power: yet we knew, and they knew perfectly well, that John Major would certainly not have resigned and called a General Election if he had lost the vote. We sustained some temporary damage where we were fighting Labour, but we had stuck to our principles.

The next key moment in the development of Paddy's strategy arose from the sudden and very sad death of Labour's leader John Smith. Although I had deplored John's stance over Maastricht, he was someone I liked and generally respected. I had worked very closely with him during the Lib–Lab pact on the first Scotland and Wales devolution bill. Our families had spent a day together on the Isle of Iona, which he loved and where he is buried – we were holidaying on Mull, and when the Smiths' kind hospitality meant that we were too late for the last ferry, we made it back from Iona in John's small dinghy. Labour had lost a leader of quality and ability in whom a lot of their hopes of recovery were invested. He had begun the attempt to make the party electable. Whether or not he could have succeeded is debatable, but the task was taken over by someone who was prepared to go a great deal further in order to make Labour electable: Tony Blair.

Tony was MP for a Northern constituency, Sedgefield, but I never felt that his heart was in the North or in constituency work. His home and family life were in London; his ambitions for himself and for the country, although more genuine and decent than many people now accept, were almost entirely concerned with national and international affairs, and a Northern constituency was, I fear, a mere stepping stone to power rather than a spur to help the North to get a better deal. His willingness to endorse Labour's unilateralist and anti-Europe programme under Michael Foot's leadership, when he stood as a candidate in Beaconsfield, was also a means to an end. As time went on, it became clear that there was no socialist sacred text which would not be burned, no trade union sacred cow which could not be slaughtered, no old Labour baby which could not be thrown out with the bath water. This man meant business. He had joined Labour to turn it into a government, and nothing was to be allowed to stand in the way.

Here was Paddy's opportunity. Despite considerable anxiety among Liberal Democrats, and before Parliament had returned that autumn, he had a lengthy discussion with the Labour leader at Tony Blair's home. He was laying the foundation of a strong personal relationship supported by a shared belief that the two parties should work together and keep the Tories out of power for a decade, during which a progressive modernisation of Britain could be carried through. Proportional representation might be on the agenda, but on that subject Blair was wary of committing himself. Blair clearly saw the Liberal Democrats as a source of both ideas and talent, and as a potential counterweight to his own left wing; Paddy was already thinking not just about a potential coalition in a hung Parliament, but also about getting Blair committed to working with us even if Labour got a majority at the next election. Behind this lurked something else – later known as 'the Project'. It was a term initially associated with the idea of a pre-election agreement with Labour, but it later became used for the belief, privately held by both Tony Blair and Paddy Ashdown, that the two parties might eventually merge. In that last sense of the term it was a concept wholly opposed by virtually all Liberal Democrats and had no support in the Parliamentary party; there were very few who would even have supported any general pre-election agreement. What did emerge from these discussions and the closeness of this relationship, however, was extremely important and valuable. It was the process leading to the Cook–Maclennan agreement.

Although the increasing press talk was unhelpful to us,[13] what was quietly being prepared was something very different, and it was good not only for us but for the country. It was a firm commitment on the part of the likely next Prime Minister to a whole series of constitutional measures, worked over in some detail by a team led by Robin Cook for Labour and Bob Maclennan for the Liberal Democrats. The list included securing PR in time for the next European Elections, incorporating the European Convention on Human Rights into British domestic law, carrying through devolution for Scotland and Wales with proportional electoral systems, and a Freedom of Information Act. Its one weak link was PR for Westminster, where agreement was limited to a Commission. That reflected not only Tony Blair's uncertainty but also the virtual impossibility of pulling his Shadow Cabinet any further in our direction on the issue at that point.

I was, therefore, happy to work with Paddy to back the achievement of things in which I strongly believed, by means of a process whose ultimate objectives I did not share. Precisely because so many of my colleagues knew of and shared my reservations about Paddy's ultimate destination, it was helpful to him to have my support. I was often reminded of the saying attributed to his days in the Marines –

'The men would follow Captain Ashdown wherever he took them, if only out of curiosity to see where on earth he was going'.

Much of the job of being Deputy Leader, which I combined first with the Treasury spokesmanship and later with Home Affairs, was the day-to-day business of chairing parliamentary meetings, talking through with Paddy some of the lines he was taking, alerting him to any concerns among the MPs, and attending bodies like the party's Policy Committee. As he devoted an increasing amount of time to events in the former Yugoslavia, where he was way ahead of the other politicians in perceiving what was going to happen and what needed to be done, more responsibilities fell on me, including further opportunities to take on the Leader's role at Prime Minister's Questions.

Deputising also involved taking his place at a mixture of events from banquets to funerals. In the latter category came the funeral of President Mitterand in January 1996. Paddy was in the Balkans, so I was despatched to Northolt airfield in the Prime Minister's convoy. We set off from Downing Street in early-morning darkness with police motor cyclists riding ahead of us to each junction: one of them fell off, happily without injury. I boarded a small RAF Queen's Flight aircraft with Ted Heath, Jim Callaghan, John Major and Tony Blair, while Prince Charles set off in a separate aircraft. From a French military airfield we were driven in a fleet of cars to Nôtre Dame cathedral. Tony Blair and I shared a car, and he quickly demonstrated the impressive command of colloquial French he had learned from working in a Paris bar. I gather that the Foreign Office did not consider it suitable for use in intergovernmental discussions.

When we arrived at the Cathedral there was unbelievable chaos. After the immaculate precision of British state occasions, I could hardly believe it. We were greeted by the harassed but resourceful British Ambassador who reported that some other country had taken our seats, but his officials were guarding two seats in the chancel for Prince Charles and John Major, and he had grabbed Azerbaijan's seats for the rest of us. Among this most extraordinary mêlée, which must have been a security man's nightmare, Boris Yeltsin appeared and was hustled by his own heavies to a seat near the front, and then Fidel Castro was similarly propelled through the crowd to a seat. Requiem Mass got under way, with a sermon from Cardinal Ratzinger which referred discreetly to Mitterand's rather distant relationship with the Catholic Church. When the Communion began, Tony asked 'Are we going up to take Communion?' I said 'But we're Protestants – they don't allow us to'. 'Oh, I do regularly when I go to Mass with the family – the priest in London doesn't mind at all'. (This was long before Tony's post-Prime Ministerial conversion to the Catholic church.) Actually, we had little hope of getting anywhere near the officiating priests, so that idea was abandoned. Then it was back to the plane. Nowadays I hope we would have gone by Eurostar.

Meanwhile, we were building up for the General Election which came on 1 May 1997. We had produced some sensational by-election victories, starting in Newbury, then Christchurch, Eastleigh and Littleborough and Saddleworth. The party was in relatively good shape, and we fought a strong campaign. We won 46 seats, more than doubling our numbers; Labour, however, had a 177-seat majority, and Tony Blair's arrival at Downing Street was accompanied by extraordinary media euphoria. Some of it was carefully stage-managed by Peter Mandelson and Alistair Campbell, but a significant part of the media and the nation seemed to be convinced that our new Prime Minister could walk on water. People who a decade later had not a good word to say about Tony Blair were equally over the top in their initial euphoria.

While I concentrated on helping the 46 Liberal Democrat MPs to become an effective team, Paddy was busy making sure that the Prime Minister kept to his commitment; Tony Blair, even in his moment of triumph, was still nurturing ideas about 'mending the schism that split apart the progressive forces in British politics'.[14] In other words, he was thinking about merger, which even Paddy was now telling him would never happen while he (Paddy) was still around. But it was a good atmosphere in which to get through the constitutional measures in the Cook-Maclennan agreement. Agreement was reached on setting up a Joint Cabinet Committee, on which I was to serve, to see these changes through, and for a Commission on Electoral Reform for Westminster to be chaired by Roy Jenkins. None of this got under way until Blair and Ashdown had brought themselves to the brink of publicly advocating an immediate coalition between Labour and the Liberal Democrats. Although I would have been a Cabinet Minister in such a coalition, I regarded the idea as hare-brained in a situation where the Government had a majority of 177, would never depend on our votes, and could therefore discard us at any time. But the Joint Cabinet Committee, although it involved some risks, was a much more acceptable proposition and one which could keep a head of steam behind the constitutional changes. My job was to do what I could to keep the Parliamentary Party on board for this much more specific objective.

The Joint Cabinet Committee met for the first time on 17 September 1997. Not since the war had Liberal Democrats sat in the Cabinet room with ministers in a Cabinet Committee to plan the carrying through of policy commitments. On the Government side of the table were Tony Blair, Robin Cook, Peter Mandelson, Jack Straw and Ann Taylor. Blair got in an early dig at my 'acerbic' comments on that day's *Today* programme. Although my task was primarily to set out clearly and unambiguously what we believed needed to be done to carry the constitutional programme forward, I was quickly cast as the tough guy. 'So what?' said Paddy in his *Diaries*:[15] 'There has to be a hard man in all this, and Alan makes a very good one'. It was to prove a productive process, putting energy behind constitutional commitments on some of which the Cabinet were lukewarm, divided or hostile, and the Committee remained useful only as long as that work was being carried through.

The following month I was caught up with a striking illustration both of the Blair–Brown tensions and of the culture of spin which the new government was developing. It was Friday night: I was in my London flat with my son Chris, packing to fly to Dayton, Ohio, next morning, as I was due to give a lecture at Earlham College, a Quaker Foundation, on religion and politics. I had bought a ticket for Chris to come with me, and friends had arranged for him to visit farms in the area. As I was closing the suitcase at about 9.30pm, the Liberal Democrat press office rang. Paddy was on holiday in France, and they needed a response from me for the ten o'clock news. Gordon Brown was publishing an article in the following day's *Financial Times* keeping open the possibility of Britain joining the European Single Currency during the current parliament; but his press officer, Charlie Whelan, had been in the Red Lion pub (opposite the Treasury in Whitehall) phoning journalists to brief them that what Gordon Brown meant was precisely the opposite of what he had said in the article. Joining the Euro in the current parliament was out. This bizarre briefing was given in the full hearing of a Liberal Democrat press officer who was having a drink in the same popular bar, and he alerted the BBC. We had laid bare an aspect of the tension at the heart of the government, and cast a light on its capacity to say one thing and mean another.

Why did 'spin' become such a feature of the Labour government, and was it as bad as was claimed? In part it was the response of Tony Blair and his key advisors, Alistair Campbell and Peter Mandelson, to what they saw as the almost unlimited capacity of a predominantly Tory press to block Labour's election or, if they could not achieve that, to destroy a Labour government. Hence Blair's shameless and successful courting of Rupert Murdoch, but the tacticians saw a need for more than that. Everything was viewed through the distorting glass of the next day's newspaper headlines, and an army of 'spin doctors' was required to feed journalists with stories and interpretations which would favour the government. Journalists are remarkably open to being fed a line: sometimes they will be seduced by a 'scoop', a story on which they and their paper or programme are given the chance to be ahead of the field, but often they hunt in a pack. I have seen them gathered at the end of a press conference discussing how to interpret what has been said. Going out on a limb with a different interpretation would be questioned by their editors and was not a risk most of them wanted to take.

In this environment the spin doctors plant stories and 'explain' what is not said in the minister's words, and for a long time the government's growing army of press officers seemed to be able to sell stories as easily as giving sweets to children. But there was one thing which, more than any other, wounded Labour and exposed the system: once the weapons of spin had been developed, they were just as likely to be used by ministers against each other as they were for the general good of the government. Whether authorised by nod and wink, or unauthorised and pursued by over-zealous aides, a civil war by press briefing became a characteristic of Labour government. Once a weapon has been invented and marketed, it is very difficult to control its use and impossible to disinvent it.

Clearly there is a proper role for press officers in presenting the government's views and policies to the media and responding to questions and criticism, but journalists should be the first to question and expose deception and 'hype'. Party colleagues should also recognise that they all sail in the same boat, and once they start shooting at each other they are likely to shoot holes in the boat, which will be liable to sink with all on board.

To a very large extent that lesson had already been learned by the excellent team of Liberal MPs with whom I was working. It was a step change to be working in a party of 45, quite different from the constant struggle to represent millions of voters with a handful of MPs. The new team contained people of real expertise, including Vince Cable, former Chief Economist of Shell; Steve Webb, who had massive specialist knowledge of the benefit and welfare systems; Richard Allan, an IT expert; John Burnett, a tax lawyer; and three doctors (one a GP, one a hospital doctor and one a doctor in community health). We also had the young economist Edward Davey, who as my researcher had worked with me to develop our policy of Bank of England independence on monetary policy, which Gordon Brown had publicly opposed during election debates but which he sensibly implemented as soon as he came into office. I was also delighted to have another Liberal Democrat in the Tyne-Tees TV area, Harrogate's Phil Willis. We set up a system of policy teams to make full use of the talents we now had in the Parliamentary Party, and it worked well.

While we in the Parliamentary Party were vigorously challenging the Government on Gordon Brown's rigid adherence to the Tory spending plans, on the need for resources for education, and on civil liberties issues, Paddy and Tony Blair were still nurturing their coalition project. We were engaged in what was officially termed 'constructive opposition' – an odd term, designed to reflect the fact that we were co-operating on the constitutional agenda. I have always believed that opposition should be constructive, and practised that principle. At the same time, Paddy and Tony Blair were circling endlessly around the proposition that, in return for a commitment to implement PR following a report to come from the Commission set up under Roy Jenkins, we should form a coalition. Paddy had made quite clear to me what he was doing, and he knew that I was supporting him because, although I thought that the coalition was never going to happen, it was well worth getting as far as we could along the road to proportional representation. There was a lot of unease in the Parliamentary Party and outside about being 'bounced' into a coalition but, despite some differences in our views, Paddy and I both believed that as a party we could afford to be much more self-confident in a situation where we had much to gain: it was far better to be negotiating with the Government for things we believed in than to be out of the picture. This, after all, was the Parliament in which Labour's huge majority was supposed to make us irrelevant, and here was the Prime Minister spending a great deal of his time and energy trying to find a way of meeting our policy demands.

It all came to a head when Roy Jenkins' Commission published its report in October 1998, recommending a system in which most MPs would be elected for single constituencies on the Alternative Vote System, while 15–20% of MPs would be elected by a list system to produce greater proportionality. It was a compromise, supposedly better for winning the support of sitting MPs, but not as proportional as the Single Transferable Vote (STV) system. STV has the added benefit that it puts much more power to choose individuals in the hands of the voters rather than the party organisers. Blair's failure to promise clear backing for the Jenkins proposal in a referendum, and the open opposition to it of some of his ministers, killed off the coalition project. The death throes involved a rather odd joint statement signed by Tony Blair and Paddy in which I was charged to work with Jack Cunningham (then Leader of the House) on a review of the Joint Cabinet Committee. At the same time I was involved in holding Jack Straw to the commitment that he would carry through the European Elections Bill to introduce PR for European elections, even if it meant using the Parliament Act. The votes of Liberal Democrat peers were crucial in getting it through the Lords. Although we disagreed with Labour over the choice of 'closed lists' in the new electoral system, we still wanted the bill – it was far better than the previous system, which was completely unproportional, producing grotesque under-representation, and was itself a 'closed list' system, but a closed list of one.

The Joint Cabinet Committee mechanism, following our review, hung on to deal with European foreign and security policy (where there was at that stage very little disagreement) but there was no real life left in it. The end of the Project meant the end of Paddy's enthusiasm for leading the party. He had long intended not to continue to the following General Election, and now he was determined to go. He was still deeply engaged in the Balkan issue, where his advice, rooted in his military experience, was rightly sought by the Prime Minister. He did much to draw public and international attention to the atrocities and the human catastrophes which were going on in our own continent of Europe day by day.

In January 1999 Paddy announced his resignation as Leader, to take effect later in the year. He had done a brilliant job. After a very bad start he had learned from his mistakes and had gone on to achieve what all Liberal and Liberal Democrat leaders in my lifetime have had to do: to overcome the massive handicap of a system which denies to nearly a quarter of the voters the parliamentary strength to which they are entitled. He had kept the party and its policies relevant, overcoming some of the limitations created by our unfair under-representation. In doing so he had championed children in under-funded schools, British passport holders denied residence in Britain, minority communities, civil liberties, the rights of the invaded people of Kuwait, and the lives of those facing genocide in the Balkans.

He had encouraged a process by which Liberal Democrats had helped to secure Parliaments in Scotland and Wales, elected by proportional systems, as well as Freedom of Information, the incorporation of the European Convention of Human Rights, and fair elections for the European Parliament. He had come pretty close to getting the Prime Minister to back and get through a partly proportional election system for Westminster, but on that he failed in the end. He remained in office long enough to see Liberal Democrats join a coalition government in Scotland, where careful preparation and hard bargaining ensured that the party was able to achieve a much better deal for students and, later, for the elderly in need of personal care. He still had the opportunity to lead the party to very good results in the first proportional European Elections.

It was a very good record, and, despite all the anxieties about his getting too close to Labour and his plotting with Tony Blair for unrealistic coalition and merger, the party was in a much stronger position than when he became leader. He had vindicated their choice, and I do not believe that I would have done better or even as well if I had won that leadership election a decade earlier.

There were plenty of candidates to replace Paddy, not all of whom actually got to the starting gate. In the end, with five candidates on the ballot paper, the contest was really between Charles Kennedy and Simon Hughes, with Charles, as expected, emerging as winner despite Simon's formidable popularity among party activists. Once again the electorate for the Liberal Democrat leader – the full membership – had accurately reflected the likely preference of the wider national electorate.

I stayed on as Deputy Leader to Charles, whose task was to establish himself and re-establish the party's standing under new leadership for the next election, which came in June 2001. For part of 2000 I had been doing relatively little in national party affairs because of the death of my son, Chris, and even now the political events of that year remain a blurred memory.

However, in October 2000, I stood in the election for Speaker to replace Betty Boothroyd. It was a bizarre election, with 12 candidates, and a tortuous and previously untried electoral process in which MPs spent most of a day walking through the division lobbies to vote for or against each candidate, one after another. I had some support on both Labour and Conservative benches and strong support from my own party and from the minority parties. I was not helped by the decision of my colleague Menzies Campbell to stand: I knew that his real ambition was to lead the party, an ambition temporarily thwarted by the diagnosis of cancer from which he made a courageous and marvellous recovery. However, that scarcely mattered because the whole election was being sewn up for Michael Martin by trade union Labour MPs, who saw it as a licensed opportunity to rebel against Tony Blair. The Prime Minister was thought to be favourable to an Opposition Speaker, whether it was a Liberal Democrat or a Conservative. Here was a chance for old Labour to defy their leader without provoking a crisis.

Charles showed his ability by leading the party to further success in the 2001 election, which saw our numbers go up to 52, the highest since the 1920s. This further increase in numbers had implications for our position in the House of Commons, where the Labour and Conservative parties had for years united in a pretence that there were only two parties. We had gradually broken down the barriers with the introduction of funds for opposition parties, for example, in which we were recognised both for our seats and for our votes in the country. Liberal Democrat MPs even took to queuing up at seven o'clock in the morning to book seats for prayers so as to claim the front bench below the gangway as our front bench. One of the relics which remained was that there was no Liberal Democrat among the Speaker's three deputies, who chair debates in his absence, and this was a symptom of the attempt to marginalise Liberal Democrats in the Chamber. Being a Deputy Speaker, although it carries a salary, is not a hugely inviting job, but it should be shared amongst the parties as it is in most other parliaments. Our numbers justified our claim, and my colleagues believed that I should take it on. Robin Cook had become Leader of the House, and on a promise that he would take the matter forward we did not block the initial appointment of Deputy Speakers when the session started. Robin Cook had envisaged creating an additional Deputy Speakership. This proposal was batted around for weeks and then months with no outcome, and in the end Labour failed to deliver. It was a battle we would have to fight another day.

Charles Kennedy knew that he was seen by some as a pragmatist leader without a strong ideological identity, except on the issue of Europe. He therefore commissioned me to lead a group defining and setting out Liberal Democrat philosophy and making clear what the party was about. *It's About Freedom* was the answer we gave in the title of the document we produced, and I set out more of these ideas in Chapter 11 below. I had a very good group to work with, including two future MPs, Sarah Teather and David Howarth, and we had lively and productive debates around the issues of liberty, social justice and internationalism.

Charles knew full well that Paddy's project and his close co-operation with Labour had delivered all they could in terms of Liberal Democrat policy and were past their sell-by date. The Joint Cabinet Committee was ended, and he quickly made the Parliamentary Party more comfortable about its independence and its ability to challenge both of the other parties.

During this Parliament, Charles had to lead the party through a tough decision on the Iraq invasion early in 2003, about which I have written in another chapter; his leadership in opposing the war was an example of the sound judgement which he so often showed. I enjoyed working with him, and I never had any problem about access to him, although others felt that his staff over protected him from colleagues whom he needed to keep on board. A curious problem he had was an apparent unwillingness to sit down with his colleagues in the dining room or the tea room, traditionally the places where leaders need to keep in touch. In our party the dining table was the place where colleagues could, in a jocular and friendly atmosphere, air some of their concerns and build up bonds of friendship which could survive through disagreements and tensions. I regularly sought to coax or drag Charles to the tea room or the dining room without success. Whether it arose from his drink problem I do not know, but it did not help him, even though he remained well-liked by colleagues.

I stepped down from the position of Deputy Leader when the opportunity arose to become Chairman of a newly created Select

Committee to oversee the Lord Chancellor's Department. It was extraordinarily delayed while two Labour committee chairmen disputed its intended name, the Constitutional Affairs Committee; although the Government gave in and dropped the title, it came back automatically when the Lord Chancellor's Department itself later temporarily became the Department of Constitutional Affairs, so it was a typical fuss about nothing. Then the name changed again to the Justice Committee.

Charles once again led the party very successfully in the 2005 General Election, bringing our numbers up to 65 – another record. We had moved on a long way from the 12-member Parliamentary Party I had joined, and we also had a formidable and hard-working team in the House of Lords, to one of whom I was now married. Our peers not only had massive expertise in their ranks but also had the voting power, if Conservatives, Labour rebels and cross-benchers voted with them, to defeat the Government. On civil liberties issues they regularly did. Our strength in local government was considerable, and we were running Northern cities like Newcastle, Liverpool, Durham and Hull which were once completely dominated by Labour.

For a Leader with this success to be under threat might seem surprising, but threat there was, and for three reasons. One was that others had ambitions to succeed him and did not want to wait too long. Another was that he seemed to lack a clear sense of direction about where the party was going next, and perhaps lacked the energy to move the party on: success is good, but it must be accompanied by planning to achieve the next objective. Finally there was the drink problem, which only rarely surfaced but was very damaging when it did. In the whole time I served as Charles' deputy I hardly ever saw him impaired in his thinking or actions by alcohol, although I was aware of the lurking problem which he had promised to deal with. From the more detached back-bench position I occupied in late 2005, I was aware that Archy Kirkwood and others were trying to bring matters to a head, and I made clear to them that I was opposed to what they were doing: my own belief was that Charles should be given until early the next summer to demonstrate that he was fit, able and committed to take the party into the next General Election, by which time, if we were going to make a change of leader, we would need to be doing so. The self-indulgent and malevolent interviews of one MEP, Chris Davies, and one former MP, Jenny Tonge, between Christmas and the New Year were deplorable, and were not even necessary to force the decision which Charles then made and announced. His genuine qualities shone through in his moving resignation speech. It was a sad day, but he did the right thing for the party.

Following another well-conducted leadership election it fell to Menzies Campbell to pull the party back from the damage inevitably done by the very public way in which Charles' resignation had been brought about: he set about doing so methodically and with determination to promote many of our able young people to key posts and to sharpen the party's machinery for the task ahead. But at the same time he had to cope with Prime Minister's Question Time, a task he has never found easy, with several hundred MPs in both Labour and the Conservative parties actively wanting him to fail. He set out to prove them wrong, particularly by avoiding boring partisanship and taking a firm line on those issues on which he is most knowledgeable and confident.

However, he faced a virulently ageist press campaign against his leadership, with cartoonists regularly and ludicrously depicting him in a wheelchair or needing a stairlift. When the *Guardian*'s Steve Bell was later asked on the BBC *Today* programme why his cartoons of Menzies Campbell were so vicious, he replied 'Well, he got his "come-uppance"' over what Bell regarded as his role in the removal of Charles Kennedy. Gordon Brown's decision, after much dithering, not to hold an autumn election created a new situation, because an election was unlikely for as much as two years. The ageism, deplorable though it was, would clearly continue, and Campbell took colleagues by surprise with a quick decision to allow the party to choose a new leader, Nick Clegg.

By this stage, however, running a party was no longer my job: I was enjoying being a constituency MP, chairing an active committee, and pursuing my specialised interest in intelligence and security.

A VIEW FROM THE NORTH

—11—

WHAT'S IT ALL ABOUT?

You might well ask, what is this all about? What is the purpose of maintaining and managing a third political party in an electoral system which severely under-represents such a party whose support is widely spread around the country, and which erects huge barriers against such a party being admitted to government? The answer, in short, is that it's about freedom. It is about the need for there to be a political party whose guiding principle is freedom. It is an answer to the failure of the other two national parties to hold to any consistent and enduring set of principles which can guarantee the protection of freedom. I am as keen as anyone that Liberal Democrats should take part in government, and I welcome the involvement the party has had in government in both Scotland and Wales, with real practical results which have benefited, for example, the elderly in need of personal care and students unable to cope with high fees. But the party exists not in order to turn itself into whatever is most likely to be elected into government, but in order to be an effective instrument for furthering fundamental values. It can do this in government, and it can do it by challenging government. The Liberal and Liberal Democrat Party has survived through bad times and good because there is a manifest need for such a party, and that need is not being fulfilled by others. It has grown because that need is ever greater.

People are often advised, when considering how to vote, that they should study the manifesto of each party. The policies set out can be compared and a judgement made about which set of policies will best serve the country, or will meet their own particular concerns. That advice is at best inadequate, and at worst downright misleading. It is not so much that parties renege on their manifesto promises, although they sometimes do: it is that what determines the behaviour of a party is much more likely to be how it responds to changing circumstances – 'Events, dear boy', as Harold Macmillan put it. How they respond will depend on what corpus of belief or philosophy, if any, the party and its leaders have. In order to predict the moves a party might make, you need to understand what its instincts are, and whether they arise from a philosophy which you can share or support.

Therein lies the most striking difference between Liberal Democrats and the other two parties. Tony Blair was a master at handling or deflecting difficult parliamentary questions, but the question which completely threw him was one put by one of his own backbenchers, Tony McWalter, who gently inquired if he could give a brief characterisation of the political philosophy underlying his policies.[16] He could not, and he was reduced to quoting meaningless health service statistics. His mission had been to discard Socialism as a philosophy and make the Labour Party electable: having done so, his approach was to take up ideas, react to problems and promote policies according to what his advisers suggested, his ministers proposed or his focus groups approved. No framework of principles or beliefs conditioned these responses and initiatives. A change of leadership after Tony Blair may have brought a willingness to revert occasionally to a little of the older Socialist language, but, given Gordon Brown's long involvement in the Blair government's policies, no reversion to the old ideology is in prospect.

British Conservatism was traditionally anti-ideology, except in its belief that the established order of things should not change unless change was unavoidable. That it is still a party without a framework of belief is, paradoxically, demonstrated both by the Heath government and by the Thatcher years. Ted Heath made the Conservative government a pro-European government which secured Britain's entry into the EEC. Labour was the fiercely anti-European party at the time, despite the views of a minority within Labour who later founded the SDP. The complete role reversal which has since taken place demonstrates that neither of these positions was based on a firm framework of belief.

Mrs Thatcher took the Conservative Party to an ideology which was neo-liberal in economic terms, but not at all liberal in terms of social or constitutional issues. Lacking a genuine liberal basis, it contained no instinct to counter the growth of centralised state power, and no instinct for individual liberty. The fact that so much of the Thatcher ideology is now rejected under David Cameron's leadership confirms that it did not take firm root in the party. There has, therefore, remained a real need in British politics for a party which knows what it is about. Part of my purpose in politics has been to make sure that the Liberal and Liberal Democrat Party never forgets what it is about.

Liberalism grew up in the history of challenge to oppressive power, from the English civil war to the nineteenth century battles for the right of non-Anglicans to take part in public life and non-owners of property to vote. It was defined and refined in a tradition of philosophical writing from Milton to Mill. It was John Stuart Mill, following the argument of John Locke's *Letter Concerning Toleration*, who most systematically and memorably encapsulated Liberal thinking in his essay *On Liberty*. Out of that document comes the insistence that the state or the community has no right to restrict the actions of individuals to live as they choose unless the actions of those individuals take away the freedom of others to live as they choose. 'The liberty of the individual must be thus far limited; he must not make himself a nuisance to other people'. And, following Milton's argument for freedom of expression, he argued: 'If all mankind, minus one, were of one opinion, mankind would no more be justified in silencing that one person than he, if he had the power, would be justified in silencing mankind'.[17]

The essential elements of political liberalism include democratic government, accountability, the diffusion of power, toleration of minorities, freedom of speech and expression, the rule of law and the right to a fair trial. Authoritarian government despises freedom; anarchy is incapable of protecting it. Democratic government is the system in which freedom is most likely to flourish and be protected, but by itself it is no guarantee of freedom and can become the tyranny of the majority. For much of our country's history, we have claimed to have democratic government despite the fact that people without property had no votes; having remedied that failing, we continued to claim to be a democracy while women had no vote; and we still claim to be a democracy despite retaining a system in which a party can claim majority power when a large majority of the voters voted against it.

Even if we get to the point when the system by which we choose governments is as genuinely democratic as we can make it, the defence of freedom requires much more. Once installed, those elected must be subject to effective processes of open accountability: there have been many regimes around the world which genuinely enjoy majority support but which exercise power unfairly, intolerantly, irresponsibly or oppressively. A powerful legislature with effective means of scrutiny is a vital part of the mechanism of protecting freedom in democracy, and of improving the quality of government. All experience suggests that the more power is concentrated, the more it is open to abuse: decentralisation of power to democratic and accountable institutions of local government is therefore a highly desirable protection for freedom, as well as being a means of dealing with the different needs of different parts of the country. The rights of minorities need to be built into the system by mechanisms such as a Bill of Rights, now effectively provided by the European Convention on Human Rights and its incorporation in United Kingdom domestic law. Even if, as some suggest, Britain repealed the so-called European Bill of Rights, we would still be bound by its provisions because we have been signatories to the European convention since the 1950s – it would simply mean that British citizens would once again have to go to Strasbourg to enforce their rights. Freedom of speech and expression are among those rights, and need to be protected from the instinct, even of some leaders of democracies, to silence their critics or deny them access to means of expression such as mass media. The rule of law is of fundamental importance. It means that a majority government cannot rule arbitrarily or capriciously, because it can be challenged in the courts for failing to act within the law. The fact that this safeguard regularly prevents governments from by-passing other constitutional safeguards such as the right to a fair trial, although inconvenient and irritating to ministers, is a vital protection against the erosion of such rights in times of tension and genuine difficulty.

Even in the nineteenth century, Liberals realised that securing political freedom did not by itself ensure that people were free. Severe poverty, ill health or lack of opportunity made freedom an empty vessel for many: they had no freedom to choose because there were no choices they could make – the course of their lives was wholly dictated by the conditions in which they lived. So free education, health facilities, social welfare provision, better housing and public health improvement came to be seen as essential to individual freedom. Liberal political activity through local government became the vehicle for achieving many of these freedom-enhancing improvements. These 'social liberal' policies were incorporated into Liberal political philosophy by writers such as L.T. Hobhouse, and they had a strong champion at national level in Lloyd George. Some Liberals joined the Labour Party in the belief that it offered a greater opportunity to pursue measures of social improvement, and many of the SDP members who joined the merged Liberal Democrats were heirs to that tradition. The inter-war depression demonstrated that in a modern industrial economy the freedom of many could be dramatically circumscribed by loss of employment. J. M. Keynes provided Lloyd George with a programme for tackling unemployment, and the unemployment insurance and old age pensions which Liberal governments had introduced were further developed into a framework of ideas by Sir William Beveridge. Beveridge wanted to set people free from the evils of poverty, ignorance, disease and idleness (by which he meant lack of employment), and he proposed a system intended to do so without robbing people of their sense of responsibility for themselves or their freedom of choice.

The use of collective powers to provide freedom-enhancing goods such as education and public health poses problems in the protection of freedom. It involves the assembling of considerable additional power in the hands of the state, such as the power to force parents to ensure that their children receive education, and the power to restrict activities which pose a threat to health. A liberal framework for accountability and for challenging the misuse of power is an essential counterpart of the extension of state or local government activity. It is part of a liberal society that the exercise of powers, even powers intended to enhance freedom, should be subject to rules and processes which can prevent those powers being abused or used oppressively.

The concept of freedom is similarly relevant to economic activity. Free enterprise and free markets are desirable in principle as well as being generally effective as a means of allowing the efficient provision of goods which consumers wish to buy. Free markets, however, are neither automatically self-sustaining nor sufficient to provide for all those things which society considers desirable. Institutions are needed to keep markets free and to defeat the tendency to monopolies or cartels and break up concentrations of power which make choice less free. Other mechanisms are needed to give individuals access to a range of goods, including aspects of health care or of culture, which markets alone are unable to provide.

The environment is a freedom issue: the ability of future generations to enjoy freedom will be dramatically curtailed if we in our lifetime do permanent damage to the planet. It is a classic case for John Stuart Mill's principle that our freedom may justifiably be restricted if its exercise in a particular way destroys the freedom of others. However, in considering the measures we can use to limit environmentally damaging activity we need to look for those means which do least to erode individual freedom. A financial incentive to switch from road or air to rail is far preferable to a ban on cars or flights.

'Globalisation' is seen by many as threatening, and as something which we ought in some way to be resisting. In reality it enhances freedom for many people, who avidly make use of the opportunities to travel, to communicate through the Internet, and to buy and sell things across national boundaries. It can be an answer to monopoly at national level, breaking the barriers of national censorship or restrictions on freedom of expression. But globalisation itself allows even larger concentrations of power at international level, and it is therefore essential for there to be an effective system of international law and institutions to control these new centres of power and to defend the freedom of individuals and people. Those who are critical of the United Nations or the World Trade Organisation need to recognise that without such institutions, imperfect as they are, those who are strongest on a world scale will have nothing to prevent them dictating their terms to the weak.

Freedom is a concept which we project beyond our shores: there is nothing new about that. Britain has housed exiles from oppressive foreign regimes through the centuries. The abolition of the slave trade and, later, of slavery in the British colonies was a moral and political crusade. Gladstone fulminated against the Turkish atrocities in Bulgaria. The anti-apartheid movement in Britain mobilised a wide range of people in support of the oppressed black majority in South Africa, and Liberals like Jeremy Thorpe and David Steel took political risks to make it a high-profile issue for the party. Liberals were much more willing to speak out over oppression in Soviet Russia than many people in the Labour Party, where the view lingered for too long that Russian communism was an essentially good idea which had unfortunately gone wrong or been misapplied. In reality, Communism, by its nature and profession, is a doctrine which has no room for freedom: it asserts what is good for people and assembles a system of unchallengeable power to ensure that no other choices can be made. It is intrinsically illiberal.

In our own time, the application of the concept of freedom on the international scale has found expression in action outside our own borders to prevent the overthrow of democracy in Sierra Leone, for example, or to end genocide in the Balkans. There is now international recognition that the threat of genocide justifies the international community overriding the national sovereignty of a state by military intervention. Failed states with no order or authority can provide the base from which terrorists attack and destroy the freedom of people on other continents: the 9/11 attacks required us to find means to establish order in Afghanistan. But freedom has also been spuriously used to provide justification for actions for which there were other motives, retrospectively in the case of the invasion of Iraq. It was only after Saddam Hussein was found not to have had weapons of mass destruction that Tony Blair took to arguing that the war was justified in order to depose a brutal dictator. Few in Britain would accept that, even if we could, we should employ military means to replace various degrees of authoritarianism to be found around the world with democratic systems enforced by our military power. Those in the US who have argued in these terms have been suspiciously selective in their choice of proving grounds for such a doctrine.

Rights and freedoms regularly conflict with each other, and the political philosophy of Liberalism does not automatically resolve such disputes – it requires them to be examined, and it provides a basis of principle for doing so. Religious freedom may conflict with anti-discrimination provisions as it did in the issue of whether religious-based adoption agencies were entitled to confine their services to married couples. Freedom of speech may conflict with legislation to prevent the publication of material designed to promote hatred between races or to advocate terrorism. Freedom to smoke in a pub conflicts with the freedom not only of other customers but also of staff to breathe unpolluted and safe air. Any philosophical Liberal considering such issues can do no better than to apply the Mill principle with rigour and care: it is failure to do so at all which is the cardinal sin. Neither our prejudices nor our preferences are proper grounds for imposing restraint by law on the freedoms of others.

Indeed, the test of a true Liberal is willingness to defend the rights of those with whom he or she fundamentally disagrees. I have often had to point out both to evangelical Christians and to gay rights groups that it is possible to be opposed in principle to homosexual practice while at the same time defending the right of homosexual people to live as they choose without fear of persecution, discrimination or intimidation. It is no kind of Liberalism to tolerate only those things of which you approve. Nor is it a principle of Liberalism to deny rights to those whose views or doctrines deny the principles of liberalism: only if their actions pose a real and credible threat to the freedom of others are we justified in invoking powers of restriction or prohibition.

There is a particularly dangerous line of argument which claims to 'balance' freedom with other 'good' things, as if this 'balancing' provides some means of comparing the value of utterly different things. It is a commonplace in discussion about the undeniably difficult issues of dealing with terrorism that we must 'balance' freedom and civil liberties with security, and that 'the right to life' is 'more important' than civil rights. But this is to pose an unreal choice, and to do so in misleading terms. If people are not secure from terrorism, their freedom is endangered; if they become the victims of bomb attacks, their freedom is destroyed. Security is not an end in itself, it is the means of protecting freedom. But there is no certainty that the removal of particular freedoms, such as the right to a fair trial or the right to walk the streets without a national identity card, will prevent a bomb. It follows that, in removing those rights, we are not 'balancing' freedom and security, we are further restricting the freedom of the same people whose freedom has already been restricted by the fear of terrorist attack. At the same time we are helping the terrorists to achieve their objective of provoking an over-reaction which, as they intend, will lead to greater dissent and disruption in the society they are hoping to destroy. Freedom belongs to everyone. The denial of an innocent person's right to free speech or a fair trial cannot be weighed in any measurable way against the risks both that person and everyone else face from terrorist attack.

My argument is not that we are prevented from taking any exceptional measures to deal with what is an immediate and severe threat to our liberty from terrorists: it is that the simple equation 'less freedom equals better security' is wrong. If you take something off the freedom side of the scales, the balance does not then tip in favour of more effective security. It is worse than weighing apples against pears – it is like trying to weigh air against water. 'Balancing' is useless as an analytical tool for examining the merits and dangers of anti-terrorism powers. You have to examine each proposal in order to establish:

1. how likely it is to assist in preventing attacks which destroy freedom;

2. whose freedoms it restricts, and in what ways;

3. whether its restriction of freedom can be reduced, or subject to controls which can determine the relevance or proportionality of its use in a given case; and

4. how readily it can be removed if it cannot be shown to be needed any longer, or to have proved ineffective.

In that way the argument is therefore cast wholly in terms of freedom and its protection, not in terms of a generalised security justification for the abrogation of freedom, still less the all-too-prevalent desire of ministers to be seen to be 'doing something' in response to a fresh attack.

I come to this view because of the importance I attach to safeguarding freedom, not because I harbour any doubts about the reality of the terrorist threat or the need to deal effectively with it. I come to this issue having spent time, in the course of my oversight duties, examining security-classified material on terrorist activity, listening to intercepts of the conversations of people who have been convicted of terrorist offences, and interviewing those who are in the front line of investigating and preventing terrorist activity. I have observed too many instances of politicians wanting to be seen to be tough. Powers are too often promoted which assist the terrorists more than they assist those who are protecting our freedom from terrorism. The whole concept of a 'war on terrorism' adds to the confusion: terrorism is the tactic, not the enemy, and it needs to be fought with understanding and skill, and cannot be defeated by rhetoric or gesture. There is no substitute for rigorous analysis of the effectiveness and implications for freedom of new powers, and powers are no substitute for well-resourced, well-trained and well-coordinated security and policing.

Another dangerous diversion or dilution of the principle of freedom comes with the argument, also favoured by New Labour ministers and Conservative spokesmen, that rights 'must be matched by responsibilities'. What a wolf in sheep's clothing this is. Of course it is desirable that people behave responsibly. If people break the law, they are liable, on conviction, to lose part of their freedom, whether by a prison sentence, a community punishment or a fine. But should rights be dependent more generally on responsible behaviour?

Clearly, if everyone behaved responsibly and considerately it would be much easier to maintain a free, harmonious and comfortable society. It is highly desirable that they should. But there is no way in which we can calibrate what rights individuals have according to how responsibly they live, except by the due process of law. Where law can reasonably be applied to control behaviour which is a threat to the freedom of others, as in the case of driving without due care and attention, there can be a defined range of penalties including loss of the right to drive a car. But no one seriously suggests that even persistent failure to check on the health of neighbours, refusal to contribute to the social life of the community or unwillingness to engage in voluntary activity can be dealt with by diminution of the right of free speech, or the right to a fair trial. It conjures up some kind of people's court or village soviet which can decide that some local residents are not fulfilling enough social responsibility to have earned the right of free association. If it is more than mere rhetoric, it is another misleading and potentially dangerous attempt to diminish freedom. I challenge those who toy with this concept to explain how they believe that taking on responsibility can become a condition for the enjoyment of rights. You can be a bad-tempered recluse if you want to. Society might benefit if you took a different approach to life and helped run the Scout troop, but doing so is not a condition for the possession of rights or the exercise of freedom.

As a political movement the Liberal Democrats do not confine themselves to protecting, preventing the concentration and abuse of power, and enhancing freedom by the removal of those things which reduce it, like the lack of education or good health care. We are keen to create a better society, and have traditionally had a vision of what a Liberal society can achieve. Community politics, an aspect of Liberalism developed in the 1980s,[18] was based on the belief that giving people in local communities power to shape those communities will unleash aspirations, commitment and creativity which are stultified by a system of centralised power. Liberal Democrats do not have a minimalist view of society. People who are Liberal in their beliefs want a society in which others share that openness and generosity of spirit. That is part of the evangelism of the Liberal tradition. But such a society cannot be legislated into existence. Laws do not make good citizens. What is more, Liberal Democrats cannot claim to have the only blueprint of how life should be lived: all we can claim is adherence to a set of principles which enable people of different views to live together in freedom, and a determination to give priority to those principles.

It is no part of my argument to suggest that Liberals or Liberal Democrats fight a lone battle for these principles, although that is how it sometimes feels. Non-party organisations like Liberty, Amnesty and Justice fight resolutely on nearly all of the key freedom issues. Moreover, there are individuals in both Labour and Conservative parties, and among the cross-benchers in the House of Lords, who share many of our concerns and have regularly voted with us to uphold these principles. The point about the Liberal Democrats is that as a party we seek to make these principles the basis for all our policies, and to judge our response to events in the light of them. If we brought no other added value to the political system, this principle of putting freedom first would justify our existence. It has sustained us through politically unpopular campaigns, for example on behalf of Ugandan Asians or Hong Kong Chinese who held British passports. It has been put into practice by Liberal Democrats in power in local government, who have carried through measures which limited their power and increased their accountability. It is what we are about.

—12—

RELIGION AND POLITICS

Alistair Campbell notoriously said 'we don't do God': he appeared to be speaking on behalf of the Blair government, but may well have been reflecting his own views. In reality, religion and politics have been intertwined throughout the centuries, and show every sign of continuing to be closely engaged with each other, whether in mutual support or in conflict.

Christian belief was undoubtedly one of the impulses which led me to become involved in politics, as it has for many other people. Some of my closest colleagues in my own party have been strongly committed Christians, such as Richard Wainwright, David Steel, Jim Wallace, Simon Hughes and, among more recent arrivals on the scene, Steve Webb and Tim Farron. Shared religious beliefs have generated and deepened friendships with colleagues in the other parties. The House of Commons contains more religiously observant people than any random collection of 650 British people would be likely to do, and, in particular, more practising Christians. Across the world we see Islam, in several forms, and American evangelical Christianity engaging with political systems, for good or ill. Religion cannot be ignored, least of all by those who are opposed to it. The critics of religious commitment in politics are frequently confused about the religious groups they dislike, assuming either that all

Islamic religious groups have as their objective Islamic domination of the state, or that politically active Christian groups share the views of the 'creationist' right in the United States. It is wrongly suggested that ethnic diversity requires a diminution in the public role of Christianity in Britain, when many in ethnic minorities are themselves Christians, and most Muslims have no desire to diminish the public role of Christianity, with whose adherents they share many concerns. So what has Christianity to say to the political world, and what should be the extent and limitations of religion's role in politics?

Firstly, it cannot involve a take-over of the state as an instrument for the enforcement of a particular religious view. Those forces within Islam who seek such a course need to be opposed as vigorously from within Islamic communities in Britain as they will be by Christians and secularists alike. Christianity has, of course, had a go at the same thing in the past, particularly in the form of the established Church in England. Until Catholic emancipation, all Members of Parliament had to swear an oath against the Roman Catholic doctrine of transubstantion, asserting that the adoration of the saints and the mass 'as they are now used in the Church of Rome are superstitious and idolatrous'. Nonconformists, unless they maintained a minimal adherence to the Church of England, were excluded from public office and from the universities until well into the nineteenth century.

Secondly, religion should not assume a role in which it becomes so subservient to the state that it cannot issue a prophetic or ethical challenge to the actions of those in power. It has been the objective of rulers as diverse as Henry VIII and Stalin to control the structures and personnel of the Church so that they posed no threat and promoted no dissent.

Thirdly, the relationship of religious organisations and politics should not be dominated by their sectional interests, legitimate though some of these may be. Roman Catholic cardinals are understandably assiduous defenders of the Catholic school system and the state funding it receives: the Church of England over the years has been fiercely defensive of the privileges it enjoys in marriage legislation – with the result that it is still bizarrely prohibited to choose religious poetry or music for a civil ceremony in England. In the past, nonconformists had a tendency to believe that when their very necessary campaign against alcohol abuse failed to convince everyone, the state should step in with total prohibition. If religious organisations are conditioned to look for favours from government, their capacity to challenge authority will be undermined.

Christians have found and should find the basis for their impulse for political action in Christ's insistence on care for the sick, and hungry, the poor and the imprisoned. This cannot simply be a calling to individual charity. We know that effective medical care requires hospitals and medical training. We have discovered that the relief of world hunger requires concerted international action on trade and debt. These are legitimate arguments about how extensive the role of the state should be. Scripture offers no guidance on the merits or failings of private sector health care or final salary pension schemes. But what is abundantly clear from Christian belief is that, seeing distress, we cannot pass by on the other side.

A further impulse is the Biblical tradition of righteous anger at what is plainly wrong. Christian denunciation of slavery and of racism follow in a prophetic line from the denunciation by the prophets of corruption among the Old Testament Kings and from Jesus' anger at the activities of the temple money-changers. Christians, and Muslims equally, feel a sense of anger at selfishness and materialism, and the glorification of these trends in the media. 'Never waste good anger' is a wise precept in politics. Anger fuels Christian campaigns on world poverty, Darfur and climate change, and it is right that it should.

The interest in climate change issues also reflects a clear Biblical concept that we are but stewards of this planet. The earth is the Lord's, and we will be held to account for polluting it and wasting its resources.

Then there is a recurring Biblical theme that God's kingdom is a kingdom of justice and peace. It is a theme which involves Christians, pacifists and non-pacifists, in peace movements and the promotion of alternatives to violence in conflict resolution. It is a theme which gets Christians involved in supporting asylum-seekers who appear to be facing unjust treatment and threats to their lives and families. It is a theme which prompts Christians to look beyond our shores at injustice, oppression and violent conflict in other lands.

There is also a willingness on the part of many Christians to undertake public responsibilities which others are unwilling to shoulder. We are called to 'bear one another's burdens' and to 'go the extra mile'. I think particularly not of those of us who have the privilege of earning our living from politics, but of the many thousands of people who in their leisure time voluntarily carry out a huge amount of work which is essential to the functioning of a democracy, quite a lot of them because of Christian convictions. One Liberal Democrat MP colleague told me that whenever he was in need of more people to help in leaflet delivery his best course was always to turn to the Baptists, amongst whom willing deliverers would quickly be found.

So is there a Christian programme for government, or a need for a Christian political party? Not in my view. There can be Christian

The Parliamentary Liberal Party: from left to right, David Penhaligon, Stephen Ross, Richard Wainwright, Jo Grimond, me, Russell Johnston, David Steel, Clement Freud, Cyril Smith, David Alton, Geraint Howells.

Serving on committees as the only Liberal had to be combined with paperwork, rather untidily. Left of me is Neil Kinnock, then Labour's education spokesman.

The Alliance with the SDP worked reasonably well at Westminster, thanks to a good partnership with Roy Jenkins and John Roper, their Leader and Chief Whip.

Merger was more of a challenge!

Cyril Smith, with Paddy Ashdown on one side and me on the other, could be wondering which of us is going to end up as leader.

Speaker George Thomas seems to be concerned about my blue tie (blue was the old Liberal colour in Berwick). It was a Methodist occasion, and Donald Soper is visible behind us.

RIGHT, SAID BEITH

(Words: Simon Titley
Tune: Right said Fred)

Right, said Beith, economic spokesman
This Green Paper'll bring the voters in;
Esoteric
To punters up in Berwick,
He was getting nowhere
And so, we, had a cup of tea.

And right, said Beith, give a job to Charlie,
Up goes Charlie to the studio.
Not one soundbite
On Channel 4 or Newsnight.
We was getting nowhere
And so, we, had a cup of tea.

So Alan had a think and he thought we ought
To free the Bank of England -
It'll go down well in Richmond.
But it did no good,
Well I never thought it would.

Alright said Beith, monetary system,
To join that system wouldn't take a mo.
Joined the system -
Economic bedlam -
Should have got us somewhere, but no
So Beith said let's have another cup of tea
And we said, Righto.

Alright, said Beith, central bank of Europe -
That there bank is the end of all our woes.
Loads of Germans,
Economic sermons,
And it got us nowhere
And so, we, had a cup of tea.

And right said Beith, time to go for EMU
Monetary Union is sure to win us votes.
No enjoyment,
Rising unemployment.
We was getting nowhere
And so, we, had a cup of tea.

And Paddy had a think and he said, Look Beith
You're causing an imbroglio -
I'm changing your portfolio
In a month or two
I will think what you can do.

Alright said Beith, home affairs is better,
Family values is what I will suggest.
But video nasties
Featuring pederasty
Landed on the top of his desk,
So Paddy and me had another cup of tea
And then we went home.

My fondness for a cup of tea in a crisis led to a song.

Getting the media interested in the value of Bank of England independence over monetary policy was a challenge – but I was right, and Gordon Brown switched from opposing the policy to carrying it out in his first weeks in office.

More funds for the NHS was another policy which Labour later adopted – spending more than we asked for, but wasting a lot of it.

Meeting the inspiring and formidable Mother Teresa.

Learning from older people in a constituency where they are a high proportion of the population.

What was said about colleagues when four ex-Chief Whips had an unusual get-together is forever secret. The host was former Conservative Chief Whip Alastair Goodlad (then our High Commissioner in Australia), and the others were Ann Taylor (Labour) and James Arbuthnot (Conservative).

Speculation about whether I might stand for Speaker. I did, unsuccessfully, among a large field of candidates in 2000.

Berwick, with 12,000 people, is the largest town in the constituency, and it is where we live. The river was sometimes the border with Scotland – but that was 500 years ago.

30 miles south of Berwick is Alnwick, the main centre of the southern half of the constituency, where my office is located.

priorities for government, but any Christian programme, or any political party claiming to be the party of Christians, would ignore some fundamental features of both religion and politics. Christians, Muslim, Sikhs and Hindus do not merely have points of disagreement with each other: they disagree within each religion on matters of theology, doctrine and practice. It follows that they will disagree even within their own religious denominations about the political implications of their message, or about the political programmes most likely to achieve their objectives. People sometimes launch into politics with good intentions but little understanding of the fact that decisions in politics, as in many other walks of life, are morally complex. To what extent, when elected to public office, are you entitled to act on the basis of firm convictions which are not shared by the vast majority of those you represent? The Christian politician may and should seek to persuade his constituents that there is a need for a bail hostel in the area, but the convinced pacifist cannot insist that the nation disarms in the face of an armed threat – his constituents expect him to ensure their protection.

To take another example, how far can the power of the state be used to relieve poverty before it reaches the point where it loses democratic support for the taxation it requires, or shows itself incapable of administering an over-complex network of social support? Is it legitimate to regulate lifestyles which pose no threat to others because of a religious conviction that they are wrong? How far is the state entitled to limit methods of scientific research which raise the possibility of finding cures for debilitating illness, but involve the use of embryos created for the purposes of IVF which would otherwise be destroyed? And should that IVF process itself be limited?

Politics poses innumerable questions of this kind. You soon discover that not all Christians agree about them, and that not all of those with whom you agree on these issues share your religious views. There are many religiously motivated people in politics; they are to be found in all the parties and on different sides in some of the arguments. Any attempt to pretend otherwise is likely to reflect a political attempt to harness religion for partisan ends.

A vivid example of this is provided by the partially successful attempts of right-wing Republicans to harness conservative and evangelical Christian support for Republican candidates on a platform which bizarrely joined together a pro-life commitment against abortion with a notably anti-life defence of the right to carry handguns and a commitment to support the Iraq war. It was not a programme elucidated from Christian principles: it was a political programme angled to appeal to evangelical Christians of a conservative outlook, and to dragoon them into supporting republican candidates. It harked back to the even more bizarre packaging of the Moral Majority movement in the Nixon era, which included opposition to the Panama Canal Treaty as a key political commitment for Christians. Beware of politicians who seek to sell a predetermined political programme on a spurious religious basis.

It is interesting to speculate why it has never proved possible to harness protestant evangelicals and conservative Catholics in a movement to support right-wing politics in Britain, although there have been a few Conservatives who have tried. One obvious factor is the significantly lower level of religious commitment in Britain, by comparison with the United States. But even within the proportionately smaller Christian constituency in Britain, a greater susceptibility to the appeal of the right, on US lines, might have been expected. I suggest that the difference stems to a larger extent from the fact that protestant nonconformists and Catholics both had to mount a libertarian challenge to the establishment in order to win their own freedoms, and therefore became associated with the Liberal and Labour parties rather than with the right. In addition, British Protestantism, particularly nonconformity, was not confined to the salvation of individual souls, but embraced a religious commitment to aid the poor and dispossessed: at a later period, Catholic social teaching in Britain, addressed as it was to the needs of the poor immigrants, was not amenable to a right-wing agenda, whatever the wishes of the traditional English Catholic Conservative families.

Britain's religious and political history differs markedly from that of the USA and from much of the rest of Europe. We do not have a powerful religious right, or dominant anti-clerical secularism. We are a country of relatively low religious observance, yet we have never had a wholly secular state. We have a tradition of religious tolerance which is widely accepted in principle but has come under strain because of fear, whether the current fear of Islamic terrorism, or the sixteenth and seventeenth-century fear of Catholic conquest of Britain. Christians have a duty to defend freedom of religion from threats whether they come from the state or from those who exploit fear by inciting violence.

Secularists seek to turn Britain into what it has never been: a society in which religion exists only in the private sphere. On this view even the historical impact of religion on our society has to be expunged. At Newcastle University we had a secularist Professor of Oral Pathology who fought unsuccessfully to change the names of the Michaelmas and Easter terms because of their religious origin. Misguided local authority officials have tried to re-name the Christmas holidays. You do not have to be a Christian believer to accept and enjoy the presence of Christian buildings, music, symbolism and ceremony in our society and our public life, so long as they do not take a form which bars people from taking part in public life. The presence of other religions is not an argument for the suppression or concealment of Christian religious traditions, and very few Muslims, Jews or Sikhs wish it to. Many people of all religions and none value the spiritual and ethical contribution of the churches to national life and to local community life. People who become anxious about the place of religion in public life generally do so because they are concerned about extreme and intolerant elements in Christianity or in Islam, but pushing mainstream religion out of the public sphere will only serve to leave the field open to extreme groups without challenge.

The Christian religion does not absolve its believers from the task of thinking things out for themselves. It challenges them to do so by the application of important principles in varying circumstances. It expects them to conduct themselves with integrity, as people who must give an account of their conduct before their Creator. It even requires from them a degree of humility, which is not a virtue much encouraged in politics. It expects them to be angry about evil, oppression and injustice, and to find ways of tackling these things. But it claims no divine authority for a specific political programme. Parties and states, governments and parliaments are human institutions in which we can serve our God, but they are not made in the image of God and cannot claim Him as their authority.

—13—

OVERSEEING SPIES

One day in 1994 I found myself appointed to a new and highly secretive committee to oversee Britain's intelligence and security services. I crossed Whitehall to the Cabinet Office, where I was helpfully provided with a photo-identity pass with the serial number 00007. I was provided with a rather long list of countries which I was not to visit without prior notification or, in some cases, at all. (Despite the collapse of the Soviet empire, I have never been given an updated version of this list.) Nine of us, eight MPs and one peer from the three main parties, were signed up to the Official Secrets Act and sat down to work out how to do what nobody had ever done before, except in the very different environment of the United States: namely, to subject intelligence and security services to a form of parliamentary accountability.

My lectures at Newcastle University had included several on areas of government where, for various reasons, public accountability is either limited or difficult to achieve without undermining the activity concerned: public service broadcasting was one example, because strict accountability can undermine media independence and objectivity. Policing is another, because of the need to avoid partisan control or influence over law enforcement. One of the most difficult areas has been intelligence, which is of necessity a secret activity.

At the time that I lectured on the subject, Britain did not admit that it had either a domestic Security Service (MI5) or a Secret Intelligence Service working overseas (MI6). Its signals intelligence activity was centred on a large establishment at Cheltenham which is still known as the Government Communications Headquarters (GCHQ); that, too, did not officially exist. The spending of these bodies was buried in the accounts of other departments, mainly the Ministry of Defence, whose ministers signed off expenditure over which they had little knowledge or control. There was no parliamentary accountability at all.

Only when something had gone drastically wrong would some scrutiny take place, either by a Security Commission of judges, reporting in secret, or by a single judge making a report partly in public, as in the case of Denning Report on the 'D' notice system (an arrangement still in operation whereby media editors are asked and agree to avoid publication of names, details or matters of ongoing inquiry where to do so would seriously prejudice national security). Parliamentary questioning on security matters was not permitted, and is still largely disallowed. When the Prime Minister or other ministers were obliged to make a statement about some well-publicised failure or breach of security, attempts were made to limit questioning to questions from the official opposition. I defied and effectively overturned this ban in July 1982, following Mrs Thatcher's statement on the Geoffrey Prime case, by repeatedly on points of order insisting that it could not be right for Liberal MPs to be excluded from this questioning process, until Speaker Thomas gave in.

The services were, of course, ultimately subject to ministers – the Prime Minister, the Foreign Secretary (for SIS and GCHQ) and the Home Secretary for (MI5). The system by which ministers approved warrants for telephone interception or approved overseas operations gave them some familiarity with their work, and major capital expenditure had to be considered by ministers and by the Chief Secretary or the Chancellor. But this provided no assurance of more general oversight or strategic direction, given the wide range of other responsibilities claiming the attention of ministers. Jim Callaghan conceded this point when I raised the issue with him in debate: ministers inevitably give more attention to matters on which they are being questioned in Parliament than to those on which they cannot be subjected to Parliamentary questioning. It was obvious that there needed to be some form of continuous Parliamentary scrutiny. The agencies had been anxious that their work might be destroyed by reckless release of information and blowing of cover, so these concerns would have to be met by exceptional arrangements for the Committee's appointment and methods of working.

In the end it was Mrs Thatcher who made the decision to create such a body, as part of a process generated by the much-maligned European Convention on Human Rights. The convention was not then part of British law – that happened with the equally maligned Human Rights Act – but that made no difference. We have been signatories to the Convention since it was agreed in the 1950s, and although that did not enable the Act to be applied in UK Courts, any aggrieved person could take a case to the European Court of Human Rights in Strasbourg. Such a case could include a claim that an individual's privacy had been invaded by a state agency (for example, by tapping their telephone) unless this was done 'in accordance with law' and for necessary purposes in a democratic society such as national security or the prevention of crime. But in Britain there was no law at all: governments were still nominally maintaining the absurd fiction that such agencies did not exist.

The Government would certainly lose such a case, and action therefore had to be taken. The first step was the Interception of Communication Act 1985, which created the system of warrants for interception signed by ministers, examined retrospectively by a commissioner, and a Tribunal to which individuals could appeal if they believed they were being subject to illegal interception.

These mechanisms alone provided no continuing monitoring of intelligence and security agencies. They covered only telephone and postal interception, and could give no wider assurance that the agencies were not invading civil rights, engaging in unauthorised ventures of the kind Peter Wright was later to allege in his book *Spycatcher*, or carrying out covert action with government approval which would not have been backed by Parliament. They provided no scrutiny against inefficiency, waste or incompetence. Moreover, they provided no source of parliamentary support for the good and often dangerous work which staff in the agencies were carrying out to protect their fellow citizens: it must have been galling for them to see only the most negative and hostile public or press comment about their work.

So it was that the 1994 Intelligence Services Act created the Intelligence and Security Committee to which I was appointed as the Liberal Democrat member; Tom King, former Conservative Defence Secretary, was appointed Chairman, with former Foreign Secretary Geoffrey Howe as the one peer and Dr John Gilbert, a former Defence Minister, leading for Labour. Although it was broadly modelled on a Select Committee, there were key differences. Its Chairman and members, although all MPs or peers, were appointed by the Prime Minister, after consultation with the Leader of the Opposition, so as to get over agency concerns about reliability and potential leaks: in practice this meant that, as with Select Committees at the time, the three parties' leaders and whips selected their members. The Committee met not in Parliament but in its own secure accommodation within the Cabinet Office, where all papers are kept and virtually none allowed to be taken away (occasionally an inconvenience but also a welcome change from the piles of paper around the office which most membership of committees creates). The Committee was to report annually to the Prime Minister, who was then required to publish the report to Parliament with such exclusions as are necessary to protect the functioning of the agencies: in practice it would make many more reports in addition to its single annual report, and publication of all of them would be on the same basis. Its members would be 'within the ring of secrecy', bound by obligations under the Official Secrets Act.

The Committee was not intended to deal with complaints by individuals affected by actions or alleged actions of intelligence agencies. Oversight committees which have been created in some other countries take on this role, but the UK system relies on a Tribunal to do this, and on Judges acting as Commissioners to check that interception or intrusive surveillance have only been carried out in accordance with the law. The main problem with the Tribunal is that, in order to prevent legitimate operations from being compromised, if it finds no fault it can only inform a complainant that 'no determination in favour has been made'. In other words, nothing illegal has taken place: either you are not the subject of any activity by the agencies or you are indeed being investigated, legally and for good reason. A large proportion of people who make complaints, some of whom write to committee members, suffer from paranoid delusions – it would be much easier if they could be told that there has never been an MI5 officer coming down their chimney, and that the Security Service has more important claims on its time and resources than to roam the rooftops like a disoriented Father Christmas, but openness would compromise security in other cases.

The credibility of the tribunal system was not helped by the fact that, for the first decade of its existence, it was unable to find in favour of the complainant on any occasion. It must have been with some relief that they did so on one more recent occasion, albeit on relatively technical grounds. A further problem was that, at one stage, the shared staff resources of the Tribunal and the Commissioners were almost non-existent, and complaint letters lay unanswered or even unopened because support staff had not been appointed: this was remedied after the ISC made strong representations in support of the Commissioners and published very sharp criticisms of the delay in providing the resources.

But, to return to the development of oversight by the Committee, it is worth remembering that preoccupations about intelligence agencies at the time the Committee was set up were different from those of today. In the post-war years, a succession of high-level infiltrators and defectors had been identified, in particular the Cambridge ring of Burgess, McLean, Philby and Blunt. They had been responsible for long and systematic betrayal of British secrets to Soviet Russia: Philby, for example, had sent courageous Albanians to certain death because he had alerted the Soviet authorities to the parachute drops which were landing them in their home country (this was before the Soviets fell out with the Hoxha regime). Whatever view you take of the wisdom of actively supporting the resistance to Albania's regime, this betrayal was cowardly and murderous. Blunt had not been exposed for some years after his identity had become known to the authorities, and there was public abhorrence of the fact that he had continued to enjoy a very comfortable career as Director of the Courtauld Institute and a prestigious position as Keeper of the Queen's pictures. As well as the security breaches, including the seriously damaging activities of less-glamorised figures like Geoffrey Prime, there were fears that the Security Service might still be engaged in politically motivated surveillance of democratic dissent rather than being focused on genuine threats to the security of the country, including threats to the country's armed forces, and protection against espionage by hostile powers. Later, when the Berlin Wall came down, the Soviet system collapsed and the threat of a Soviet attack through Communist-run East European satellite states disappeared, some press commentators and some among the public jumped to the conclusion that intelligence services had become largely unnecessary. There were mounting demands for a 'peace dividend' in the field of intelligence.

Contrast that with the situation a decade and a half later, when the chief preoccupation is whether the agencies are doing enough, are competent enough and have enough resources to track and defeat the threat of international terrorism. It is no longer a concern about whether agencies are doing too much, and has become a demand that they do more. At the same time, the misuse of intelligence in providing a justification for the invasion of Iraq has seriously damaged the reputation of intelligence, even though much of the blame for what happened belongs to politicians, and it has put a question mark in the public mind over any judgement which the Government asserts is based on intelligence.

When the Committee began its work in 1994 there were several things it needed to do in order to be at all effective, and they could not be done quickly. The first was to become familiar with the agencies, with the Joint Intelligence Committee which is the focus for the assessment of intelligence, and with a vast range of facilities, activities, terminology and international relationships. In large part this was information which is not in the public domain. Even ex-Secretaries of State for Foreign Affairs and Defence had only a very limited knowledge of the subject. I reckon that, given that it is an activity to which MPs cannot normally allocate more than about one day a week, it takes about two years, including much reading and many visits, to have enough familiarity with the system to be able to make judgements about the agencies and their effectiveness. When the whole Committee is new, the problem is even greater.

The second need was to win the confidence of agency heads and staff that senior politicians were entirely capable of handling secret information without any risk that it would leak. Their collective memory went back to one minor MP who was convicted of an offence under the Official Secrets Act (Will Owen, MP for Morpeth, who had been a member of the Defence Select Committee), and to a former Foreign Office minister who referred directly to methods used in intelligence-gathering in a debate on the Falklands war. They need not have worried: for the first decade of the Committee's existence, not a single leak of any kind occurred from the Committee, and the only one that ever has occurred was not of secret information, but advance information about the contents of the Committee's public report a day or two in advance of publication. It is a much better record than that of the US Congressional Committees, which have significantly better access, but have had a number of serious leaks. Nevertheless, heads of both SIS and GCHQ were brought up in an era in which their very existence had been denied and they took time to adjust to this new situation. One or two never really did, leaving it to their successors to change the culture. Younger staff, by contrast, were much quicker to welcome oversight which increased their sense of legitimacy in the work they were doing, and gave them the opportunity to talk to a small group of people outside their line management about their successes, problems and frustrations. Bear in mind that many of these are people who cannot tell their family, neighbours and friends outside the service what government organisation they work in. Some of them cannot tell their wives or husbands what assignment it is on which they are being sent away or abroad. I remember one official who told his wife, as instructed, that he had been sent at short notice to a conference in Glasgow when he was actually being sent overseas to deal with a problem. A family mishap led to her contacting his workplace, where she was told that he was not in Glasgow but abroad on holiday. It took some explaining to restore domestic harmony when he returned.

Building up trust, and thereby ensuring total frankness, is slow and is a never-completed process. There is no doubt at all that, as time went on, the Committee was able to delve much more deeply and effectively into the work and problems of the agencies. From an early stage we had the assistance of the small team of staff in the National Audit Office who are cleared to go through the accounts and financial records of the agencies. The need for thorough auditing in intelligence – which is sometimes frustrating for front-line staff recruiting and supporting agents – is obvious when the experience of the Metropolitan Police is borne in mind. Payments to informers, often themselves criminals, are crucial to much detective work, and names have to be carefully protected for fear that someone will pay with his life for talking to the police. This secretive process, parallel to the payment of agents by intelligence agencies, gave one head of finance in the Metropolitan Police – known as the Receiver – the opportunity to become very rich by siphoning off funds allegedly paid to informers. These informers did not exist, and with the proceeds he bought an estate in the Highlands of Scotland and the lordship of a manor near Berwick. Any competent internal security officer should have noticed that he was leading an extraordinary life, well beyond the reach of his salary, and should have made a few inquiries. He was eventually found out and convicted.

The Committee has always found that doors open more quickly when it has been specifically requested by the Prime Minister to investigate a matter, because it is then offered, or can set as a condition, that it is given full co-operation and access to any documentation relevant to its inquiry. That was the case when the Committee investigated what intelligence had been available on potential threats prior to the Bali bombings, and its examination of the 'dodgy dossier' and ministers' use of intelligence prior to the invasion of Iraq. It was also the case when the Committee examined the failure to prosecute Melita Norwood, whose spying for the Russians had become known when, through excellent work by SIS, Vasili Mitrokhin was brought out of Russia. Mitrokhin had supplied us with copious material from the KGB archives which it was his job to maintain, and copies of which he had hidden under his *dacha*. In the course of our inquiries the Committee met and interviewed Mitrokhin. In its leading article on the Committee's report, *The Times* said:

> 'Never before has a Parliamentary Committee been given access to documents detailing MI5's operation; never has the service been so publicly reprimanded'.

The Committee, it said:

> '...has made abundantly clear that it can be trusted with some of the most sensitive information in British intelligence, but that it can produce a report that is thorough, focused, rigorous in identifying individual failings'.

The Report was a 'strikingly successful example of public accountability'.

The Committee's scrutiny, detailed in its reports, has covered the effort against Northern Ireland terrorism, international terrorism, drug trafficking, arms proliferation and hostile espionage (which continues to be extensive). It worked closely on GCHQ's new building project at Cheltenham, perhaps the most difficult and largest PFI project yet completed, and ISC criticisms and recommendations led to significant improvement in the management of the project. In the end it was relatively successful and is a building well-liked by the staff who work in it, although the intention that it would fully meet GCHQ's headquarters future accommodation requirements was frustrated by the surge of extra work and staff necessitated by the increased terrorist threat.

The Committee commended the agencies for their work in support of British forces engaged in the restoration of peace and order in Sierra Leone, a difficult and notably successful operation, although we severely criticised the Foreign Office for its failure to support the UK High Commissioner with secure communications while he was in Conakry alongside the exiled Sierra Leone Government. Equipment was sent out which was too big to get through the door of his hotel accommodation, so it remained in a crate at the airport.

When lives are lost from terrorist actions, families and the wider community want to know why it was not prevented or whether it could have been. It is an inevitable question, and it is further inflamed by press speculation about alleged mistakes or bungling by security authorities. In such cases it is the Committee's job not to give the media the story they want but to examine the facts carefully and objectively. That was done both in the case of the Bali bombings and, in the case of the London July bombings, on two occasions, before and after the Crevice trial and the consequent removal of restrictions on material relevant to the prosecutions. In the Bali case we found that the bombing could not have been prevented on the basis of available intelligence, but that the Security Service had made a serious misjudgement when it did not raise the threat to UK interests in Indonesia generally. Both the threat assessment system and the Foreign Office travel advice system were revised as a result of these recommendations.

Serving as a member of the Intelligence and Security Committee in the run up to the Iraq war put me into a position that was both privileged and potentially difficult. I was privy in general terms to much of the intelligence gathering and assessment which made leaders of the intelligence community believe that Saddam Hussein was likely to be attempting to develop chemical, biological and nuclear warfare capacities, and that there was probably material unaccounted for which he had at the time of the first Gulf war. None of the intelligence was firm or reliably corroborated, but it was consistent with the possibility that he was engaged on such a course. It was good reason to be prudent and to pursue the inspection regime which he was clearly keen to frustrate. It would need to be taken into account in planning any military engagement with the regime. In no way, however, did it add up to a case for a perilous invasion which would necessitate the occupation of a bitterly divided country held together by determined repression. The Joint Intelligence Committee had assumed that, despite some earlier contacts between al-Qaida and Iraqi intelligence, 'there is no evidence that these contacts led to practical co-operation, we judge it unlikely because of mutual mistrust'.[19] In October 2002 they said that 'We have no intelligence of current co-operation between Iraq and al-Qaida'.[20] In February 2003 the JIC assessed that the threat to Western interests from al-Qaida and associated groups would be heightened by military action against Iraq, and that the risk of any chemical or biological warfare technology falling into the hands of terrorists would be increased by any collapse of the Iraqi regime.[21] My conclusion was that military force was being used appropriately to contain Saddam Hussein, including the maintenance of 'no-fly zones', and that al-Qaida could move in if Saddam Hussein fell or was overthrown by external attack, which is exactly what has happened.

You do not start wars on the basis of intelligence alone. If the situation is serious enough, you have to challenge the potential aggressors with some of the evidence, as Kennedy did in the Cuban missile crisis when he produced the photographic evidence which forced Kruschev to back down. You make clear that you are serious about using force if you have to, leaving the potential enemy in no doubt about your willingness to do so – it was the failure to do that by the Thatcher government which encouraged the Argentinians to invade the Falklands and led to a massive loss of life in liberating the islanders. Membership of the ISC, and familiarity with what was a genuinely worrying uncertainty about what was going on at various sites in Iraq, brought no conflict with my own party's view. This was that the invasion of Iraq was illegal, certain to be extremely costly in British lives either in the invasion or in the consequent period of administering a divided country, and severely damaging to stability in the region, as well as being a potential recruiting issue for terrorist groups in Western Muslim communities where there had previously been no love for Saddam Hussein. Some members of the Committee came to the same conclusions, while others voted in favour of the war, and the division was not on strict party lines.

We were unanimous, however, in our view that intelligence had been distorted and misused in the attempt to make a public case for invasion based on the development of weapons of mass destruction. We were also, as it turned out, unanimous in having missed something which the entire intelligence community also missed. Why was Saddam Hussein so un-cooperative as to trigger an invasion, the destruction of his regime and his own execution when he had, in reality, nothing to hide – when he had no weapons of mass destruction? He was bluffing. He was an Emperor with no clothes. But his entire position and that of his regime was geared to presenting himself as a great Arab leader, a very serious force to be reckoned with in the region. Virtually nobody thought about what is, in retrospect, a blindingly obvious point about a megalomaniac leader. It was another demonstration that intelligence is not merely about apparent facts, reliable or not, but about assessment set in the context of a wider understanding of the regional and political context. Uncertain facts and unimaginative assessment are no basis for launching wars.

A failing more common in the intelligence community of which we were aware was brought home by the tragic death of David Kelly. When we interviewed Dr Kelly, without any of the demeaning and damaging self-indulgence which marred the Foreign Affairs Select Committee's session with him, I was impressed by him but also conscious of the strain he was under. He obviously realised that he had overstepped the limits within which he was allowed to operate in briefing the press on technical matters, and it was preying on his mind. He had done immensely valuable work and was an acknowledged expert. Ironically, he genuinely believed that Saddam Hussein was successfully developing chemical and biological weapons, but his testimony had made clear that he had never seen and would never have endorsed the material on which the absurd '40-minute' claim in the 'dodgy dossier' was based. The intelligence community was not bringing to bear the resources it had to assess the soundness of intelligence material, and in this case had not used expertise readily available within the Defence Intelligence staff. It was tragic that a good man ended up taking his own life in the process through which this lesson was learned.

The David Kelly tragedy led to the Hutton report, which unearthed a great deal of material but was too narrowly conceived and focused to draw useful conclusions, and then in turn to the Butler inquiry. I was on the train down from Berwick to London when my mobile phone rang and the Prime Minister, Tony Blair, was put on the line. Was I willing to take part in a wider inquiry into the use of intelligence for the Iraq war? As a party we had been calling for such an inquiry, so my answer was yes, so long as there was agreement with party leader Charles Kennedy on its terms of reference. These were still under discussion, so it was agreed that I would consult Charles when I got to London. Apparently Tony Blair's original intention had been to use the ISC for this inquiry, but he had been persuaded to create a separate group including people from a military and civil service background, chaired by ex-Cabinet Secretary Robin Butler, with three ISC members: Ann Taylor (the ISC Chairman), Michael Mates and myself.

The discussion of terms of reference with the two opposition parties was complicated and still inconclusive by later that evening: changes had been made at the behest of the Conservatives, but the Government refused to yield on the Liberal Democrats' insistence – which I strongly supported – that the actions of ministers should be within the remit of the inquiry. When no agreement was reached, Charles Kennedy's view was that we should not take part; I agreed, although I had some concern that the press and the public would not understand why it was that we were boycotting an inquiry which we had demanded. Charles' political judgement turned out to be right, as it usually was on all the serious issues which came up during his leadership. The press strongly backed our stance. Ironically, the Conservatives fell in line with our view a week later, and announced that they, too, would withdraw from the inquiry: they had reckoned without my good friend Michael Mates, who has never been one to take orders from his party, and who was being appointed to the Privy Council on the strength of his participation in the Butler Committee. He announced that, whatever the party leader was doing, he was staying on the inquiry. In the end, the Butler Committee did a thorough job, setting out practical recommendations which have significantly improved the mechanism of intelligence co-ordination, and to a degree they went beyond the limitations in their terms of reference, to indicate where ministers had misused intelligence.

Overseeing a world to which very few people have access has been a fascinating task, and it leads me to some thoughts about how scrutiny can be strengthened and general conclusions about intelligence. The committee had to evolve as its reliability, authority and role were gradually recognised. Its public credibility – or rather more its parliamentary and press credibility – was to some extent weakened by its ambivalent status, appearing to be like a select committee but appointed by and reporting to the Prime Minister while working within the ring of secrecy. It would be possible to create an Intelligence Committee which had all the characteristics of a select committee, but its ability to scrutinise the intelligence world would be superficial or non-existent. Some compromises are essential so that the Committee can be told everything that is relevant, see everything that is relevant, and report on everything, even on issues which cannot be revealed more widely to Parliament without destroying the secrecy on which the activity may depend. It is clearly better to give explicit parliamentary approval for the Committee's membership, so long as a procedure exists for excluding anyone who cannot be relied on to keep secrets, for whatever reason, or expects to use the committee as a way of making a public reputation. Politicians have other fields in which they can make a name, and any attempt to do so in intelligence oversight defeats the process.

From day one the Committee was by its statute precluded from considering 'operations', as opposed to expenditure, policy and finance, which it has explicit statutory authority to investigate. It is a distinction which, although it was intended to protect agency operations from accidental disclosure (the fewer people who know operational details, the safer they are), is unrealistic in practice. Many issues cannot be understood without understanding the kind of operations in which they arise, and knowledge of operations is sometimes necessary for the Committee to be able to provide reassurance that agency activity is appropriate, proportionate, and sound in its assessment of the various types of risk involved. It was a limitation which became overdue for removal.

It also became clear that in some circumstances the Committee cannot be sure of what has happened unless it can see all the relevant documentation, with full access to all relevant files and stored material. We know this to be the case because there have been a number of inquiries, like the Bali bombing inquiry and our inquiry into rendition, when we have been given that power, and it has made a difference. It is not necessarily that the agencies deliberately withhold information. It is more likely that, when staff of the Agencies carry out a detailed search of their records, in order to meet the Committee's requests, their own view of events has to be modified from the version which originally filtered through the system to them. I have seen it happen.

At one stage in its history the Committee appointed an investigator, Dr John Morrison, partly with the intention that he could go through documentation and advise the Committee of items it needed to see. In practice he was used mainly to produce detailed reports on discrete subjects which were valuable but were not central to the inquiries the Committee was conducting. His departure, or the non-renewal of his part-time contract, was for a quite different reason. He appeared on television, having been advised not to do so, and gave his opinion on the Iraq dossier controversy. The fact that I largely agreed with his view made no difference to my belief, and that of the rest of the Committee, that taking such a public role made it impossible to carry out the duties of an investigator giving advice in secret, for which purpose he needed to be trusted by the agencies. I remained of the view, now widely accepted, that despite this setback the Committee needed to develop and extend its investigatory capacity.

The Committee only gained access to the important work of the Defence Intelligence Staff by informal agreement and by seeking the assistance of the Prime Minister in ensuring that this was extended after the David Kelly affair. Although much of military intelligence is tactical, the Ministry of Defence is a very important contributor to the strategic intelligence picture. This aspect of its work cannot be properly investigated by the Defence Select Committee, and has needed the involvement of the ISC.

It has also been argued that the Committee would be in a stronger position if it was chaired by an opposition rather than a government member. When Labour came to power, Tom King was left in place as Committee chairman until he left the Commons at the next General Election. I now know much more about the appointment of the next Chairman than I did at the time: it turns out that my name had been put forward, and had got as far as the Prime Minister's desk with the

Cabinet Secretary's recommendation, when Tony Blair felt obliged to find a new role for Ann Taylor, the former Chief Whip and Leader of the House whom he had not reappointed to his government after the election. Ann was a good and fair chairman of the Committee despite her long record as a Government loyalist, but that same record probably encouraged the perception of the Committee as the Prime Minister's Committee. When Ann Taylor left the Commons the chair was given to the Northern Ireland Secretary who was not reappointed after the election, Paul Murphy. Paul is an able man of great integrity, but the use of the chairmanship as a consolation prize for loss of ministerial office, although no fault of the individual concerned, has reinforced the criticisms of the method of appointment. Both Ann Taylor and Paul Murphy became ministers again, filling gaps caused by unexpected resignations, although it is fair to say that neither had expected to do so, and former Foreign Secretary Margaret Beckett became chairman. A convention that a member of one of the opposition parties should normally chair the Committee, or even a practice of appointing a non-government chairman more often, might help to give the Committee greater authority.

Looking more generally at the intelligence community, I am in no doubt of the value of good intelligence. Knowledge of the intentions and capacity of hostile powers can prevent wars or at least ensure that British forces know the threats they have to face. The work of intelligence agencies can discover and disrupt terrorist plots, and can track and frustrate illegal arms trafficking. Intelligence can uncover breaches of international agreements which protect our security, our trade or our environment. Intelligence agencies, when resources are available, can support the police in pursuit of serious and organised crime. Intelligence cannot thwart all terrorists or uncover all hostile activity, but without it we would be in much greater danger.

Intelligence is not helped when political leaders misuse or exaggerate it to defend their policies, or when they create circumstances in which agencies, in this country or any other, are tempted to tell them what they want to know rather than giving them the whole picture. Phrases like 'the war on terrorism' illustrate the sort of strategic confusion which political leaders talk their way into. Terrorism is a tactic, not an enemy; it is a tactic which cannot be defeated – you have to remove the enemy, or the cause for which the enemy is fighting, or the potential he has to recruit the fighters and collaborators he needs.

Britain 'punches above its weight' in intelligence, and its agencies are recognised and respected throughout the world for their particular skills. This is something in which as a country we can take some pride, but it is also dangerous if it lulls us into complacency. Whether in complex technology or in more traditional but very necessary human intelligence, a reputation has to be maintained by constant renewal of personnel and resources, and the maintenance of high standards. Intelligence is now much more a subject of international co-operation, and even services which have long worked against each other, like the British and the Russians, recognise common interests which make some limited co-operation possible. Co-operation with Pakistan and with Arab States is essential in tracking and frustrating terrorist networks. New democracies in Eastern Europe and South Africa's post-apartheid democracy needed to develop intelligence and security services to replace hated instruments of oppression like the Stasi, the Securitate and BOSS, and were rightly anxious to ensure democratic oversight. We have sought to help and co-operate with oversight bodies in many countries, and have built up, on the basis of an initiative from the Australians, a system of international sharing of oversight experience. It is sometimes startling to find that you are comparing notes with a South African politician who was originally trained in intelligence in Eastern Europe, and instructive to meet both South Africans and Eastern Europeans who have suffered at the hands of repressive and brutal security agencies.

For Britain, by far the most important international links it has are with the United States. Although some areas have remained 'off limits' for national interest reasons, the co-operation in the main is close, instinctive, long-standing and of enormous mutual benefit. Given the sheer size of the US intelligence establishment, cumbersome and elephantine though it can sometimes be, the UK benefits most from the closeness of this relationship, although it is of real and recognised value to the United States. If the 'special relationship' is thought to be largely illusory in some fields of policy, in intelligence it is real. Moreover, it has survived major foreign policy disagreements, and does not depend on slavish UK backing for US policy. Obviously it can come under strain at times of disagreement, but, surprisingly, it stays on track. In our report on Rendition we criticised a lack of regard by the US for UK concerns in ignoring caveats and subsequent protests in the rendition of individuals from the Gambia to Guantanamo Bay, a rare departure from normal standards of co-operation which we said 'has serious implications to the working of the relationship between the US and UK intelligence and security agencies.'[22] The same could be said of the use of the US base on Diego Garcia for rendition previously denied, which the Foreign Secretary reported to Parliament following a belated disclosure from the US authorities. However the relationship survived Suez, Vietnam and the Falklands, in each of which there was a fundamental divergence between US and UK policy. In my judgement it would have survived, with some strains, a UK refusal to support the US-led invasion of Iraq. As well as the US relationship, both we and they have a long-standing relationship with Canada and Australia which, in the field of signals intelligence, has a long-standing basis in a formal agreement.

In the period since I first became involved in intelligence oversight there have been massive changes in the intelligence environment and in the agencies themselves. Once run as very separate fiefdoms with very limited co-operation, they now work much more closely together. Many staff are seconded between them and with other related areas of government. A common IT system is gradually coming into place, to facilitate intelligence-sharing. The cultures of the different agencies are still distinct because they work in different ways, employing different skills, and if a unique organisation like SIS lost its distinctive ethos it would no longer be able to attract either the recruits or the sources which make it the envy of much larger organisations. If the Security Service lost its sharp focus on intelligence-gathering, as opposed to the very different role of the police, it would not serve its purpose. And if GCHQ were to lose its technological cutting edge, our attempts to tackle terrorism and international crime would be greatly weakened. There is no need to amalgamate agencies which have shown that they can work closely together while specialising in different roles.

James Bond is not the reality of intelligence, and the world of *Tinker, Tailor, Soldier, Spy* has largely gone. It remains a challenging and dangerous field in which courage and skill are constantly deployed for our protection. Substantial resources and considerable powers are entrusted to agencies, and they need effective parliamentary oversight, carried out in a manner which does not stop them from doing their job.

—14—

HARMONY AND HERITAGE

Being an active MP for a very scattered rural constituency, when combined with family life, leaves very little time for hobbies or leisure pursuits. I walked many more miles in the Cheviot Hills and in the Norwegian mountains in the decade before I was an MP than I have done in the several decades since. I never had the acres of time required to build up any proficiency in golf. That is a pity in a constituency with more golf courses than any other in England. I occasionally used to play my late constituency chairman, Geoff France, a farmer and holder of the Military Cross, and one of the finest men I have known. With only one leg (he lost the other thanks to an aggressive cow) he would drive like a rocket and beat me every time. I briefly resumed the sport to play my son on Wooler's amazing hilltop course, where local rules state that you must drop the ball to play on without penalty if your ball lands on a prehistoric cup-and-ring marking. But Chris could usually beat me.

For a time I kept a small boat on the River Tyne. My urge to get on the water was met at first by an inflatable with an outboard motor, which was used mainly on holiday in Sweden and on some of the North-West canals; later it was replaced by something with more all-weather shelter, the appropriately named *Freedom*, which was a 20-foot Hardy Pilot. I kept it in St Peter's Basin, which is just downstream from Newcastle's Quayside. Because I could operate it single-handed, I could spend a couple of hours out on the water at the end of a day of meetings in Newcastle: it was even handy to the Tyne-Tees studios, and I kept a clean shirt and tie on board for when I was called away for news interviews.

The Tyne is an amazingly under-used asset. The North Sea, for much of the year, is a fairly hostile environment for small boats. The Tyne, however, offers 10 miles of sheltered navigable water, from the Shields piers to Blaydon (although you need to watch the tides for depth in the upper stretches). It is a riverside packed with interest, from the landmarks of old industry to the city's quayside and the new riverside residential developments. Not a lot moves on the water between Newcastle and Tyne Commission Quay apart from a few pleasure boats. That makes it even more exciting if you turn the corner and find a large sand-carrier bearing down on you on its way to moor at the depot on the Gateshead bank or, better still, a Navy ship heading for Spiller's Wharf to tie up for a courtesy visit. Downstream you have the gigantic car transporters, or the DFDS ferries preparing to cast off, with passenger announcements in Norwegian carried on the breeze across the waters. And, except during what used to be frequent breakdowns, the yellow Shields ferry would ply back and forth; it is alarming to think that I travelled on the old car-carrying Shields ferry when coal was still being shovelled to fire her boiler. Scenically, the most enthralling stretch of the river is undoubtedly the length under the bridges from the Eye to the Redheugh bridge. There are wonderful views of Newcastle's waterfront. In recent years it has only been really busy on the water during the Tall Ships' visits, a rare opportunity not only to see wonderful sailing ships but also to sense the opportunities offered by a river buzzing with life. There are plenty of leisure boats moored along the river: many are used rarely, and mainly as a means of getting out of the river and into the sea. What the Tyne needs is more public landing stages to open up riverside attractions and encourage local and visiting boat owners to spend more time on the river itself.

The perils of mooring on the Tyne without a landing pontoon were brought home to me one day when I moored at North Shields, went to get a bite to eat and some supplies, and spent more time ashore than was wise when the tide can drop 14 feet. I returned to find my boat perilously close to being held above the water by very taut mooring ropes. Rapid descent of the ladder and drastic action with the bread knife saved the situation, but I could still see the remains of that blue mooring rope from the deck of the MS *Jupiter* as I returned to the Tyne from Norway a couple of years later.

Eventually I found I was not getting enough time on the boat to justify the cost of keeping and maintaining it, but not before it had given me and my son a lot of pleasure, and had occasionally served as overnight accommodation for me when Barbara was in hospital in Newcastle.

Many politicians do still manage to preserve what has become known as a hinterland of their own interests. In my case, apart from reading, there have been two: one is music, and the other is the development of my longstanding interest in neglected chapel buildings into what has become a movement to recognise and preserve the best examples.

I owe the delight I have had from music mainly to school, and also in part to strong musical traditions in the village in which I was brought up through the band and the chapel. There was the seed sown by my primary school headmistress in taking us to hear the Hallé Orchestra – in particular a seed of interest in the music of

Richard Strauss, which did not really grow until many years later. But it is to the music teaching and performance opportunities at the King's School that I owe most of my commitment to the enjoyment of music. I have referred earlier to the oratorio, operetta and orchestral performances in which learning to play the trumpet involved me. The village brass band, although not as well directed then as it later became, was a chance to play in contests, which are the exacting standard-setters of the brass band world. The chapel had a powerful musical tradition, bolstered by the fact that it was the centre for a Male Voice Choir. Hymn singing in Northern Chapels, as it is still in Wales, was four-part singing. Nothing compares with part-singing by a large congregation. At a Sunday evening service at our own chapel there would be at least 30 men in the congregation singing the bass part, most reading music but others following their lead. Tenors were fewer – perhaps 10 if we were lucky – with a couple of dozen contraltos. Occasionally, if the singing was going really well, the organist would leave one verse unaccompanied. The effect, to me, was exhilarating: it was as if we had been taxiing along the runway, wheels firmly on the tarmac; then, suddenly, we were flying – we had taken off. It gave me a love of unaccompanied singing which has never left me. Occasionally there would be house parties, particularly at Christmas, where conversation and a delicious supper (no alcohol, of course) would be followed by the handing round of hymn books and music sheets, as hymns, carols, songs and anthems would be sung. For years I sorely missed these opportunities to enjoy singing, until I realised that it was up to me to reinstate the tradition, so it is now at least an annual event in our own house.

The town and fishing community chapels of the North East also had a strong part-singing tradition which seemed likely to disappear completely, but with the leadership of Anne Suggate of the '20,000 voices' project there has been a determined and successful effort to interest both young and old Northumbrians in using their voices for the pleasure of choral singing.

Singing parties are one of my few opportunities to get involved in performing music. The others include playing annually at Christmas with the Salvation Army band, and filling last-minute gaps in the orchestra for local productions: second trumpet in Haydn's Creation or fourth trumpet in Verdi's Requiem. I was once asked to play in a 'celebrity' backing group for Cheryl Baker in an ITV production from Manchester in which the few notes I had to play were vastly exceeded by the pound notes of the performance fee – far more than I had ever been paid to speak on television (and most of the time politicians are not paid at all for TV appearances, on the assumption that they are hungry enough for publicity to appear for nothing).

Occasional orchestra slots have been possible for me because amateur choirs use 'scratch' orchestras of semi-professional and amateur players who are only expected to rehearse on the day of the concert. The choir will have been practising the work for months, on a midweek practice night which makes choral singing impossible for MPs.

Impossible, that is, until an enterprising group of peers and MPs including Lord Filkin and Baroness Walmsley had the brilliant idea of establishing a Parliament Choir, and the equally brilliant idea of persuading Simon Over to direct it. Around 6.30 every Monday night, in the crypt chapel of the House of Commons, 40 to 70 people assemble to practice major choral works. It is a group made up not just of MPs and peers but also clerks, researchers, secretaries, librarians, catering staff, auditors, police officers, family members – all involved in or closely associated with Parliament. Regularly a batch of MPs or peers will put down their music and dash for a vote in one House or the other. But therein lies the great benefit for us – singing regularly in a choir, although still difficult, becomes possible because it takes place in the Palace of Westminster at a time when we have to be there. Most of the performances are also midweek, and Whips have occasionally been cajoled into rearranging the order of business so that the Hallelujah chorus or the B Minor Mass are not imperilled by an exodus of singing legislators from Westminster Cathedral, St John's Smith Square or the Cadogan Hall. BT have been consistent sponsors and supporters of the choir.

I have also had enormous pleasure from listening to music of many kinds. In Northumberland we miss out on opportunities to hear full symphony orchestras, except for the periodic visits of major orchestras to the Newcastle City Hall in the past and now to the Sage, across the river. However, we have the continued delight of the Northern Sinfonia and we also have superb artists in the wonderful setting and marvellous acoustic of Brinkburn Priory every summer. There is also superb chamber music at Paxton House, just outside Berwick, and regular chamber music at Alnwick music society. Newcastle's Avison ensemble periodically visits Berwick. For someone who is stuck in London for most of nearly every week, I despair at the wealth of orchestral, operatic and chamber music I scarcely ever dip into because of evening votes, evening meetings, or the sheer unpredictability of parliamentary life. The same goes for the theatre – there are very few evenings when you can be confident of getting into the West End for a 7.15 performance and not having to leave for a vote in the middle of the last Act.

I have spoken more about performing music than about listening to it being far better performed by professionals and great artists. It puts me in mind of the fact that school music education seemed to send people on one of two completely divergent paths. One was performance; the other used to be enshrined in the description 'musical appreciation'. Schools, and music teachers, differ in the emphasis they give to each. Those for whom music means performance are happiest when they can pick up a sheet of printed music and sing it or play it. Along with performance I should include creative composition, which is now much more emphasised in school music and feeds into the rock and pop music culture which has brought out talent in young people who are not initially attracted by the classical tradition. Those in the 'appreciation' stream are happiest when they pick up a new DVD, an old vinyl or a remastered great performance and play it on high-tech equipment reproducing faithful sound. Performers discuss what it is like trying to get the fingering right or to play with some particular ensemble; appreciators compare great performances, discuss the styles of long-dead conductors as if they had been present at their concerts; they compare Björling with Bostridge, or Wagner Ring Cycles in pre-war and post-war Bayreuth. The two approaches are not mutually exclusive: every performer enjoys listening to good performances. But it is more than the conflicting time requirements of musical competence and musical connoisseurship: styles of education do tend to send people one way or the other, and for me it is performing that has meant most, despite the barriers created by my severely limited technique and limited practice time. My approach is to find music which is challenging but not impossibly difficult, and play or sing it with as much musicianship as I can manage. It is a delight to play music with others, to learn from them and to share the thrill of producing something special.

Apart from music, the one interest I have managed to keep up and, indeed, extend has been in the architectural heritage of chapels, and their inclusion within the heritage movement. I refer to it as a movement, because it has done so much to transform attitudes to this country's amazing inheritance of buildings of many types and periods. It is a movement which has encouraged people to value our built heritage, and has made sure that much more of that heritage is still around to be enjoyed than at one time seemed possible. But chapels, with very few exceptions, were late to be recognised: a chapel would be dismissed in old county guides as 'a barn-like structure', and very few even get a mention in the first Pevsner *Buildings of England* volumes. The new series is remedying that omission.

My interest began as I cycled around Cheshire as a teenager, and my scope for exploration widened once I managed to borrow the money to buy a motorbike. In our own village the chapel was the oldest public building, with only farmhouses and a few of the miners' cottages preceding its 1837 origins. Most people assumed that the Parish Church must be older: its spire was a pleasing landmark, but it was a fairly standard essay in 'Early English' from the late 1850s, whereas the chapel was an honest construction, built by miners with their hard-earned money, suited to its purpose of simple worship, and furnished and extended gradually as its membership and resources grew. Cycling brought me to the delight of 1690s Presbyterian meeting houses in Knutsford, Dean Row and Macclesfield: they were among the first fruits of the 1689 Toleration Act, and their congregations later became Unitarian. These lovely buildings had two external staircases giving access to galleries which looked down on a high pulpit around which box pews radiated. They spoke more vividly than my history books of earnest Protestant dissent among communities of hard-working artisans, whose black Sunday hats would line the chapel, hanging on pegs which were still there. They gave rise to the Northern saying 'his eyes stuck out like chapel hat pegs'.

In Macclesfield, within walking distance of my school, were the numerous towering Methodist chapels, built with almost as much competitive spirit as is shown by Tesco and Asda as they vie for places in the out-of-town shopping centres. 'Wesley's' was the oldest, from the 1790s, with Brunswick declaring its date in its loyal name, then Beech Lane and Church Street West and Park Street and Park Lane and – in the smartest Victorian part of town – Trinity, with a spire. All these and many more were to be found in a town where one of the mill owners was so caught up with Wesley's revival that he determined to capture its spirit within the established church, paying for the massive preaching box of Christ Church to be built to rival the mediaeval parish church. One chapel was even built as a speculative venture by a developer, taken on by the Congregationalists, and later bought by the Church of England. Virtually all had massive galleries. Between them they would have had room to spare even if every man, woman and child in the town turned up for Sunday worship. Gradually they fell out of use; today the Methodists use only one of the dozen or more they once had. Some have been demolished. One had been built by a Methodist mill owner as a 'Free Methodist' breakaway and in due course was incorporated into his mill. Even Christ Church was declared redundant by the Church of England, but was thankfully preserved by the Churches Conservation Trust.

In later years, exploration in the North East yielded similarly rich treasures and showed a similar pattern: in Tyneside and County Durham it was the Methodists who, with their division into Wesleyans, Primitives and the various United Methodist streams built competitively, while in North Northumberland it was divisions among the Presbyterians which ensured that small towns like Alnwick, Wooler and Belford have had at least three Presbyterian meeting houses or churches, and Berwick had eight. The Presbyterian heritage includes Branton from 1720, disused since the 1960s, and Norham of 1743, now a house. The Methodist buildings range from the simple chapel at Newbiggin-in-Teesdale, claiming to be the oldest in continuous use, and the octagonal chapel at Yarm, commended by John Wesley himself for its acoustics, to mighty Brunswick in the centre of Newcastle, the elegant Wesley Chapel in the centre of Hartlepool (rescued from dereliction to become a night club), and the grand St John's Ashbrooke, in the posh part of Sunderland which Kate Adie so vividly portrays in her autobiography. A stroll along Howard Street and into Northumberland Square in North Shields will reveal a whole string of chapels and former chapels, no less than three of them attributed to Newcastle's most prolific nineteenth-century architect, John Dobson. The Baptists take good care of a delightful 1774 Chapel at Hamsterley in County Durham, while the Unitarians have a hidden and very unusual gem, cold-shouldered by Newcastle's Central motorway, the Church of the Divine Unity. Most unusually it was built in 1940/41 to the design of Newcastle architects Cackett Burns Dick.

Back in Oxford, my motorcycle meandering had led me to a mysterious isolated Baptist chapel among the water meadows at Cote; it had an almost Dutch gable front, and an evocative graveyard. It dated from 1740. I later found a drawing of it by John Piper illustrating an essay on nonconformist chapels by John Betjeman in his *First and Last Loves*. Finding the essay was a revelation – I had previously thought I must be alone and eccentric in finding these buildings so fascinating and valuable. Now an author of repute – admittedly a reputed eccentric – had dared to

Another of my eleven General Election campaigns (so far).

Speaking in the House, supported by Phil Willis, whose election as Harrogate's MP
brought welcome reinforcement for Liberal Democrats in the North East.

Meeting First Secretary Gorbachev in the Kremlin when *perestroika* was just beginning.

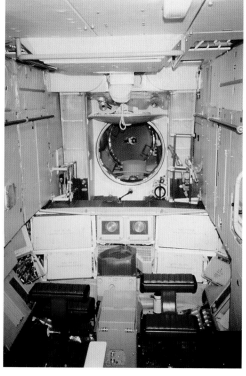

On the Russian visit, Denis Healey took photographs everywhere, so I photographed the inside of the Mir space station while no-one was looking (right).

Even a Russian who has walked in space can find something of interest in the
Newcastle *Journal*!

The Intelligence and Security Committee presents one of its reports to
Prime Minister Tony Blair in the Cabinet room.

On the footbridge over the River Aln near our home when we lived at Whittingham.

Chris came with me for a week with friends in Indiana, visiting farms while I gave a lecture at Earlham College.

Diana (who is, confusingly, both Lady Maddock and Lady Beith!) has brought renewed happiness into my life...

...and delight has come in the form of grandson Scott, seen here with Caroline and Iain.

The work of the Historic Chapels Trust has saved many fascinating buildings, and it is a privilege to be involved as chairman. Up in Coquetdale we have a Victorian Catholic Chapel (top left), which is built into a medieval pele tower. At Coanwood, on the Northumberland/Cumbria border (bottom left), we look after a peaceful and tiny Quaker meeting house dating from 1760. St. George's Lutheran Church in East London (top right) dates from 1762–3, and is the Trust's headquarters. Bethesda Methodist Chapel, Hanley, Stoke-on-Trent (bottom right) attracted nearly two thousand visitors for an afternoon open day when we completed the first million-pound stage of a major restoration.

The North's links with Norway are important, and I became chairman of the British-Norwegian group in Parliament. Here we are showing Norway's Crown Prince the portraits of his ancestors in the Palace of Westminster.

admit to this unfashionable enthusiasm. Around the same time I was given a copy of an excellent book by Rev. George Dolbey, whom I knew as a preacher in our area, detailing *The Architectural Expression of Methodism*. Only gradually did I discover that there were other enthusiasts hidden away, most notably the greatest authority and most diligent recorder of nonconformist architectural history, Christopher Stell. He had laboured for decades at the Royal Commission on Historical Monuments and had travelled the country developing the descriptions and drawings which were eventually published in the four superb volumes of chapels and meeting houses of the regions of England. An article of his in an early issue of the magazine *Interiors* showed that a Suffolk independent chapel's remarkable surviving fittings deserved attention just as must as a restored Venetian palazzo or the latest Finnish cutlery design. The writings of Kenneth Lindley, Ken Powell, Marcus Binney and Professor Clyde Binfield added to awareness of the significance of nonconformist buildings.

Meanwhile, the very buildings which had aroused our enthusiasm were disappearing before our eyes, or being altered beyond recognition. It was partly a consequence of the large decline in church and chapel attendance in the twentieth century, but that was not the only reason. As we have seen, there had been massive over-building because of splits and rivalries in the nonconformist denominations. Most had a policy of uniting in a single building, causing the loss of several others: in some cases, deplorably, they could not agree on whose building to use, and therefore abandoned all of them and put up a generally much inferior new building. Some chapels were in places which had suffered drastic depopulation: built by lead miners, coal miners or clay miners, they lost their purpose when the mines closed and the population moved on. Where chapels had lively congregations, precious interiors were vulnerable to destructive change dictated by fashions in worship. Pulpits and pews would be ripped out to be replaced by stacking chairs – allegedly for flexibility, although in practice they were rarely moved. One Anglican vicar in Whitehaven had a superb Georgian pulpit taken down because, he claimed, preaching from it gave him vertigo: the less damaging expedient of not using it and leaving it for future generations did not occur to him.

One Baptist minister's bonfire led to a change in the law: whereas in the Church of England the faculty system gives some possibility of protection to historic interiors, other denominations enjoyed the same freedom from listed building controls without any comparable internal system of scrutiny and control. The destruction of the seventeenth-century pews at the Baptist Chapel in Great Gidding led to an outcry, and to the eventual removal of ecclesiastical exemption from listed building control in all denominations which did not put in place a system of control based on suitably qualified advisory committees. It was a step forward, but there was much more to be done. The Council for British Archaeology had set up a Churches Committee in 1978, and it was in 1988 that its Research Officer, Richard Morris, asked me to chair a meeting to set up a new society to promote interest in non-Church of England religious buildings, which I gladly did.

The Chapels Society, which began with this meeting, has proved an extremely valuable organisation for sharing knowledge of and enthusiasm for religious buildings outside the Church of England. The Georgian Society and the Victorian Society also championed the cause of an increasing number of chapels threatened with destruction or damaging alterations.

But time does not stand still, and even if denominations could be persuaded to value their historic buildings and at least use some of them well, there would still be a stream of buildings which the denominations did not need and could not afford to maintain. A few could be re-used as concert or lecture halls (both St John's Smith Square and the Cadogan Hall in London are former places of worship): others could be sympathetically converted for offices, housing or entertainment. But for some, such a fate would involve the destruction of the very features which made them important, especially their interior fittings and layout. The redundancy problem was already recognised in the Church of England through the setting up of the Redundant Churches Fund (later renamed the Churches Conservation Trust), to which some of the more significant closed churches are handed over, and maintained through annual grants provide by both the government and the Church. For the buildings of other denominations in a comparable state there was nothing. English Heritage and the National Trust each had a chapel or two in their care, and there were a few local trusts looking after redundant chapels. There was clearly a gap to be filled. It was Matthew Saunders of Friends of Friendless Churches who got together Christopher Stell, Richard Morris and me over a meal at the Athenaeum Club to plan what could be done, and this led to the creation, with government support, of the Historic Chapels Trust. Sir Hugh Rossi, former Conservative minister and a Roman Catholic, became the first Chairman of a group of Trustees which included Christopher Stell and myself. Hugh gave good leadership to the Trust and used all his contacts to secure government commitment for its work, and Peter Brooke, then Environment Secretary, presided at an inaugural event in the delightful Paget Memorial Mission Hall in Islington on 15 June 1993. The Trust's achievements are in very large part due to the brilliant work of its part-time Director Dr Jenny

Freeman, whom I had first met on a Georgian Society exploration of Friends' Meeting Houses in the Home Counties. She had already played a large part in the rescue of the Dissenters' Chapel in Kensal Green cemetery, and her skill and energy in restoration projects, the recruitment of enthusiasts and in fund-raising has made the impossible become the achievable.

I took over the Chairmanship of the Trust when Sir Hugh Rossi retired in (2002). The buildings we have taken into our care include a wide range of types, including early and very simple Quaker meeting houses at Farfield on the Dales Way in Yorkshire and Coanwood (1760) in a remote corner of South West Northumberland. The 1739 Baptist chapel at Cote in Oxfordshire which had so excited me and inspired John Piper, is in our care. We have a Baptist chapel of 1877 at Umberslade, on the southern edge of Birmingham, a rare example of a landowner's 'estate' chapel, built in Gothic style by Midlands industrialist G.F. Muntz: in his declining years he remained at the forefront of technology, installing a telephone line so that he could listen to the services while confined to his sickbed in his country seat across the fields. Another manufacturer's chapel is the massive cathedral-like Unitarian church which dominates the Pennine mill-town of Todmorden, built by the sons of Liberal MP, Sunday School teacher and philanthropist John Fielden. A contrast in style although not in the significance of wealthy patronage is provided by the 1899 Wallasey Memorial Unitarian Church, with its rich and lovely 'arts and crafts' furnishings.

The Walpole independent chapel which featured in *Interiors* magazine was one of our first projects. Methodist chapels range from the tiny Penrose Bible Christian chapel in Cornwall to the massive and magnificent 1819 Bethesda Chapel, Hanley, Stoke on Trent, which featured in the BBC's *Restoration* programme and is the subject of a £2.5 million project to rescue it from 20 years of advancing dereliction. It is a very good example of a building loved by the local community, who felt that a prized asset had been taken from them and are now keen to see the doors thrown open for choir and band concerts, visits, exhibitions and occasional services. The community affection for the building was delightfully demonstrated when I accompanied a local journalist and photographer round the chapel in hard hats before restoration began. As soon as he had taken his pictures, the photographer pulled out his phone and rang his mother, with evident excitement, to tell her he was actually inside the chapel where she and his grandparents had all been christened and married, and that it really was going to be saved. When the opening of the only partly restored building was announced, queues formed all along the street and into the next street, and 2000 people visited during the afternoon.

Our function is not to look after buildings which are still in denominational use, but to rescue some which will otherwise be lost. Although the future care of the buildings will depend on wider community use, we encourage the use of the buildings for services of worship in the tradition for which they were built: big chapels like Bethesda were not built as shrines for private devotion, but to be filled with worshippers listening to stirring sermons preached from the high central pulpit, and to echo with rousing hymns. We do, however, have a shrine: among the Trust's Roman Catholic buildings is its youngest, the Shrine of Our Lady of Lourdes in Blackpool, designed by F.X. Velarde in 1955 and decorated with sculpture reliefs by David John, who – uniquely among those who have helped to create on the Trust's buildings – was able to be present when we launched the restoration project, and to meet people who remembered seeing him 50 years ago, perched on high scaffolding as he carved the statues on the façade. Other Roman Catholic buildings include the amazing Biddlestone chapel in the Cheviot Hills above Rothbury, which was attached to the now demolished home of the Catholic Selby family. It is a Victorian chapel built on the upper floor of a mediaeval pele tower, in the bottom of which is a Second World War Anderson air raid shelter – as diverse a history as a single small building could contain.

The Trust's responsibilities include two further Catholic chapels, a Yorkshire Baptist Chapel and a magnificent German Lutheran Church of 1762 in Tower Hamlets, where Dietrich Bonhoeffer's close friend Julius Rieger ministered, organising help for German Jewish refugees before and during the war. Here the Trust has its headquarters.

These buildings have to be restored, cared for in perpetuity and made available for local community use. The basis for doing so is funding from English Heritage, Heritage Lottery capital grants, energetic and exhausting fund-raising by our staff of only two people, and additional fund-raising to help with maintenance by the local friends' groups which we establish at all our buildings. The Trust badly needs some greater financial security, perhaps partly from government aid on a scale more closely comparable to that given to the Church of England's Churches Conservation Trust, and partly from legacies. A significant number of historically important and aesthetically outstanding buildings from the dissenting religious traditions have been saved, and will be conserved in perpetuity. It is immensely rewarding work. It is why I describe this bit of my life as more than a hobby: it has been and remains part of a movement to retain a physical reminder of why we are as we are. We need to know where we have come from if we are to make sensible and imaginative decisions about where we are going as a society and a nation.

—15—

LOSING LOVED ONES

'The Lord gave and the Lord hath taken away. Blessed be the name of the Lord.' These are the words from the book of Job, heard at the beginning of the burial service. I am not sure how Job managed to say them, since everything bad you could think of, and a great deal more, seemed to have happened to him. But they are words which work for me: they are how I have learned to live with losing those closest to me. When loved ones have brought joy into our lives, the reality of that joy is in the end more significant than the pain of loss. The effects of that joy are more powerful even than the questioning that comes when a life is cut short. The gap can never be filled, but the gift which that loved one has been to us, preserved in our own character and memory, can never be taken away.

Barbara and I, having for some years of marriage failed to produce any children, concluded that we should accept the situation. We did not feel that we wanted to go to great lengths to alter it. We thought that there were enough children in the world for us to be able to fulfil a role either by taking responsibility for a child in need through adoption, or by helping children in our working lives, as Barbara already did as a teacher. It happened that close friends and neighbours adopted at around this time. We applied to one of the adoption societies, the Children's Society, and waited to see what transpired.

It was a year or so later when we were suddenly alerted to a possible adoption. I was already in Parliament and Barbara was teaching at Hexham. I was summoned back from the Party Conference in Llandudno. We suddenly found ourselves caring for a beautiful fair-haired baby boy, full of life and energy. Since there had been no certainty that this would happen, or when, or what age of child it might be, we had done none of the preparation which accompanies a pregnancy, but we rushed around to get the necessary things together and we managed. Grandparents appeared from the other side of the country to give a hand; my father-in-law delighted in pushing the pram and was amazed by the generous local custom of neighbours and villagers slipping a silver coin into the baby's hand. We were able to enjoy what all parents enjoy in bringing up a baby. He was baptised Christopher Ian at our little chapel in Corbridge Market Place, and by the age of two he was running around with ever more energy and enthusiasm. Adoption proceedings went without a hitch.

We began to notice that Chris was drinking very large amounts of liquid and seemed constantly thirsty. Late one evening, when I was changing him, a sickly sweet smell reminded me of something I had read years before. Luckily our doctor was our next-door neighbour, and she immediately tested him for diabetes. The test result made the diagnosis unavoidable, so we went straight to the Royal Victoria Infirmary in Newcastle for him to be stabilised and for insulin-based therapy to begin. He was in the care of a doctor who will long be remembered by parents of sick children treated in Newcastle, Professor Michael Parkin. Chris formed a bond with him which lasted until Mike Parkin's early death: Mike had a heart attack as he was walking to unlock his Methodist Chapel for the Sunday morning service. In a short life of phenomenally hard work he saved many lives, healed many sick children and helped many children to live a full life whatever their condition.

Coping with a diabetic child is more complicated than it looks. Not only does it involve several injections a day, which in those days were with a glass syringe. It was often impossible to keep a glass syringe still while holding a struggling child. Diabetes involves constant monitoring of blood sugar levels. It also involved, at that time, very rigorous measuring of carbohydrate intake: this was not too difficult at home, but very difficult when travelling or buying food out. At that time in Britain there was no labelling of nutritional content of food, and that was another plus point for holidays in Norway and Sweden, where you could read the carbohydrate content of an ice cream or a biscuit on the packet. Then there were the problems of having to refuse the sweets given with kind intention at parties or even church services. Being late for meals – or finding that food was not served at the expected time – would produce hypoglycaemia. Falling blood sugar levels bring mood swings and drastic behaviour changes which are at first difficult to distinguish from normal childhood bad temper, bad behaviour or boundary-testing.

There are conditions and illnesses which place much heavier physical and emotional demands on parents than diabetes, but I have deliberately listed some of the problems we faced in order to speak up for a group of parents whose difficulties are not always recognised or understood, and for young diabetics. They sometimes find themselves in serious trouble because of unexpected behaviour changes whose medical cause will not be understood by people who do not know them. Coping with insulin-dependent diabetes is not just about avoiding sweet drinks (which can actually be needed in the event of a 'hypo' attack), or never being allowed to have the pudding after school dinner. It is actually, in part, about the healthy eating patterns which in more recent years have been promoted for everyone, but coping as a teenage diabetic involves a very high degree of self-discipline.

None of this stopped Chris from being a frenetically active child, and he managed to break a leg just as we were packing to move from what had been a very happy house in Corbridge to our new home in the middle of my constituency. It was a terraced brick cottage in the lovely village of Whittingham, which is set in its own beautiful vale. In the 1970s the village had a shop, two pubs, and several buses a day on the long-distance service that ran between Newcastle and Edinburgh, giving you a choice of two cities at either end of the route. The neighbouring village of Glanton had a grocer's, a bank, an ironmonger, a draper's, a post office, two pubs and a district nurse. Both villages had schools, and there were places of worship for the Church of England, the Presbyterians, the Roman Catholics and the Plymouth Brethren. The Presbyterian Minister, who served the village for over 30 years, was a great friend of the Roman Catholic priest; in earlier times a long-serving vicar had rented a pew in the Presbyterian church and attended evening services there to hear good sermons. The Catholic chapel dated from the 1870s, when Callaly Castle passed from an old Catholic family into Protestant hands, and no longer maintained its own Catholic chapel. Major Brown of Callaly Castle was a churchwarden at Whittingham, where the Callaly pew stood on one side of the church with the Ravensworth pew on the other. Lord Ravensworth was a regular attender at church. He was a former BBC sound engineer who had unexpectedly inherited the title and the estate which, although much of it had been sold off, still owned many of the cottages on our side of the village. It was to be another happy house, with Chris and later Caroline, having close friends of their own age who were also adopted living at the farm along the road.

214

Caroline had appeared on the scene three and a half years later: she was six months old when she came to us, a lovely baby girl. When the adoption hearing took place in the County Court judge's chambers in Alnwick, the three of us filed in, not knowing what to expect, but before the judge or anyone else could say anything, Chris spoke out. 'Can we keep her?' he demanded, and that set the tone for the proceedings. We did keep her. For most of their childhood, despite the age gap and all the customary jealousies and conflicting demands of sister and brother, they got on very well and, in a crisis, would take care of each other. Chris was alert but not academic, and sports of all kinds were his real love. Caroline, although a good runner and quite capable of sporting success, was more into school work and was artistic. I think they both suffered from some of the weaknesses of the education system of that time and some of the problems of the 3-tier system. Both were happy in the 9–13 middle schools, Chris at Wooler and Caroline later at Berwick, but both suffered from the delayed adjustment to High School at 13 and the culture of under-achievement which prevailed in Berwick High School at that time.

Being a country parent involves ferrying your children around the countryside to cubs, brownies, playgroups and other activities which are usually miles away. That and the fact that we were cramped for space both inside and outside led us to look for a bigger house, and you got a lot more house for a modest mortgage in Berwick than in the Alnwick area. Berwick was still largely undiscovered. So we moved to coincide with the children's change of schools. Barbara, who had helped found and run a playgroup in Powburn, returned to teaching at Berwick Middle School and, later, at Lindisfarne Middle School in Alnwick. She was a wonderful mother, and although she was equally supportive of both our children, Chris had a special dependency on her because of his diabetes.

Much is written and said about the pressures on the family life of MPs. It is a case that can be overstated, because there are many parents whose work takes them away from home just as much as mine did; one of our friends worked as a long-distance lorry driver, and was regularly away all week. Others had to move jobs, working away from home rather than uprooting the family. For RAF and other service families it is a choice between constant moves, every two years or so, from base to base, or serving away for months at a time while leaving the family at home. A Falklands posting, for example, meant six months without seeing the family at all. The one difference is that MPs who live in their constituencies – and I cannot imagine doing the job any other way – are just as busy at home at weekends as they are during the week. Instead of 'quality time' there is likely to be absence at the other end of the constituency, or children being compulsorily taken round all the coffee mornings, fêtes and shows. Shopping could sometimes be difficult, because it is often interrupted by friendly chat from constituents or urgent problems: someone's housing case details would often have to be written on the back of my shopping list or cheque book. Chris used to delight in sneaking up behind me in the supermarket, tapping me on the shoulder and saying 'Mr Beith, can I have a word with you?' But we still had some time and opportunity as a family to get fantastic enjoyment from our two children and their friends. Holidays, with uninterrupted time together, were marvellous. Often we camped, graduating to a motor caravan: it also did duty as my 'mobile surgery', which I took round every village in my constituency each autumn.

Barbara was a brilliant and inspiring teacher: I have had endless testimony to this from pupils and ex-pupils whom I met not only locally but all over the country. She enjoyed almost every day of her teaching life, despite the frustrations that go with the job, and apart from periodic sore throats (an occupational hazard) she had the health and energy to keep up her teaching while running the home, which she had to do single-handed between Monday and Thursday. Childhood rheumatic fever, which was always thought likely to present heart problems later on, seemed to have done no lasting harm. Then some problems started to arise, and one of the indications was breathlessness. I noticed that she was having some difficulty as we hurried up the hill to catch a train home from Durham station. At the same time I was conscious that she was hiding something, some fear or anxiety, which was not at all characteristic of her. Although she was far better at coping with pain than I was – unlike me she was not in the least scared of the dentist – and as a biologist she was not at all squeamish, she did have a real fear of doctors and hospitals. It was therefore with some difficulty and insistence that I got her into the doctor's surgery. The provisional diagnosis of breast cancer was immediate and shattering. Later that day we saw a consultant in Newcastle; surgery, he decided, was not an option. It had to be chemotherapy and radiotherapy, and the prognosis was not good. We were probably on borrowed time.

The children had to be the first to know: by this time they were teenagers, and Caroline was coming up to GCSE exams. They were shaken by the news, and we did not conceal how serious it was. For all our sakes, Barbara was determined to fight for more time, but she had first to get over her deep phobia about hospitals, and I thought I would never get her either into the ambulance, or out of it at the Newcastle General Hospital for the first round of treatment. The cancer wards of the General, where wonderful staff worked, were in a tired 1960s building on a hospital site from which most in-patient services were disappearing as other buildings were demolished. We were to get to know it well: Barbara was an in-patient there on 14 occasions and, in addition, she regularly made the exhausting 135-mile round trip to attend there for radiotherapy. There was an extraordinary moment when almost all my family were in different hospitals: Barbara was receiving chemotherapy in Newcastle, Chris had been taken to the Borders General Hospital after a minor rugby injury which had disrupted his diabetic control; and Caroline was having her tonsils removed in Berwick Infirmary. Only my mother, then 80 and living with us, seemed to be healthy, although it was not long before she, too, was in the Infirmary for a few days. I was driving between hospitals, visiting three in one day, with distances of over 60 miles between each of them. We seemed to have quite a lot of overnight stays at the hospital around public holidays – I have curiously happy memories of us celebrating New Year in the General Hospital: the staff created a delightful midnight party for the small number of patients who had not been able to go home.

Barbara may have been terrified of going into hospital, but she was a hugely courageous patient, and was constantly helping and encouraging other patients in the ward. There were times when the diamorphine she was given left her confused, and one of my lowest moments was finding her completely confused about where she was and about whether the children were young or grown up and married. I was so overcome that Chris had to drive me home, although underneath he was just as upset as I was. It brought home forcefully to me the anguish which serious mental illness and dementia must bring, with the feeling that the person you know so well is changing into a different person.

But we had good times. We knew the days were numbered, so every day mattered. Barbara was adamant that I should not give up my work as an MP and, although she had retired on health grounds, she returned to her school whenever she was fit on a purely voluntary basis because she loved teaching and wanted to continue. When she was not fit enough for school we would play Scrabble and she would watch *Countdown* each afternoon in a determined attempt to keep her mind clear and active: I remember telling Richard Whiteley how much this had meant to her, just before his own untimely death.

We had plenty to laugh about when it came to choosing a wig, and I enjoyed seeing her hair grow again in its lovely original golden auburn colour. As Christmas approached I booked a week in Tenerife so that Barbara could enjoy the warmth, and not have to think about all the usual preparations. She had already ordered Christmas presents by mail order; I left Chris and Caroline with a long food shopping list, and when we got back I got out Delia Smith's book and studied how to cook Christmas dinner. The truth is that for most of my life I had hardly cooked anything beyond breakfast. Thanks to Delia I now have a bizarre cooking repertoire consisting mainly of Christmas dinner, Sunday roasts and grilled fish.

We were also able to take a wonderful two-week summer trip on the Norwegian coastal steamer, at a time when Barbara was able to enjoy it. Being on a ship meant no worries carrying luggage about, and the opportunity for a rest or a sleep whenever she needed it. She loved being among the dramatic scenery and the kind people of Norway. It would have been marvellous trip at any time but in these circumstances it was even better: it was sheer bliss.

For nearly two years the effects of cancer ebbed and flowed like a tide, and the hospital periods came and went in consequence. Home was where Barbara wanted to be. Normally I was able to spend nights in London, when I really needed to, without any problems; on one or two occasions when I was not so confident, we got the help of a Marie Curie nurse to stay overnight. One weekend in April 1998 we were due to go to the wedding of my God-daughter in Durham, after which she and her husband were leaving to live in Panama. Barbara had hoped to come, but did not feel too well on the day. I arranged for two friends to sit in with her for the afternoon. When I got back she seemed weaker, and it was a struggle to get her to eat some supper. The next morning she got up but was reluctant to get dressed, even with help. I asked for a visit from the community nurse, and although this did not lead to any conclusion about further help being needed, Barbara seemed more content. That night she slept very restlessly; I got up in the night and then fell asleep in a chair. It was a beautiful, bright, sunny April morning and the light woke me. Barbara had got out of bed before me, and fallen to the floor, where she lay lifeless. It was over. The Lord had taken away. I rang for the doctor, rang Chris, who I knew would be devastated, and woke Caroline with news which was shattering for her. And then I remembered that it was my birthday.

You have many things to organise when someone dies. They fill in the time in the following days, while you try to support your grieving family. The funeral was clearly going to be too big for our small chapel, so we held it in the nearby Church of Scotland church in Wallace Green, where we were made very welcome. Barbara loved flowers, so I told the undertaker that, unlike many funerals nowadays, there was to be no discouraging of floral tributes (but, as Barbara always insisted, the wrappings had to be taken off – I could imagine her grimacing at rows of flowers concealed by paper and cellophane). The church was packed, and the second row was filled with children from her school class. They were around 10 years old, and most had never been to a funeral in their lives before. They were so good, and such a boost to me. They had sent her marvellous notes in the previous weeks, saying things like 'you are a fab teacher'.

Barbara had supported me in so many ways, including listening to my speeches and sermons more often than anyone ought to have to do, so I was determined to give the address at the funeral. I had a contingency plan for the minister to take over if I was unable to continue. In a strange way it was an address which wrote itself, and the delivery of it was a massive piece of therapy for me. Each morning, between Barbara's death and the day of the funeral I would wake up at about 4.30 with my head full of memories, and immediately start writing on any scrap of paper I could find. The memories become the reality – they have an existence of their own, filling some of the gaps which the loved one has left. They are more precious than jewels.

Barbara was buried in Whittingham's peaceful churchyard, within sight of the cottage where we had lived. We had to settle down to life without her. It was hardest of all for Chris and Caroline, hitting them both in different ways. Caroline had been working as a dental nurse. Chris had left school and gone on to pursue his interest in farming by becoming a student at Kirkley Hall College, Ponteland. Diabetes had not stopped him from pursuing all manner of physical activities, from sport to farm work. He played regularly in rugby, cricket and five-a-side football – he even managed to be the highest scorer in the defeated South of Scotland under-18 cricket team in a match against the North at Linlithgow. He threw himself into his sport, and was consequently prone to injury – I have several times chased the ambulance or dashed to the hospital where Chris would be treated for an injury and a consequent loss of diabetic stability. When he was not playing sport he would be working on a farm, first helping a local cattle breeder, then working from very early hours at the

Maxwells' dairy farm at Doddington, famous for its cheese and its ice cream. He would think nothing of milking over 200 cows single-handed. He loved farm work with the exception of shepherding: he had to do it, and had done plenty of lambing, but managing ewes tried his patience. Success at Kirkley was hard-won, because he was not comfortable with much academic work, and was impatient to get on with the practical. At Kirkley, as well as organising sports teams, he became the first student President. Barbara and I were overcome with delight at hearing him making a speech at the awards and graduation ceremony. He quite deliberately made it all his own work, without reference to Dad, and it was a delight to me to have our roles so effectively reversed.

After leaving Kirkley he took a demanding job on a hill farm on the edge of the Cheviots, with his sheep dog, and we helped him set up his own home in a farm cottage. He was working there when Barbara died, but some time later, undoubtedly in part because of the problems posed by his diabetes, he left. He started on a new career as a tool salesman for Snap-on-Tools; he underwent training and was employed and provided with a van and stock. He had real natural talent for the work: he was well-liked, an easy conversationalist, and a person people rightly felt they could trust. But it, too, had its pressures, and he became very depressed following a break-up with his girlfriend. Both children were still desperately missing their mum, and Chris would regularly take flowers to her grave in Whittingham and spend a long time there remembering and grieving.

Around this time, death seemed to stalk our family. Chris and I went to see Barbara's mother, who had gone into residential care and was clearly weakening. Within days she had died, having lived not quite as long as her own mother did, but within sight of 90. A greater surprise was a sudden deterioration in the health of Barbara's only sister, in her early 60s – Chris and I went down to Macclesfield to see her in hospital, but it was a terrible shock when she did not recover, and died shortly afterwards. My own mother seemed to be in much better health: she had made the decision to go into one of Berwick's two Abbeyfield houses. Without Barbara at home she was lonely in our house while I was in London, but at the Abbeyfield she had company, and was in amongst the shops and activities of the town centre. She thoroughly enjoyed it, and it had been a great idea to make the move: then, without warning and peacefully in her sleep, she died. It could not have happened in a nicer way for her, but it was yet another loss for us. Caroline had lost every female close relative she had: her mother, two grandmothers and her aunt, all of whom had been devoted to her. It had mostly happened during important years of school, college and starting work, and was undoubtedly a real setback and the cause of very troubled and difficult times for her. She left school early and took a business studies course at the very small annexe which was all Berwick had to offer in the way of further education. She worked first as a dental nurse, then at one of the local holiday parks and at the newly opened J.D. Wetherspoon pub in the town.

Two years after Barbara's death I decided to go with a group of MPs and peers from the All-Party Heritage Group for a long weekend holiday to Austria and Southern Germany, including the Oberammergau Passion Play. The weather was beautiful, the scenery was wonderful, the play was an experience not to be missed, and the company was very enjoyable. We were rounding the visit off with a meal in a restaurant private room; the weather had broken in a noisy thunderstorm, and the conversation noise level was high. I suddenly realised that my mobile phone was ringing, but I was too late to answer it. A quick check revealed that Caroline had been trying to ring me for the last hour. I dashed outside and rang her. The news was devastating. She had found Chris dead, in his room on the top floor of the house. It was so noisy, and my mind so disbelieving, that I had to get her to say it again. The ambulance and police were there. Her best friend, who was also living in our house, was beside her in what used to be my mother's flat.

Those who have shared the experience of losing a son or daughter know how deep is the abyss into which you feel you are falling at that moment. My fears for Caroline, my own devastation, and the memory not only of Barbara's death but also of her love for Chris were all swirling around me as I seemed to fall deeper and deeper. My colleagues rallied round to organise the earliest possible flight back, which was by way of Vienna, early the next morning. The police very helpfully met me at the airport. We drove straight to the smallholding outside Berwick to meet Caroline where her boyfriend's parents lived. After we had talked I walked outside by myself and simply howled in anguish. Then we set off home, with the police car craftily avoiding the press cameras set up outside. Since then I have watched families who have lost a child giving immediate and inevitably tearful TV interviews – for all my experience of TV interviews, I just could not have done it. All we wanted to do was to hide away in our own home with our grief, and that is what we did.

Chris had been depressed, and when that is combined with diabetes – which itself contributed to the depression – there is a constant underlying risk. An insulin-dependent diabetic lives each day close to the threshold of life and death. Once insulin has been injected, it must be balanced by eating sufficient carbohydrates for the body to derive the necessary sugars from it or, in an emergency, sugar must be provided directly by drinks or injection. Once hypoglycaemia sets in, a normally rational person will start to behave irrationally, and without regard to their own good or their own safety. This will sometimes take the form of refusal to take the very step which will deal with the situation, by having a sugary drink or glucose-based injection. We had seen it happen with Chris. When we were with him we could quickly deal with it, but you cannot always be there.

He had taken insulin, more than he should have done, and not bothered to eat. He was planning to go out that night – he had a ticket for a barbecue in Kelso – and had made various plans for the following week. He had been working on the Friday, but the people at his last call had noticed that he had a slightly puzzling way of speaking; even at that point in the day his balance must have been going badly wrong.

In that state of mind he did not care what happened to him.

Barbara's death was a severe blow, but it was one which the three of us knew was coming, and there was time to prepare for it. This was a loss without warning, and without preparation. The Lord had taken away again, and what had been taken away was His most precious gift to us. Caroline and I were all that was left of our extended family. But again and again I came back to the thought that what had been given, our years with Barbara and Chris and with all the family members we had lost, could not be taken away. The gifts had been received, and had brought delight; they had helped to make us what we were; they were now part of us.

The proof of that, amongst all the pain, was the way we could talk about what Barbara would have said, or what Chris would have said – and how often we could laugh about it. We would recall past occasions, and the memories would be projected into present events. It was not easy, and Caroline's life had been so traumatic that she needed help. We were able to get it from the community psychiatric nurse, who helped her to talk through it all. The initiative to organise some help came partly from her boyfriend Iain, who was a real support, and they got engaged. Iain, a young gamekeeper, had fairly recently arrived on the scene prior to Chris's death; they were getting to know each other, and with similar interests, he and Chris were clearly likely to get on well. Caroline gained a new family through the kindness of Iain's parents, and later, thanks to Iain and Caroline, came the gift of Scott, a delightful grandson.

Through this latest crisis I had the support of Diana Maddock. I had worked with Diana some years before, when she was MP for Christchurch from 1993 to 1997 which she had won with the biggest ever swing of votes from the Conservatives. She had helped me on the Finance Bill Committee when I was Treasury spokesman. She has always regarded this as my rather cruel method of giving her a knowledge of parliamentary procedure by throwing her into the pool at the deep end with very little guidance on how to swim. However, the experience showed its value when she successfully promoted a private member's bill. In the previous session I had tried and failed to get through the Energy Conservation Bill. I would probably have succeeded but for the sudden departure of a sympathetic minister, Tim Yeo, because of troubles in his private life: he was replaced by Robert Atkins, who seemed to have no sympathy at all for environmental issues, and did everything he could to block the bill. He ensured that scores of government amendments were tabled for the Report Stage. This tactic, which must take up a good deal of expensive time of civil servants in the drafting of unnecessary amendments, relies on the strict limits on private members' time to ensure that a Bill makes no further progress. My bill therefore fell. In the next session Diana came first in the ballot for private members' bills. The cause of energy conservation was one which Diana had long championed: we re-named the Bill the Home Energy Conservation Bill, she got it through with much skill and the assistance of the late Robert Jones, a more sympathetic minister. It has been the foundation of much of what has been achieved in improving the energy efficiency of homes throughout the country.

Diana had become the MP for Christchurch in 1993 in one of the most spectacular by-election victories ever. In the 1997 General Election she only narrowly lost the seat, which had been the safest Tory seat in the country. A couple of years later she was nominated by Paddy Ashdown to serve in the House of Lords as a working peer, which she has certainly been. Diana had separated from her husband and they later divorced. Her support at the time of Chris's death was immensely important to me; and we decided to get married. Confusingly, Baroness Maddock became Mrs Beith in June 2001. To have been happily married once, and for 33 years, is something for which to be deeply thankful. To be happily married for a second time seems like a miracle. The Lord has taken away, but He continues to give.

—16—

FAITH IN THE NORTH

Religion has been a powerful and visible part of the life and history of the North. For people without any religious commitment as well as those with faith, it is a fascinating story. Current interest in Celtic spirituality, the Lindisfarne Gospels and the Northumbrian Saints can lead to an assumption that there was only a short period of religious excitement and inspiration in the region, although a very fruitful one, but the real story is a much longer one.

The remains of religious or ritual expression from Northumberland's prehistory are still visible in Neolithic carvings such as Bellshiel Law in Redesdale, Bronze Age cup-and-ring markings at Doddington and Hesleyhurst, standing stones at Yeavering and stone circles at Duddo and Threestoneburn. The Romans left behind a temple to Mithras south of the Wall near Housesteads, and Temple to Antenociticus, in what is now a suburban road in Benwell. By the time they left, Christianity was a significant presence in the North.

Although Paulinus, as Bishop of York, had set about converting Northumbria to Christianity and had baptised many people at Yeavering, Christianity in the North was effectively secured by Oswald's victory at Heavenfield in 634. Oswald looked to Iona, Columba's headquarters, for missionary help. Thus came Aidan's move to Lindisfarne and Cuthbert's celebrated years there, which have given us the indescribably beautiful Lindisfarne Gospels. There has been a long battle with the British Library to get the Gospels returned to the North-East for at least some of the time, where they could still be cared for and displayed by the British Library's staff. Reluctance in London to allow this to happen has been seen as characteristic of southern attitudes to the North.

Within a few years of Oswald's victory there had developed the dispute between the Roman and Celtic traditions in the Church which was resolved in favour of the Roman view at the Synod of Whitby in 664. Although the dispute centred on the date of Easter and was fuelled by the question of whose authority should be recognised, some see its resolution in Rome's favour as causing the loss of Celtic traditions of spirituality and Celtic emphasis on the presence of the Divine in nature and in everyday things. Christianity, in this tradition, was thought to be more closely bound up with daily living. After Cuthbert's death, Holy Island was sacked by the Danes and Cuthbert's remains began a long, slow journey to Durham. It was three centuries before they were finally placed on the site of the present cathedral in 995. There the Normans built the structure which remains the most dramatic and least altered tribute in stone to the Christian faith of that period to be seen anywhere in Britain.

Meanwhile Benedict Biscop and Bede had established monasteries at Monkwearmouth and Jarrow, and we can still see at Escomb the essential features of the church established there in Bede's time. Monastic centres including Durham, Tynemouth, the re-established Lindisfarne, Hexham and Brinkburn provided centres for the mediaeval consolidation of Christianity in the North: parish churches were built, subject to and in some cases fortified against Border raids. Small cells and hermitages provided centres of prayer and pilgrimage in such places as Ovingham, Alnwick and, in a later period, by the river at Warkworth.

Much has been written about Christianity in the North up to the time of the Reformation but, apart from the 1715 rebellion, with the defeat and execution of the Earl of Derwentwater, popular history makes little mention of what happened to Christianity in Northumberland thereafter. It is an omission which ignores the distinctive way in which Christianity developed in the North-East, and the influence it has had on the life of the region.

The Reformation had left a number of prominent Catholic landowning families who remained loyal to their old faith and survived to tell the tale. The Selby family, the Charltons of Hesleyside, the Haggerstons, the Claverings – with priest's holes and private chapels, they kept the tradition until toleration and inward migration from Ireland enabled the Roman Church to rebuild in the nineteenth century.

The Reformation itself and the Elizabethan settlement, briefly interrupted by the civil war and the reign of Catholic James, set the pattern for the established church. The North, however, had a very significant dissenting element which did not accept that settlement.

After the Civil War, many Puritan and Presbyterian vicars who had been appointed during the Cromwellian period were excluded from the churches and towns in which they had served, and replaced with conformist clergy. At Bolam in Northumberland, Dame Katherine Babington, an ardent dissenter, conspired with the local blacksmith to have the new vicar pulled out of his pulpit. The punishment, when she died a few years later, was to be denied a burial in the churchyard. Her tomb can be found carved out of the rock in the grounds of the family home, Harnham Hall, near Belsay.

Presbyterianism provided the largest element in the dissenting tradition, with many congregations which have continued to the present day as part of the United Reformed Church having their origins in the sixteenth and seventeenth centuries. The strength of Presbyterianism in Northumberland has sometimes been attributed to its proximity to Scotland. John Knox was at one time vicar of Berwick, and in the nineteenth and early twentieth centuries many congregations recruited ministers from Scotland, where supply exceeded demand. The movement of farmers and farm labourers across the border, and later the migration of skilled shipyard workers from Glasgow to Tyneside, strengthened these congregations, but in their origins most of them were native to Northumberland. Many Baptist congregations in the region can also trace their history back to the same origins in the Reformation and Civil War periods.

When John Wesley and the preachers he recruited came to the North-East, they found an industrial population which was largely alienated from religion, and it was in the coal and lead mining areas that Methodism mainly took root, filling the gap left by an increasingly complacent Established church and by nonconformist congregations which attracted artisans and farmers with little impact on the growing population of industrial workers. Wesley was a frequent and tireless visitor to the region, with the Orphan House in Newcastle serving as one of his three principal bases of operation along with London and Bristol. He came close to marrying a Newcastle woman, Grace Murray, but his hymn-writer brother Charles was set against the match, and conspired to marry her off to another preacher. Within a year, on the rebound, John married a widow but neither of them was ever happy in the marriage – he would have been much better off with Grace.

However, this unhappiness at home probably made it easier for him to keep up the travelling ministry which had such a huge impact. By the time of his death Wesley had established congregations and seen chapels built from Berwick to Yarm, and indeed through much of England and parts of Wales, Scotland and Ireland. Most significantly for the region, he had brought religious faith into the lives of a significant proportion of the manual and skilled workers in the growing industrial areas. This task was to be continued by breakaway Methodist groups. One was started by an Alnwick-based minister, Alexander Kilham, who demanded a more democratic structure for Methodism, complaining in an Appeal to the Methodist Societies of the Alnwick Circuit in 1796 that Methodist people had "no voice in the choice of their own officers, the formation of their own laws, or the disbursement of what they give to carry on the work".

He set up the Methodist New Connexion, and his call for democracy was echoed in Methodist support for political reform and, in later decades, in Methodist involvement in the organisation of trade unions in the North. This was particularly marked among the Primitive Methodists, who started in Staffordshire in 1807 and became strong in the mining communities of County Durham and some of the fishing villages of the North-East coast. The "Tolpuddle Martyrs" included Primitive Methodist local preachers, and the history of North-East trade unionism contains countless examples of men who learned their skills as speakers and organisers in the chapel, and applied them to achieve the betterment of their fellow-workers through the trade union movement. The town of Peterlee commemorates in its name one such man - a local preacher, union executive member and eventually County Council Chairman, Peter Lee. Religion, and particularly Methodism, had equipped people in the region to tackle the industrial and social problems of their time and given them a zeal to do so.

Meanwhile, the older dissenting tradition was having an influence in a rather different way. Throughout England a proportion of

Presbyterian congregations had moved to a much more liberal theological position, and had become known as Unitarians or Free Christians. Their Newcastle congregation in Hanover Square attracted many of the prosperous and influential of the City. One of its members had founded the Dispensary referred to in the song "Blaydon Races". Their remarkable Minister, whom they appointed in 1782, was the Rev. William Turner. He served in that capacity for nearly sixty years and had a profound impact on the city. So great was his commitment to science and scholarship that, influenced by his mentor Joseph Priestley, he introduced the middle classes of Tyneside to the latest developments in chemistry and metallurgy while also campaigning against slavery and pursuing a ministry of theologically advanced preaching, and lecturing week by week.

His permanent achievement was the establishment of Newcastle's Literary and Philosophical Society, still housed in its fine library premises of 1822. He helped to found schools, a Mechanics Institute and the Newcastle Savings Bank, and tried unsuccessfully to establish a university. Here religion was an educating and civilising force, accepting and promoting scientific discovery as evidence of a Divine Creator, seen in the wonders of the created universe, and using scientific knowledge as a tool for the service of mankind.

Turner also worked with Quakers and Methodists to produce massive North-east support for the petitions against the slave trade. Meetings were held throughout the region and help was enlisted from Charles Grey, later to become Earl Grey, Prime Minister and reforming politician whose monument looks out over the City of Newcastle from his column at the top of Grey Street. The campaign was a model for the campaigns of Churches Together two centuries later. It was one of many influential campaigns in which Northumbrian Christians played a key role: Josephine Butler from

Glendale campaigned against the oppression of women, and W.T. Stead, born at the Embleton Presbyterian manse, campaigned with the Salvation Army's General Booth against child prostitution.

The Established Church had by now stirred from what is rather simplistically portrayed as its eighteenth-century sleepiness into separate streams of evangelistic endeavour. Evangelicalism had a prominent Newcastle church, St Thomas's, and a leader in Richard Clayton, whose supporters later decamped to build a church in Jesmond in his memory: it remains a stronghold of evangelical preaching today. Outside the Established Church, conservative evangelicalism was a force in the Baptist Churches and in the Christian "Plymouth" Brethren, who had a significant place in some of the farming communities. The growth within the Church of England of ritualism and Anglo-Catholicism bred a missionary effort in areas of urban poverty, such as Byker and Rye Hill in Newcastle, and spread out into some of the mining villages through the efforts of dedicated clergy. In a different and more colourful way, they sought to make religion a force in the lives of some of the most disadvantaged people of the region.

At the other end of the social scale, rich patrons made some of the Churches showpieces of architecture and art, such as Pearson's St. George's Church, Cullercoats, paid for by the 6th Duke of Northumberland, and even more dramatically, St. George's in Jesmond, where the wealthy Charles Mitchell recruited a group of talented artists to achieve a sumptuously decorated interior. The most notable example of this kind of artistic patronage in the Church is to be found in Sunderland: in 1906 at St. Andrew's, Roker the self-made shipyard millionaire John Priestman paid for an Arts and Crafts masterpiece adorned with Morris and Burne-Jones designs, and work by Ernest Gimson and Eric Gill. Religion enriched the region's artistic heritage.

The engagement between religion and society in the North-East continued to throw up challenges. When Bishop Hensley Henson was nominated by Prime Minister Lloyd George to be Bishop of Durham, it was against the wishes of the Archbishops of both York and Canterbury. Lloyd George, a rather lapsed Welsh nonconformist, knew Henson not only as a powerful preacher but also as a man who had in the early years of his ministry worked among and championed the urban poor. In the diocese of Durham he found over 100,000 miners, with the lowest pay in the entire mining industry and some of the most overcrowded living conditions, as well as growing unemployment.

Initially he got on well with the miners, and the idea grew that, like his predecessor Bishop Westcott in the 1890s, he could be a mediator between miners and the owners. But it was not to be: invited to speak at a large meeting in Hartlepool by the miners and the owners in 1921, he revealed so rooted an objection to strikes and to a minimum wage, that there began a long-running stand-off between the miners and the Bishop. On the Miners' Gala day in 1925 miners attacked the Dean of Durham (perhaps mistaking him for the Bishop) and tried to throw him in the river. He was rescued by a motor launch as his top hat floated downstream. Bishop Henson was an individualist, who seemed unable to come to terms with the necessity of trade union organisation to deal with the relative weakness of employees in an exceedingly hard industry. He had understandable concerns about intimidation of people during strikes, and about the need to keep the industry viable if there were to be jobs for future generations in Durham. But the picture which he presented to the North-East of Christianity was not coloured by his conscientious and devout character or his intellectual and rhetorical skills: it was coloured by his inability to respond adequately to the realities of conditions in the industrial North-East. It was an unattractive picture of Christianity which others have had to strive to dispel.

In more recent years the Church of England, following a tradition strengthened by William Temple during Henson's time, has sought to take a very different approach, manifested particularly in the "Faith in the City" report of 1986, and by the "Faith in the Countryside" report of 1990. Each examined in detail issues such as housing, employment, health, social care and public safety and proposed measures involving both government and the churches. The North-East features in both reports.

Immigration from Ireland vastly increased the Roman Catholic strength, particularly in Teesside and South Tyneside, while in a few rural areas it built on traditions which had survived throughout the periods of persecution and proscription from the Reformation until the early nineteenth century. Roman Catholicism had become a serious force within Christianity in England, and Newcastle gave it one of its most respected national leaders of modern times, Cardinal Basil Hume.

Immigration brought other faiths into the region. The Jewish community, although long-established, grew in strength as persecution drove Jews first out of Eastern Europe and then out of Germany. Newcastle's Jewish community produced no less than two successive and outstanding holders of the post of Lord Chief Justice, Lord Taylor and Lord Woolf. Gateshead has long been the home of a strictly orthodox Jewish community and a centre for its teaching. At the same time South Shields can boast one of the oldest Muslim communities in Britain, as a result of its sea links with the Middle

East. The West End of Newcastle is now home to Muslims, Sikhs and Hindus, each community maintaining active places of worship. Leaders of all faiths are working together to address the problems and build on the strengths of a religiously and culturally diverse city.

Will religion, and in particular the Christian religion, continue to play a significant role in the life of the region, given that less than ten percent of its population are regular worshippers and many churches are closed or empty? The United Reformed and Methodist churches have seen the most significant drop in numbers, from a time when the majority of worshippers in many parts of Northumberland were to be found in these denominations. However, even at the peak of church and chapel attendance, between two thirds and three quarters of the population were not attending Sunday services. The impact of religion on society has been greater than its numerical strength, and the active churches and faith communities of the North are likely to continue to exercise an influence beyond their numbers.

Initiatives like the Churches Urban Fund are having a direct effect on poor communities in the North-East, while a DEFRA-commissioned research project has revealed the extent of the support which churches offer to the countryside. A 2004 government-supported report on "Faith in the North-East" revealed 4,762 separate community projects involving 13,439 volunteers, and similar research in the North-West found 5,000 projects with over 45,000 volunteers. 75% of churches in the North-East provide facilities which are used by the wider community.

In order to continue this level of support for the wider community, the churches and faith groups will need to nourish and expand the spiritual foundations on which it is built, challenging future generations to recognise that there is a reality beyond our daily lives and that there are ethical principles derived from religious belief which make for a better society. Christianity has been a force in the North for nearly 2,000 years: in different ways, from Celtic saints to charismatic preachers and Christian social reformers, faith has served the people of the North.

—17—

WHAT FUTURE FOR THE NORTH?

Our home in Berwick is close to the northernmost point of the most northerly constituency in England, and it is further North than a large slice of Scotland. The house is Victorian, semi-detached and stone built, and only a short walk from the railway station. It was the childhood home of a now sadly forgotten playwright, lyricist and broadcaster, Alan Melville. His autobiography provides a fascinating record of life in the house and the local community in the 1920s and 30s, when he was growing up with his piano teacher mother and his apparently ill-tempered heavy drinking father, a director of the local woodyard. Melville began his career travelling by train to Manchester to feature as a child actor on BBC North Children's Hour programmes, making a strange link with my own childhood listening to the same programmes years later. He travelled my route in reverse. The apex of his career was probably his co-operation with Ivor Novello. He wrote the lyrics for Novello's last show entitled – without irony because it had not yet acquired its modern meaning – *Gay's the Word*.

Melville was one of many who left the North to pursue a career – in his case one which necessarily involved being closer to the London theatres and studios. The worry common to many Northern parents is that their children will have no alternative but to move out of the region in order to make a living. Some of that movement is natural, inevitable and healthy: in parts of our region it is to some extent balanced by the inflow of students to the region's universities. One of Northumberland's problems is that there is no higher education institution north of Newcastle, and no further education institution north of Ashington. Some of those who are educated here adopt the region enthusiastically, make their home here, and use their skill to its benefit. But this raises the question of how we can strengthen and diversify the economy of our region so as to enable a higher proportion of our young people to find careers here, and so as to offer a more rewarding future to the whole population of the North.

The story of the job losses in the North's heavy industries – coal, steel, shipbuilding and chemicals – is often told, well documented, and not in need of repetition in these pages. It was certainly mishandled by governments, both Conservative and Labour, but most of it was inevitable sooner or later. Agriculture and fisheries have also seen large job losses.

The North needed to rebuild its economy on different foundations. There have been some successes: the arrival and recent expansion of Nissan's car production, for example; less obviously, the biggest industry in the City of Newcastle is now higher education. Tourism to the region has grown significantly. The employment rate in the North-East is rising, but remains below national levels for England. In fact the region's population has been declining and is projected to remain no more than static, while the population of England as a whole is rising, and the age profile of the region is significantly older than the rest of the country.

The temptation for those of us who have an income and a home which enable us to enjoy living in the North is to pull up the drawbridge and tell each other how good it is to have fine scenery, two world heritage sites and quiet roads with no-one getting in our way. Even from a narrowly selfish point of view that is actually unsustainable. There is no excuse for narrow selfishness. The region belongs to all its people, not just the comfortably off and those who have moved here to retire – although many of the retired contribute significantly to the quality of life here.

So what holds the North back? What obstacles stand in the way of achieving an economy which can meet the needs and aspirations of all its people? Geography plays a part – we are further from London than any other part of England. It did not matter when the South needed the North's coal: ships and trains carried it southwards. But in the absence of the competitive advantage given by a raw material in high demand, it certainly makes a difference that we are on the edge of the motorway system – or beyond its reach in the case of Northumberland. We may not like the fact that national and international businesses look for the blue lines of motorway on the map, but there is no mistaking the fact that they do. A significant element in South Yorkshire's bid to recover from the collapse of coal mining has been its place at the heart of a motorway network where distribution and warehousing business want to be located. Development in much of the North-East is undoubtedly hindered by the lack of dual carriageway for much of the A1 in Northumberland: instead of being part of an East coast economy in both England and Scotland, we are seen as beyond the end of the road.

In other aspects of communications we do better – we have the fastest long-distance rail link from the South-East for both passengers and freight, but it has almost reached the limits of its capacity. We have growing large ports on the Tees and the Tyne, as well as smaller ports such as Blyth and Berwick. Air services from Newcastle, and to a lesser extent from Durham Tees Valley, cover an increasing range of destinations, and when Emirates flights to Dubai from Newcastle were introduced, the outbound freight capacity was filled within days. Sustainable transport policies will require serious investment to increase rail capacity, and while road expansion in general is not a sustainable option, the gap in the basic network left by the undualled A1 clearly has to be filled. Ports investment will need to continue. Government investment in transport in the North-East should be above the national average, not 17% below it.

Geography is a fact of life, but centralisation such as we have in England was an unwelcome development of the twentieth century. If you look far enough back in history, although London was the undisputed capital of the country, Berwick was one of the busiest ports, and Durham was a major centre of political and ecclesiastical power, as well as becoming the home of England's oldest university outside Oxford and Cambridge. For much of the nineteenth century Manchester mattered more than London, and Middlesborough's rapid expansion demonstrated its crucial role in the national economy. This alternative pre-eminence and power of Northern cities was reflected in the national importance accorded to their newspapers, as is still the case with major European cities like Frankfurt and Zurich. Under Embleton-born W.T. Stead, the *Northern Echo* achieved national campaigning importance from its Darlington base. The *Manchester Guardian* under C.P. Scott reflected a distinctive and powerful Northern liberal view, and the paper earned long-standing resentment in the North when its editorial staff slunk away shamefacedly to London in the 1960s, and dropped Manchester from the paper's title in case it offended southerners.

We have in England a London-centred national culture, encouraged by the modern economic dominance of the South-East, which needs to be countered. With the exception of the BBC's current move of several departments to Manchester, the broadcast media are far more heavily centred in London than they were either in the early days of the BBC or during the first decades of independent television. ITV was deliberately structured and licensed on a regional basis but is now highly centralised. Because of this highly centralised broadcasting structure, creative talent in regions such as the North has lost some of the opportunities and outlets it had, and local production is increasingly confined to a small element of regional news and current affairs. Even in the field of news, despite the fact that it has become technically so much easier to feed into live programmes from anywhere in the world, centralisation rules. I am often contacted by TV news programmes asking me to give interviews who then discover to their obvious amazement that I am in the North-East and not in London. I am sometimes reduced to saying: "People live here and work here – have you not noticed?" It is an attitude of mind we must work to change. There are still parts of the BBC, and of ITV and Sky, which could benefit from locating in the North-East and getting a less London-centred view of life.

Another problem which holds us back is an undoubted skills gap. Almost a quarter of the unfilled job vacancies in the North-East result from a shortage of applicants with the necessary skills, qualifications and experience. More employers in the region are funding or carrying out training in the region than is the case in the rest of the country, but the region needs to go further and create a skills advantage over other regions so as to counteract the geographical factors which weaken our growth. We also have a particular problem with providing new skills and opportunities for people over 50 – only six out of ten over-50's in the North-East are in work, compared with over seven out of ten across the country. We are wasting talents we have within the region.

Another problem for the North-East has been high dependence on the public sector, with a less active enterprise culture than prevails in the south, shown in a significantly lower level of small business start-ups. It may take a generation to change that, and to do so will require a significant additional effort to spread understanding of business and its opportunities among young people in the North.

In the past, the North-East has called for much more decentralisation of Government departments to the region. The most striking and long-lasting instance of this was the move of the central pensions administration of what was then the Ministry of Pensions to Newcastle after the war. The move of National Savings to Durham in the 1960s was a more modest but valuable sequel. However, the vaunted ambitions of Gordon Brown as Chancellor to move many thousands of jobs out of London have had no beneficial impact on the North-East. At the same time, centralisation within government departments such as the Department of Work and Pensions and HM Revenue and Customs is taking jobs away from many of the smaller towns to central processing centres. Even when these are within the region, for example in North Tyneside, they lead to a loss of employment in places where it is difficult to replace, and to excessive travel to work for staff who are relocated. Government shows an unimaginative inability to identify units of work which can be transferred out to small town offices, where, although the functions may not be local, thirty or forty jobs can be retained for the local economy. I have already quoted the example of the then Ministry of Agriculture agreeing to relocate central functions to its Alnwick office when it was no longer needed as a regional office – there has been no systematic attempt to develop this kind of initiative, which could be of great benefit to rural market towns.

The North-East has great opportunities in fields in which its universities have taken a lead, such as life sciences and renewable energy. Some of the potential is already being seen and developed, but it is worrying that the region still has the lowest spending on research and development of any region, both in the private and in the public sector.

I have left to the last two of the biggest handicaps the North-East has had in moving forward. One is, bluntly, the politics of the region. Throughout most of my 35 years in Parliament, Labour has held almost all the parliamentary seats in the region. Labour councillors have run most of the councils, and Labour nominees have dominated many of the vast array of "quangoes" – supposedly independent bodies – which Labour and Conservative governments have created. This is partly a product of the absurd electoral system, which has left Liberal Democrat and Conservative voters in County Durham with no parliamentary seats, while Labour voters have been unrepresented in Surrey and Somerset. It is a system which Liberal Democrats are fighting to change, but until it is changed the party seeks to win under the present system, with notable success in the City of Newcastle, wrested from decades of Labour control, in Durham City and in Northumberland.

One-party dominance has proved harmful to the region. Among this large regiment of Labour politicians there are, of course, many who have worked diligently for the good of the region and some who have made an outstanding contribution on issues important to the region. Among the phalanx of Labour-run councils there are occasional examples of imaginative and successful effort, such as Gateshead's securing of substantial cultural investment in the Baltic and the Sage. But taken as a whole, the region's predominantly one-party state has been part of the problem and does not look like part of the solution. We have seen decades of unrestricted Labour power at local level and over a decade of Labour power at national level, with Tony Blair and many Cabinet members representing North-East constituencies. These ministers should, between them, have achieved a lot more for the North. Labour in London has shown remarkably little interest in a Labour regional machine which has been unambitious, unimaginative and unlovely. It has been too easy to take the North-East's Labour votes for granted and get on with other priorities; it has been too convenient to rely on votes in Parliament from North-East Labour MPs without anything in the way of tangible benefits for their constituents. Most notably, the Government kept in place the Barnett formula, which guaranteed an increase in Scottish public spending every time spending in England rose, but gave the North-East no comparable mechanism to help it deal with the same rural and social problems for which Scotland has been able to use the money.

To the extent that general management of the economy improved under Blair and Brown, the North-East benefited from increased employment, but a gap remained between the region and more prosperous parts of the country. Opportunities which could have been of real help to the North such as the Energy Technologies Institute, an obvious fit for Newcastle, have gone to other regions. The local government funding formula penalised both Northumberland and Durham, and Northumberland found itself at the back of the queue for capital to build new schools.

This leaves the question of whether things could have been different if the North-East had been given devolved government, capable not only of making decisions within the region, but also of bidding more effectively for national and international projects. Scotland, Wales and London all have the ability to allocate resources in accordance with a locally determined view of the needs of the area. The London Mayor and the First Ministers in Scotland and Wales all have a clout that no-one is able to exercise on the North-East's behalf. But did the region not turn down just such an opportunity when we were offered it in the 2004 referendum? Indeed it did, despite the best efforts of Liberal Democrats and others to make the case. There were reasons for the defeat: what was on offer was a distinctly underpowered model of devolution. It was not attractive to people in the business community who might have supported a devolved assembly with powers which could make a real difference to the things which mattered to them. And it came too late in Tony Blair's premiership, when people were becoming much more suspicious of anything the government claimed to be offering them. Labour's regional predominance was a handicap, even in the referendum; despite the promise of a proportional voting system, there was a belief that the Assembly would be a talking shop of predominantly Labour politicians, costing money without delivering real benefits.

I am more than ever convinced that it was a missed opportunity. Those of us who backed it did so in the belief that, once established, the Assembly would gain more power, as has happened in Wales, and would become more widely accepted, as has happened in London, Wales and Scotland. It is now hard to imagine a referendum in any of those three supporting the abolition of bodies whose creation was so deeply controversial and bitterly contested. They have been seen to work to the benefit of their citizens, even by those who are opposed to the parties currently in power. The Conservative party, which opposed the creation of all three, is not now in favour of abolishing any of the devolved administrations.

What the North has instead of devolved government is a complex structure of appointed bodies which are not accountable in any democratic way to the region. The unelected regional assembly has been abolished, leaving the regional development agency (One North-East) the Government Office for the North-East, the Association of North-East Councils (representing the local authorities), two "city region" boards based on Tyne and Wear and Tees Valley, and numerous "partnerships" at regional, and local level. Newcastle and Gateshead, in innovative and welcome co-operation, have set up a joint City Development Company. The Northern Way is a joint initiative with Yorkshire, Humber and the North West, with so far not much to show for North-East involvement. Gordon Brown designated one of his Ministers to be regional Minister for each region alongside other duties, with no budget and hardly any ability to have an impact on departmental decision-making.

Some would argue that this largely unelected structure will enable professionals to take initiatives with less bureaucracy, although, with such a complex system, that is far from evident. Conservatives have usually argued that most of these bodies should be abolished, giving local authorities more responsibility: that ignores the fact that Conservative governments have not been willing to give local authorities either the power or the tax base to operate with real autonomy, and it ignores the fact that like all governments, they found it necessary to have some kind of structure at regional level.

Regional devolution to an elected body for the North-East will force its way back on the agenda. Voters in this region and other regions will not for ever be content to have unelected bodies determining what happens to housing and transport in their area, and will get fed up with the fact, unlike them, Scottish and London voters can see decisions taken in their own areas about where money is to be spent.

Facing up to the region's problems should not lead us to undersell or undervalue the North. It is a wonderful part of the country. The scenery, the history, the life, the people, the sport and the culture – these are tremendous assets. I started life where England begins to be northern, and moved to its northernmost county, and then to its northernmost town. I have gained much from the North. I have brought up my family here, and my view of life is Northern. There is a magnetism in the North which, once experienced, takes hold of those who come from elsewhere to live here. It brings others back here as soon as their careers allow. It is worth the effort to make life in the North, in every sense, sustainable for the future.

NOTES

1   The only other Beith ever to be an MP came from the same sort of dissenting Presbyterian background, but I have found no trace of a link between our families. Gilbert Beith was member for Inverness Burghs, Glasgow Central 1885–86 and Inverness District of Burghs 1892–95, and was the son of the Rev. Alexander Beith, one of the most notable preachers among the ministers who broke away to form the Free Church in 1843.

2   Sir Arthur Harvey, Conservative MP for Macclesfield 1945 to 1971 and Chairman of the Conservative 1922 Committee.

3   D.E. Butler and Anthony King, *The British General Election of 1964*. Macmillan, London, 1965.

4   Kate Adie, *The Kindness of Strangers*. Headline, 2002.

5   For a full description of the NVA, see Beith, A. J. 'An Anti-Labour Caucus: The Case of the Northumberland Voters' Association' in *Policy and Politics*, (1973) Vol. 2, No. 2, pp.153–165.

6   Bob Wareing, MP for Liverpool West Derby since 1983.

7   See *Tragedy of the Salmon*, by David Shaw, Highfields Press, 1995, which sets out the parliamentary debates on salmon fisheries legislation in detail, and gives a vivid picture of a parliamentary battle between North-East and Scottish interests in which I was largely on my own. The decline of salmon fishing on the Tweed in Berwick was beautifully recorded by Jim Walker in *By Net and Coble: Salmon Fishing on the Tweed*.

8   *Northumberland Gazette*, 5 March 1992.

9   See *Hansard* 15 January 2004, Col. 924; Report of the Committee on Standards and Privilege, 1st April 2004, and Government response, 16 September 2004.

10 Pitchford, Rachel and Greaves, Tony, *Merger: The Inside Story*.

11 In *Journal of Liberal Democrat History*, Issue 18, Spring 1998.

12 Daniel Finkelstein, who later left the Owenite SDP for the Tories, recalls the spoiling tactics involved in canvassing in a by-election for a deservedly hopeless SDP candidate 'all just to stop the Liberal getting in'. He added: 'There is a nice Yiddish word for what I was – *meshugener*. It means lunatic'. *The Times*, 5 September 2007.

13 See, for example, *The Sunday Times*, 7 May 1995.

14 *Ashdown Diaries*, Volume II, p. 15.

15 Volume II, p. 92.

16 *Hansard*, 27 February 2002.

17 *On Liberty*, Ch. 3.

18 See *The Theory and Practice of Community Politics* by Bernard Greaves and Gordon Lishman.

19 Quoted in *Review of Intelligence on Weapons of Mass Destruction*, Report of a Committee of Privy Counsellors, Chairman The Rt Hon Lord Butler of Bracknell, HC 898, July 2004, para 481.

20 *Ibid.*, para 482.

21 ISC Report on *Iraqi Weapons of Mass Destruction – Intelligence and Assessments*, September 2005, Cm5972, paras 126–127.

22 Intelligence and Security Committee report on *Rendition*, July 2007 Cm 7171, para 137, conclusion V.

BIBLIOGRAPHY

ADAM, D. (1997) *Flame in My Heart: St. Aidan for Today*. London: Triangle, SPCK.

ADIE, K. (2002) *The Kindness of Strangers*. London: Headline.

ASHDOWN, P. (2000 and 2001) *The Ashdown Diaries*. Volume I: 1988–1997; Volume II: 1997–1999. London: Allen Lane, The Penguin Press.

BEITH, A. (2006) *Religion, human rights and politics, 1906–2006*. Lecture at Robinson College, Cambridge 21 October.

BEITH, A. (2002) *It's About Freedom*. The Report of the Liberal Democracy Working Group Policy Paper 50. Liberal Democrats.

BEITH, A. (2001) Introduction to *Berwick in Parliament. A history of the representation of Berwick in the House of Commons 1529–2001*. Berwick: Berwick-upon-Tweed History Society.

BEITH, A. (1998) *Merger Hopes and Fears: Were they Realised?* Journal of Liberal Democrat History, Issue 18, Spring.

BEITH, A. (1988) *Leadership and Freedom*. Hebden Bridge: Hebden Royd Publications.

BEITH, A. (1987) *Faith in Politics: which way should Christians vote?* (with John Selwyn Gummer and Eric Heffer). London: SPCK.

BEITH, A. (1987) *The Fullness of Freedom: Policy priorities for achieving a Liberal society*. Liberal Challenge Number 9. Hebden Bridge: Liberal Party Publications.

BEITH, A. (1983) *The Case for the Liberal Party and the Alliance*. London: Longman.

BEITH, A. (1976) *The M.P. as a Grievance Chaser*. Public Administration Bulletin Number 21, August.

255

BEITH, A. (1965) Chapter 11, 'The Press', in Butler, D.E. and King, A. *The British General Election of 1964*. London: Macmillan & Co.

BEITH, A. Journal of Liberal Democrat History, especially issue 18, Spring 1998, *Ten Years On: The Legacy of the Alliance and the Merger*.

BETJEMAN, J. (1952) *First and Last Loves*. John Murray.

BINNEY, M. and Burman, P. (1977) *Chapels and Churches: Who Cares?* British Tourist Authority in association with Country Life.

BRADLEY, I. (1981) *Breaking the Mould. The Birth and Prospects of the Social Democratic Party*. Oxford: Martin Robertson.

BURLEIGH, J.H.S. (1988) *A Church History of Scotland*. Edinburgh, Hope Trust.

CHADWICK, O. *Hensley Henson: A Study in the Friction between Church and State*. Oxford: Clarendon Press.

COOK, C. (1989) *A Short History of the Liberal Party 1900–88*. Third Edition. Macmillan Press.

COOK, R. and Maclennan, R. (2005) *Looking Back, Looking Forward. The Cook Maclennan Agreement, Eight Years On*. London: New Politics, Network.

DAVIES, P.H.J. see Glees, A.

DE WAAL, E. (1991) *Celtic Light, A Tradition Rediscovered*. London: Fount/Harper Collins.

DOLBEY, G.W. (1964) *The Architectural Expression of Methodism: the First Hundred Years*. London: The Epworth Press.

Faith in the City: the Report of the Archbishop of Canterbury's Commission on Urban Priority Areas. London: Church House Publishing.

Faith in the Countryside: Report of the Archbishops' Commission on Rural Areas. Worthing: Churchman Publishing.

FOOTE, G. (2005) *The Republican Transformation of Modern Politics*. Palgrave Macmillan.

GLEES, A., Davies, P.H.J. and Morrison, J.N.L. (2006) *The Open Side of Secrecy: Britain's Intelligence and Security Committee.* The Social Affairs Unit 2006. London.

GREAVES, B. and Lishman, G. (1980) *The Theory and Practice of Community Politics.* Association of Liberal Councillors Campaign Booklet Number 12, Hebden Bridge.

GREAVES, T. see Pitchford, R.

GUBBINS, B. (1991) *Generating Pressure: the campaign against Nuclear Power at Druridge Bay.* Ryton, Tyne and Wear: Earthright Publications.

HARBOTTLE, S. (1997) *The Reverend William Turner, Dissent and Reform in Georgian Newcastle upon Tyne.* Newcastle: Northern Universities Press.

HATTERSLEY, R. (2002) *A Brand from the Burning: The Life of John Wesley.* Little, Brown.

HEMPTON, D. (2005) *Methodism: Empire of the Spirit.* New Haven: Yale University Press.

HOGGART, S. see Michie, A.

IGNATIEFF, M. (2004) *The Lesser Evil: Political Ethics in an Age of Terror.* Princeton University Press.

JONES, SIR HUGH (2007) *Campaigning Face to Face.* Sussex: Book Guild Publishing.

JOSEPHS, J. (1983) *Inside the Alliance. An Inside Account of the Development and Prospects of the Liberal SDP-Alliance.* London: John Martin Publishing.

LEIGH, I. (2005) Accountability of Security and Intelligence in the United Kingdom in *Who's Watching the Spies: establishing Intelligence Service Accountability.* Washington D.C.: Potomac Books, Inc.

LINDLEY, K. (1969) *Chapels and Meeting Houses.* London: John Baker Publishers Ltd.

LISHMAN, G. see Greaves, B.

MACLENNAN, R. see also Cook, R.

MICHIE, A. and Hoggart, S. (1978) *The Pact: The Inside Story of the Lib-Lab Government, 1977–8*. London: Quartet Books.

MORRISON, J.N.L. see Glees, A.

PEVSNER, N. and Richmond, I. (1992) *The Building of England: Northumberland*. London: Penguin Books.

PEVSNER, N. revised by Williamson, E. (2002) *The Buildings of England: County Durham*. New Haven and London: Yale University Press.

PICKERING, W.S.F. (ed.) (1981) *A Social History of the Diocese of Newcastle upon Tyne*. Stocksfield, Northumberland: Oriel Press.

PITCHFORD, R. and Greaves, T. (1989) *Merger: The Inside Story*. Liberal Review, Colne.

SHAW, D. (1995) *Tragedy of the Salmon: The Scottish Fishery and the 1986 Salmon Act*. East Grinstead: The Hillfield Press.

SLESSOR, T. (2002) *Ministries of Deception, Cover-ups in Whitehall*. London: Aurum Press.

STEED, M. (1983) *The Alliance: A Critical History*. New Outlook 1983. Guildford: Prism Publications Ltd.

STEEL, D. (1989) *Against Goliath: David Steel's Story*. London: Weidenfeld and Nicolson.

STELL, C. *Nonconformist Chapels and Meeting Houses*. 4 volumes: Central England (1986); South Western England (1991); North of England (1994); Eastern England (2002). Published by Royal Commission on Historical Monuments/English Heritage.

WALKER, J. (2001) *By Net and Coble; Salmon Fishing in the Tweed*. Blackhall Press.

WEARMOUTH, R. (1937) *Methodism and the Working-Class Movements of England 1800–1850*. London: The Epworth Press.

INDEX

religion
  in AB's childhood, 10, 23–29
  at Oxford, 39–40
  and politics, 138, 165–172
  in the North of England, 229–239
  chapel and church buildings, 202–210, 214
  see also Christianity, Methodism and other individual religions

Rippon, Geoffrey, 54

Robertson, Sue, 103

Robson, Allan, 59

Rodgers, Bill, 102, 114

Roper, John, 102, 103

Ross, Stephen, 95, 99

Rossi, Sir Hugh, 207, 208

Saddam Hussein, 127, 159, 184–186
  see also Iraq war

Salford, 2, 3, 11

Saunders, Matthew, 207

Scotland, 2, 57, 60, 77, 121, 129, 130, 232, 238
  devolution and Scottish Parliament, 68, 74, 98, 129, 134, 143, 151, 249

Scott, Norman, 93

SDP (Social Democratic Party), 101–120
  merger with the Liberals, 112–120

Owenites reject merger, 119, 125
  see also Alliance of Liberals and SDP, Liberal Democrats

Security and Intelligence Services, 173–194
  see also Intelligence and Security Committee

select committees
  role of, 83–85
  Treasury and Civil Service Committee (AB served on 1987–94), 84
  Justice Committee (and its predecessors: AB has chaired since 2003), 84–85, 88
  Liaison Committee (AB currently a member), 86
  see also Intelligence and Security Committee

Short, Edward, 86
  introduces "Short Money" for opposition parties, 86

Sierra Leone, 159, 183

Slessor, Tim, 82

Smith, Cyril, 62–64, 71, 93–95, 103, 122

Smith, John, 132

Smith, T. Dan, 49, 68

Social and Liberal Democrats, *see* Liberal Democrats, name of

Sorton, Doris (née Harty; AB's aunt), 5, 6, 41